CW00543821

A General System of Horsemanship

William Cavendish
Duke of Newcastle

Facsimile reproduction of the edition of 1743
Introduction by William C. Steinkraus
with a technical commentary by E. Schmit-Jensen

J.A. Allen
London

Reproduced from the 1743 edition published by J. Brindley, London.
Foreword and technical commentary from the J. A. Allen edition of 1970.

Allen Classic Series edition 2000

British Library Cataloguing in Publication Data
A catalogue record for this book is available from the British Library

ISBN 0-85131-759-6

Published in Great Britain in 2000 by
J. A. Allen & Company Limited,
1 Lower Grosvenor Place, Buckingham Palace Road,
London SW1W 0EL

Printed by Dah Hua International Printing Press Co. Ltd., Hong Kong
Designed by Nancy Lawrence

FOREWORD

More than two and a quarter centuries have passed since the Duke of Newcastle's *A General System of Horsemanship,* which is reproduced in facsimile in the following pages, last appeared in print. This is a curious fate to have been suffered by a work long cherished by bibliophiles for the excellence of its typography and the quality of its illustrations, a work esteemed by countless generations of horsemen and revered by such masters as La Guérinière, Comte d'Aure and Steinbrecht, and a landmark of equestrian literature susceptible to description even within the past decade as "still the only really outstanding work on the subject written by an Englishman.[1]"

The *General System's* present oblivion can be attributed primarily, of course, to the substantial evolution of equestrian theory and practice which has occurred since Newcastle's time. Its eclipse is probably also partly due, however, to the rather disparaging treatment Newcastle has received from the pens of various historians and commentators on the history of equitation, especially those of the nineteenth century. The former have delighted in ridiculing his personal vanity and unshakeable loyalty to the Royalist cause, while the latter have accused him of relying far too heavily on force and even cruelty as training methods. Admittedly it is not difficult to find passages which appear to support these charges in some degree. But surely it is necessary to largely ignore both the context of Newcastle's own life and times, and the major thrust of his writings about horsemanship, in order to endorse them fully.

Indeed, one is tempted to believe that Newcastle's most scathing detractors have often been content to accept and repeat the opinions and citations of others without troubling to evaluate his works for themselves. This may be due, in turn, to the increasing difficulty of locating and gaining access to copies of the rare original editions, locked away in rare book rooms as they so often are. In any case, the present writer must confess also to having parroted second-hand views of Newcastle's significance for some time before the occasion finally presented itself for him to examine the works personally. To his astonishment, what then seemed remarkable was not the extent to which Newcastle's ideas in fact proved invalid, primitive or cruel, but quite the opposite: it was the degree to which Newcastle had divined, three hundred-odd years ago, principles of training sound enough to have served as the foundation for so much subsequent progress in the art, and the vigor and wit of his elaboration of them.

It is hoped that the present facsimile of the *General System,* by affording today's riders and students of equestrian literature easier access to the full context of Newcastle's thought, will finally enable them to judge for themselves his proper place in the history of equitation.

[1] R. S. Toole-Stott, *Circus and Allied Arts: A World Bibliography,* Derby, 1960. Vol. II p. 87. This excellent work includes a comprehensive selection of works on equitation, including careful collations of the various editions of Newcastle's works.

FOREWORD

The author of *A General System of Horsemanship,* William Cavendish (1593-1676), the earl, marquis and duke of Newcastle, was one of the most accomplished men of his era and a figure of considerable historical importance. A nobleman of great wealth—his grandfather had been treasurer to both Henry VIII and Edward VI—he was knighted while still in his teens, and educated at Cambridge. Though perhaps better suited by temperament to action than to scholarship, Newcastle was a cultivated man with broad humanistic interests; he enjoyed music, poetry and painting as well as martial sports, and gave both friendship and patronage to such men as Descartes, Hobbes, Jonson and Dryden. He himself published both plays and poetry. An outspoken man with a shrewd wit and a gift for pungent expression, Newcastle was seldom obliged or inclined to call a spade anything but a spade, and his reluctance to temper his opinions with conventional pleasantries must have irked many during his life, as indeed it has seemed to do ever since.

In 1638 Newcastle was appointed governor to the young Prince of Wales, afterwards Charles II, and the following year he was named a privy counselor to Charles I. When the Scottish insurrections that later evolved into the Cromwellian rebellion first erupted in 1642, Newcastle mustered forces to suppress them, largely at his own very considerable expense, and he was ultimately appointed Commander in Chief of Charles' Northern Army. Initially he was skillful and successful in this role, but the reversals at Winceby in 1643 and Marston Moor the following year clearly foreshadowed the eventual fate of the monarchy, and in July of 1644 he was obliged to flee to the Continent.

For several years he endeavored, unsuccessfully, to obtain support for his beleaguered king from foreign courts,but the establishment of the protectorate and the execution of Charles I finally put an end to these activities. Banished from England, his estates confiscated, Newcastle retired to private life in Belgium where he rented from Rubens' widow the painter's house in Antwerp.

Today it seems almost *de rigeur* for defeated generals to occupy their declining years by writing memoirs, in which they are finally enabled to deliver to their enemies with the pen what they could not with the sword. How strikingly different was the diversion Newcastle chose for his own years of exile: the training of dressage horses, and the writing of a book about his methods. Fortunately, his second wife had considerable literary talents and was quite prepared to settle with her husband's enemies, as her biography of him attests.[2] She also touched upon his riding activities:

"My Lord lived there [in Antwerp] with as much content as a man of his condition could do," she wrote, "and his chief pastime and divertisement consisted in the manege of . . . horses . . . in which he took so much delight and pleasure, that though he was then in distress for money, yet he would sooner have tried all other ways than parted with any of them; for I have heard him say that good horses are so rare as not to be valued for money, and that he who would buy him out of his pleasure (meaning his horses) must pay dear for it . . ."

The book that was the fruit of these equestrian pursuits represents something quite remarkable, hardly to be compared to the typical treatise of the retired riding master, no matter how expert—it constitutes nothing less than a labor of love by one of the ablest minds of its age at the height of its powers, applied, through a stroke of fate, to the problems of the horseman instead of weightier matters of politics, war or diplomacy. The splendid production Newcastle lavished upon his book testifies eloquently to the importance he placed upon his equestrian activities and his supreme confidence in the eventual restoration of the monarchy, as well as reflecting very favorably (considering

[2] Margaret, Duchess of Newcastle (1625-73) was a maid of honor to Henrietta Maria, queen consort to Charles I, when the widowed duke married her in Paris in 1645. Her biography of him, *The Life of William Cavendish, Duke of Newcastle,* was published in London in 1667.

his straitened circumstances at the time) on his relations with his creditors.[3]

With the restoration of the monarchy and the accession of Charles II to the throne in 1660, Newcastle was able to return to England. His estates had suffered severely during his sixteen years of exile, but most were restored to him. He became a privy counselor to Charles II, his former ward and riding pupil, and he was created duke in 1665, but his prime of life was past, and he had little influence at court. He continued to devote himself both to riding and to writing, publishing a second volume on horsemanship in 1667, but failing health finally obliged him to give up even his own horses. He died in 1676 at the age of eighty-three, having survived his wife by three years, and was buried beside her in Westminster Abbey.

The *General System* was first published in a French translation with the title *La Méthode Nouvelle et Invention Extraordinaire de Dresser Les Chevaux* in Antwerp towards the end of Newcastle's exile there.[4] Inspired no doubt by the elegant volumes on riding published thirty years earlier for Antoine de Pluvinel (1555-1620),[5] the Ecuyer to Louis XIII of France, it was opulently produced and sumptuously illustrated with 43 double-page plates after Abraham van Diepenbeke, a pupil of Rubens.

The first printing cannot have been very large, and Brunet[6] relates that part of it was destroyed by a fire in the booksellers' shop. Many of the copies that survive today apparently were presentation copies given by the author to personal friends in England and abroad, and it is unlikely that much of the first edition ever found its way into what might be considered normal channels of distribution. It was probably in order to rectify this situation that the Duke published his second book,[7] this time in English, after his return from exile. Its title—*A New Method and Extraordinary Invention to Dress Horses*—was a literal translation of that of the earlier book, and the general scope was similar. In detail, however, the text differs substantially. "This is neither a translation of the former [book] nor an absolute necessary addition to it," wrote the Duke in his preface, "and [it] may be of use without the other as the other has been hitherto and still is without this; but both together will questionless do best."

The *New Method* was handsomely printed in imperial folio, but contained no illustrations at all. This circumstance no doubt lent credence to the belief that the original plates for *La Methode Nouvelle* had been destroyed, as La Guérinière[8] stated, but fortunately this was not the case. The plates had remained in Newcastle's estate after his death, and his granddaughter, the Countess of Oxford, was able to furnish them intact to the London printer John Brindley for his reprint of *La Methode Nouvelle,* still with the French text, in 1737.

Brindley's reprint was a handsome one on splendid paper, the impressions of the plates even surpassing those of the original edition. Apparently the undertaking was a financial success, for six years later Brindley brought out the work again, this time in an English translation with the title *A General System of Horsemanship,* complete

[3] In fact, the printing alone cost £1,300, a sum which the Duke obliged to borrow from two friends.

[4] The engraved title of the work is dated 1658. On the printed title, however, the final "i" is invariably added in manuscript, suggesting that some copies may have been issued in 1657 before the engraved title was finished.

[5] The two works *La Maneige Royale,* Paris 1623, and *L'Instruction du Roy en L'Exercice de Monter à Cheval,* Paris 1625, were published posthumously by Pluvinel's disciple, René de Menou. Both are highly sought after today for their magnificent plates by Crispin de Pas, le vieux.

[6] J. C. Brunet, *Manuel du Libraire,* Paris, 1860-5.

[7] Published by Thomas Milbourn in London in 1667. Milbourn also published a rather unsatisfactory French translation (London, 1671 and 1674), which was reprinted in Brussels in 1694. A corrected translation was produced by Jacques de Solleysel for Clouzier's Paris edition of 1677. A German text was published in Nuremberg (1700 and 1764) and a Spanish translation was issued in Madrid in 1786-7.

[8] Francois Robichon de la Guérinière, *Ecole de Cavalerie,* Paris, 1733, Vol. 1, p. 60. La Guérinière was a warm admirer of Newcastle and both of his "two excellent books." Already in 1733 he noted that the first edition of *La Méthode* had "become so rare that one can scarcely find it."

with all of the engraved illustrations. It is this first English-language edition of 1743 that has been reproduced in present facsimile.

In preparing his English edition of 1743 Brindley went further than simply providing the full Newcastle text; he also appended an index, and a "Dictionary explaining the technical terms that belong to the stud, stable, manage and farriery, or whatever else relates to horses." The dictionary remains of interest, since it provides the modern reader with contemporaneous definitions of many French technical terms that appear in the Newcastle text, and it has been included in the present facsimile. Brindley also added, as a second volume, a translation of a then-recent French veterinary text, Gaspard de Saunier's *La Parfaite Connaissance des Chevaux*. This "farriery" was a rather derivative work even for its time and is of only moderate interest today.[9] It has not been retained in the present reprint.

Brindley's *General System* seems also to have met with success, for it was issued again five years later by the London printer C. Corbett. This 1748 edition was to be its last appearance in print up to the publication of the present facsimile.

W. C. STEINKRAUS

[9] Jean de Saunier (†c. 1700) was in charge of the royal stables of Louis XIV. His son Gaspard (1663-1748), Ecuyer at the University of Leyden, first published his treatise at the Hague in 1734. Though ostensibly its contents are largely drawn from his father's notes, the book owes more to the *Parfait Maréchal* of Newcastle's friend Jacques de Solleysel (1617-1680), which was first published in Paris in 1664 and reprinted more than thirty times.

TECHNICAL COMMENTARY

The name Newcastle has come down to us as one of the most illustrious in the entire history of equitation. To understand why, and to properly evaluate the true significance of his works, we must first relate them to the historical context within which they were written.

In ancient Greece the art of riding, like other arts, attained heights that were not to be equalled, much less surpassed, for centuries. Xenophon's *Hippike* (Treatise on the Horse), dating from the fourth century B.C., has been translated into countless languages and remains in print today. One has only to read it anew to verify how much of its value endures. With the fall of Greece, their art passed over to the ancient Romans, but there, alas, it languished or even retrogressed. Indeed, riding as an art almost disappeared during the "Dark Ages" that preceded the renascence that started in Italy during the Fifteenth Century.

This renascence, even when it came, was not quick to flower. At the beginning of the Seventeenth Century riding masters everywhere were still more or less groping in the dark, following the primitive and often cruel methods that had been advocated by Grisone and Blundeville,[10] which are of solely historical interest today. Then within a span of fifty years three stars appeared in the equestrian sky: Georg Englehard von Löhneysen (born c. 1550) in Germany, Antoine de Pluvinel (1555-1620) in France, and William Cavendish, Duke of Newcastle (1593-1676) in England. Among them these three masters reestablished a firm, rational foundation for the training of horses, and each of them, fortunately, left a written record of the methods he employed.

Although these methods differed somewhat in specific detail, all achieved the same general result: a horse systematically trained up to the level at which what we now term the airs of classical Haute Ecole could be obtained.

The first of these masters to publish a summary of his methods was also the oldest, Löhneysen, whose *Della Cavalleria* first appeared in Remlingen in 1609. His work is valuable not only for his discussion of riding, but also for the fascinating picture it affords of the whole range of equestrian activities of his time, the second volume being devoted entirely to carousels and breeding.

The second method to appear was that of the Ecuyer to the court of Louis XIII, Antoine de Pluvinel. Pluvinel's works deal primarily with the individual horse and rider, and his text, which is cast in the form of a dialogue between himself and his pupil the King, was prepared posthumously by his pupil René de Menou (1578-1651). The first published version, which appeared as *Le Maneige Royale* in 1623, employed a corrupt and apparently unauthorized text, and a corrected version appeared two years later, using the same superb plates, under the title *L'Instruction du Roy en l'Exercice de Monter à Cheval.*

It is the third of these masters, however, with whom we are primarily concerned, because of the lasting influence many of his innovations have exerted upon the development of the whole art of schooling horses. It is interesting to trace the course of this influence through succeeding generations down to the present day.

[10] The *Ordini di Cavalcare* of Frederico Grisone (fl.c.1525), first published at Naples in 1550, was the first serious book on riding as such to appear since Xenophon. An abridged paraphrase, considerably recast, was published by Thomas Blundeville as *The Arte of Ryding* in 1560? and later incorporated into his *The Fower Chiefyst Offices Belonging to Horsemanship,* 1565-6. These are generally considered to be the first works on horsemanship in the English language.

TECHNICAL COMMENTARY

The next great book to appear, François Robichon de la Guérinière's *Ecole de Cavalerie* of 1733 (which still forms the basis of the instruction given at the Spanish Riding School in Vienna), pays frequent tribute to its debts to Newcastle. Eleven years later the first of many editions appeared of the most popular riding book of the eighteenth century, the anonymous *Le Nouveau Newkastle,* actually the work of Claude Bourgelat, which undertook to clarify and condense Newcastle's principles, while praising them for having opened "a surer, easier and shorter route than all of those previously cleared for us."

A century later the great French masters d'Aure and Baucher were continuing to quote from Newcastle in their works, and the German equestrian genius Gustav Steinbrecht regarded Newcastle's book as the most important in the literature. He presented his own copiously annotated copy to his pupil Plinzner, along with the manuscript copy of his own book, *Gymnasium des Pferdes,* which Plinzner published in 1885, after his master's death. The *Gymnasium* (which unfortunately has never been translated into English) later formed the basis for the German Cavalry Manual of 1912, due largely to the efforts of Col. Heydebreck, a fervent adherent of Steinbrecht.

Heydebreck's own book, *Die Deutsche Dressurprüfung,* was published in 1929, and during the 1950s, when this writer was a member of the Dressage Committee of The Fédération Equestre Internationale, it served as the basis for revisions of the FEI's *Definitions of Paces and Movements for Dressage.* Thus after more than three hundred years Newcastle's influence still exists, even if in scarcely recognizable form, in the pedigree of modern competitive dressage.

Turning to a more concrete examination of the substance of Newcastle's methods themselves, we are first struck by the importance he attaches to the use of a special cavesson for the initial training of the young horse. This cavesson had three rings, the reins being attached to the outer two, and Newcastle employed it in conjunction with the curb reins in order to obtain the lateral effect of the reins. He advocated the use of the snaffle for the same purpose, as well as for raising the horse's head.

Along with the cavesson, Newcastle used running reins that were fixed to the saddle or girth and passed through the cavesson rings back to the rider's hands. These were later to become known as "Weyrother's running reins" after a Viennese master who popularized their use in the early nineteenth century. Through the use of these reins Newcastle obtained and kept a pronounced lateral flexion of the horse's neck, the nose pointing towards the point of the shoulder. This is the only position in which it is possible to flex the *whole* neck, rather than simply part of it.

Having thus established a flexed position of the head and neck, Newcastle proceeded to supple the horse's shoulders, and then its hindquarters. To supple the shoulders he worked the horse in diminishing circles using lateral aids, thus foreshadowing the *épaule en dedans,* or shoulder-in, which La Guérinière was to advocate almost a century later. Such exercises were performed at the walk, trot and canter as well as the rein back. To supple the quarters he worked first on straight lines, using diagonal aids to hold the quarters in (producing a sort of *travers*), and then worked on a small circle around a pillar both in this position and its opposite (i.e. a sort of *renvers*). The canter was developed gradually into a *terre-à-terre,* or two-beat canter.

Newcastle has often been criticized for this extreme flexion of the horse's head and neck, but it is obvious that he knew how to employ it advantageously and could achieve quick results by so doing. (Indeed, he claimed to be able to school a five-year-old in only three months' time.) In addition, though he speaks only of suppling the horse's shoulders and hindquarters, it is clear that he also succeeded in suppling the horse's back; and since the function of the back muscles always determines, in the final analysis, the horse's action, this is the prime criterion of all correct schooling. (When a horse contracts its back or contemplates bucking, one cure is to force it to continue straight forward while establishing a pronounced lateral flexion of the head and neck, thus isolating the neck from the back and inhibiting the horse's ability to contract it. This is obviously the effect Newcastle obtained, and judging from the rather heavy type of horse portrayed in the book, his mounts had backs that were difficult to supple!) Once the horse's back functions properly, everything else in training becomes comparatively easy.

Newcastle's subsequent principles are largely a matter of methodical routine. He gradually substitutes the action of the curb reins for that of the cavesson, then replaces the cavesson with a snaffle, and finally employs the curb alone, holding the reins in both hands at first, and later in only one—the left—in the classical way. The final schooling of the horse is concerned with the development of such airs of Haute Ecole as the Pirouette, Courbette, Ballotade and Capriole.

E. SCHMIT-JENSEN

HONI SOIT QVI MAL Y PENSE
HONI SOIT QVI MAL Y PENSE
HONI SOIT QVI MAL Y PENSE
LA METHODE NOUVELLE
&
Invention extraordinaire de dresser les Chevaux les
travailler selon la nature, et parfaire la nature par la
subtilité de l'art; la quelle n'a jamais été treuvée que.
Par
Le tres-noble, haut et tres-puissant
PRINCE GUILLAUME MARQUIS ET COMTE DE NEWCASTLE,
Viconte de Mansfield, Baron de Bolsover et Ogle, Seigneur de Cavendish,
Bothel et Hepwel; Pair D'Angleterre, Qui eut la charge et l'honneur d'estre
Gouverneur du Serenissime Prince de Galles en sa jeunesse et maintenant
ROY DE LA GRANDE BRETAGNE; Et davantage qui est Lieutenant
pour LE ROY de la Comté de Nottingham et la Forest de Sherwood;
Capitaine general en toutes provinces outre la Riviere de Trent et autres
endroits du Royaume d'Angleterre, Gentil-homme de la Chambre du
Lit du ROY; Conseiller d'Etat et Prive; Et Chevalier
de L'ordre tres-noble de la Iartiere etc.
Traduit de l'Anglois de l'Auteur en Francois par son Commandement
A ANVERS
Chez
IACQUES VAN MEURS
l'an M. DC. LVIII.

A

GENERAL SYSTEM

OF

HORSEMANSHIP

IN ALL IT'S

BRANCHES:

CONTAINING A

FAITHFUL TRANSLATION

Of that moſt noble and uſeful WORK of his Grace,

WILLIAM CAVENDISH, Duke of *Newcaſtle*,

ENTITLED,

The Manner of Feeding, Dreſſing, and Training of Horſes for the Great Saddle, and Fitting them for the Service of the Field in Time of War, or for the Exerciſe and Improvement of Gentlemen in the Academy at home: A Science peculiarly neceſſary throughout all *Europe*, and which has hitherto been ſo much neglected, or diſcouraged in *England*, that young Gentlemen have been obliged to have recourſe to foreign Nations for this Part of their Education.

WITH

All the original COPPER-PLATES, in Number forty-three, which were engrav'd by the beſt Foreign Maſters, under his GRACE's immediate Care and Inſpection, and which are explained in the different Leſſons.

And to give all the Improvements that may be,

This Work is ornamented with HEAD-PIECES and INITIAL LETTERS, properly adapted to the ſubſequent Chapters; and enlarged with an INDEX.

VOL. I.

LONDON:

Printed for J. BRINDLEY, Bookſeller to His Royal Highneſs the Prince of WALES, in *NewBond-ſtreet.*

M.DCC.XLIII.

To His GRACE

CHARLES

DUKE OF

Richmond, *Lenox*, and *Aubigny*,

Maſter of the Horſe to HIS MAJESTY, *&c.*

MAY IT PLEASE YOUR GRACE,

THE Dignity of the moſt noble Author, the great Reputation of the Work, and the Office YOUR GRACE enjoys under HIS MAJESTY, will, I hope, juſtify my laying at Your Feet, *The new Method of Dreſſing Horſes*, written by CAVENDISH *Duke* of NEWCASTLE.

After having been encouraged ſome Years ago, to publiſh a New Edition of that Nobleman's Works, then out of print in the original *French*, and ſupported in the Undertaking by the Right Honourable the COUNTESS of OXFORD, Heireſs of that Branch of the Illuſtrious Family of CAVENDISH, who had in Poſſeſſion all her Grandfather's Plates; I was ſoon convinced, that I ſhould farther oblige the Lovers of Horſemanſhip if I procured a *Tranſlation* of the Book, and printed it with the ſame Advantages as the *Original.*

This *Tranſlation*, MY LORD, with the Addition of ſeveral ornamental Prints, is what I now offer to YOUR GRACE as the *Firſt Volume* of *A Complete Syſtem of Horſemanſhip*, a Work that, I preſume to hope, will be found no leſs curious, uſeful, and ſatisfactory to the Reader, than it has been tedious and expenſive to the *Undertaker*.

YOUR GRACE as Maſter of the Horſe, has an undoubted Claim to the Patronage of this the *Fineſt Treatiſe* of Horſemanſhip extant; it is therefore I appear, MY LORD, as an humble Suppliant that you would, on this Occaſion, take me under Your Protection, and permit me to ſubſcribe myſelf, MY LORD,

Your GRACE'*s moſt obliged,*

moſt obedient, and

moſt Humble Servant,

JOHN BRINDLEY.

CONTENTS.

BOOK III.

Teaching how to dreſs a Horſe in all ſorts of Airs, by a new Method.

BOOK IV.

Which treats of all the Vices belonging to Horſes, and the ſureſt Ways to cure them.

The Epitome of Horsemanship.

Chap.

ADDITIONS.

After this Work of mine was all printed some very necessary Lessons came to my Mind, which I give you here in Form of Appendix, or Additions, and particularly recommend them to your Study. They treat of the Actions of a Horse's Legs; for without a perfect Knowledge of these, it is impossible for any Man to dress a Horse well, unless by mere Chance.

INTRODUCTION.

THE underſtanding of a Horſe is infinitely degraded below that of a Man by ſeveral, who notwithſtanding, by their actions, ſhew, that they believe the Horſe to be the more intelligent of the two. And indeed, a boy is a long time before he knows his alphabet, longer before he has learn'd to ſpell, and perhaps ſeveral years before he can read diſtinctly: and yet there are ſome people, who, as ſoon as they have got upon a young horſe, entirely undreſſed or untaught, fancy, that by beating and ſpurring they will make him a dreſs'd horſe in one morning only. I would fain aſk ſuch ſtupid people, whether, by beating a boy, they could teach him to read, without firſt ſhewing him his alphabet? Sure, they would beat the boy to death, before they would make him read. Don't then expect more underſtanding from a horſe than a man, ſince the horſe is dreſs'd in the ſame manner that children are taught to read. The horſe is taught firſt to know, and then by frequent repetition to convert that knowledge into habit. It is in like manner in what men learn: for example, a boy is a long time before he can play perfectly on the lute; but when once he is become perfect, his fingers move without his thinking on every note, or every point. There is juſt as much to be ſaid for a managed horſe. It is true, that the hand and the heels are all that is required to make a perfect horſe; but there are other things requir'd to make him perfectly obedient to the hand and heels.

It might as well be ſaid, that to be a good ſcholar one needs only underſtand Latin, Greek, and Hebrew, and know how to make uſe of thoſe languages;

guages; and, to play upon the lute, to preſs with one hand, and touch the ſtrings with the other: but a great deal more is requir'd before one becomes a good ſcholar, a dextrous player on the lute, or an able horſeman.

There are but two things that can make an accompliſh'd horſe, *viz.* the hope of reward, or the fear of puniſhment, which all the world are influenc'd by; and, as far as we know, God has no other means of exciting his people to virtue, but by the largeneſs of his infinite rewards, and the terror of the pains that are prepar'd for their crimes.

A horſe muſt be wrought upon more by proper and frequent leſſons, than by the heels, that he may know, and even think upon what he ought to do. If he does not think (as the famous philoſopher DES CARTES affirms of all beaſts) it would be impoſſible to teach him what he ſhould do. But by the hope of reward, and fear of puniſhment; when he has been rewarded or puniſhed, he thinks of it, and retains it in his memory (for memory is thought) and forms a judgment by what is paſt of what is to come (which again is thought;) inſomuch that he obeys his rider not only for fear of correction, but alſo in hopes of being cheriſh'd. But theſe are things ſo well known to a complete horſeman, that it is needleſs to ſay more on this ſubject.

Altho' horſes do not form their reaſonings from the ABC, which, as that admirable and moſt excellent philoſopher maſter HOBBS ſays, is no language, but the marks and repreſentation of things, he muſt notwithſtanding give me leave to think, that they draw their reaſonings from things themſelves. For inſtance; that I obſerve the clouds to darken, I ſee it lighten, or hear it thunder, and that I have been once wetted after having made theſe obſervations, and that a horſe at paſture has been likewiſe wetted: tho' he knows not theſe words, *dark*, *cloud*, *lightening*, *thunder*, both he and I will notwithſtanding take to our heels to ſhelter ourſelves from the rain under the trees. So far the one is as wiſe as the other. I am reaſoning by marks expreſs'd in language, and he is reaſoning from the preſence or abſence of things without theſe marks. The ſame judgment is to be made in a thouſand other things. It is true, the horſe cannot expreſs his reaſoning by a propoſition, not knowing the marks A, B, C; whence he has at leaſt this advantage, that he never errs as men do.

Many are of opinion, that the reaſon why men ſpeak, and not the beaſts, is owing to nothing elſe, but that the beaſts have not ſo much vain-glory as men, which produces language in them; and we ſee that the rarity of things among many *Indians* occaſions their uſing language very little; therefore the beaſts do not amuſe themſelves with bracelets, enamel'd rings, and innumerable baubles of that kind, but follow nature ſimply, without having, like men, their heads crouded with a multitude of thoughts and buſineſs, of which horſes are not ſolicitous. Some too are pleaſed to ſay, that horſes are void of underſtanding, becauſe men get the better of them: but when the horſe gets the better of the man, which frequently happens, is the man then void of underſtanding? Force ſubdues men, as well as beaſts. If the wiſeſt man in the world were taken by a ſavage people, and put to draw in a cart proportion'd to his ſtrength, and if he were beaten when he refuſed to do his duty, would not he draw juſt as a horſe does when he is threaten'd? And in like manner when he felt hunger, would he not be very uneaſy till he got victuals?

Some-

Somebody will perhaps ſay, that he is ſo proud he would ſooner die than draw a cart, and ſo full of reſolution, that he would rather throw himſelf down than ſtir. A horſe will do as much as all that, and will (I believe) bear beating ſomewhat longer than the mighty man that talks at this rate. We call the horſes of that temper *reſtive*, and the men *obſtinate*, 'tis all one.

Many men are too ſtrong for one horſe, and many wild horſes a little too untractable for one man. One perſon can drive ſeveral horſes before him, but it muſt be ſuch as are bred to it, and not ſeveral horſes that are wild in a wood. I have in like manner ſeen a few men drive two thouſand priſoners before them. The learned will hardly be brought to allow any degree of underſtanding to horſes; they only allow them a certain *inſtinct*, which no one can underſtand; ſo jealous are the ſchoolmen of their rational empire.

If a man was locked up from his birth in a dungeon till the age of twenty, and afterwards let out, we ſhould ſee that he would be leſs rational than a great many beaſts that are bred and diſciplin'd.

What makes ſcholaſticks degrade horſes ſo much, proceeds (I believe) from nothing elſe, but the ſmall knowledge they have of them, and from a perſuaſion that they themſelves know every thing. They fancy they talk pertinently about them, whereas they know no more than they learn by riding a hackney-horſe from the Univerſity to LONDON, and back again. If they ſtudied them as horſemen do, they would talk otherwiſe: for example, if a man has loſt his way in a dark winter's night, let him leave the horſe to himſelf, and the horſe will find the way to the place whither he ſhould go; whereas a man, tho' ſober, would ſpoil his horſe, and not be able to compaſs his journey. This is fact, for I have been in the ſame circumſtances; and I believe I ſhould have loſt my way, had it not been for my horſe. As for men of letters, tho' they ſtudy, they don't ſtudy horſemanſhip, but their ſtudies turn to better account, by procuring themſelves to rule over the reſt of mankind, till ſuch time as they are ſubdued by the ſword; wherefore it is not ſurprizing, if they be ſomewhat miſtaken in what is not their profeſſion, and which they do not ſtudy; nay, what is more, have not the leaſt knowledge of. This puts me in mind of what the great and excellent doctor EARLE ſays in his characters, that a ſcholar and a horſe are very troubleſome to one another; and ſo I leave them, without giving them or myſelf any farther trouble.

All that I have ſaid hitherto is only to ſhew, that a horſe's reaſon is to be wrought upon; towards which this book upon Horſemanſhip is very much to the purpoſe, and may ſuffice for the preſent. As for the paſſions, a horſe knows as much of ours, as we do of his; becauſe we know perfectly the paſſions of one another; as love, hatred, thirſt of revenge, envy, *&c.*

I have ſeen very few paſſionate horſemen get the better of a horſe by their anger; on the contrary, I have ſeen the horſe always get the better of them: and ſince the weakeſt underſtanding is always the moſt paſſionate, it is probable that the horſe will always outdo the man. In this act there ſhould always be a man and a beaſt, and not two beaſts. Indeed, a good horſeman ought never to put himſelf in a paſſion with his horſe, but chaſtiſe him like a kind of divinity ſuperior to him. If the horſeman ſpurs his horſe rudely, the horſe will anſwer in the ſame manner, by flinging maliciouſly. Don't we ſee men in play give each other blows without being angry with one another? but when they

are

are in earneſt, the leaſt jeſting occaſions a duel. It is juſt the ſame with a horſe; if the rider be angry with him he will be malicious, but otherwiſe will take all in good part, and never be offended: ſo that patience is one means of dreſſing a horſe. It is true, that patience without knowledge will never do, as knowledge will ſeldom do without patience: you muſt therefore treat him gently, and not exert your full power; but the thing is difficult; for if he takes it into his head to rebell, you muſt either let him maſter you, or elſe venture a bold ſtroke to reduce him. If you let him maſter you, you have done with him; if he ſubmits, you muſt alight that moment and cheriſh him. If he does not yield, you had better ſtay till next morning, than ſpoil him. Reduce him by degrees, mixing gentleneſs with helps and corrections. From hence you will learn how to fit a horſe either for uſe or pleaſure.

Some wagg perhaps will aſk, what is a horſe good for that can do nothing but dance and play tricks? People of that character (who from a wrong turn and for want of judgment) are good for nothing themſelves, and laugh at all the world, and at every thing; they therefore ſtrive to reduce every thing to their own way of thinking, that it may reſemble themſelves.

If theſe gentlemen will retrench every thing that ſerves them either for curioſity or pleaſure, and admit nothing but what is uſeful, they muſt make a hollow tree their houſe, and cloath themſelves with fig-leaves, feed upon acorns, and drink nothing but water, for nature needs no greater ſupport.

When a commonwealth is to be form'd, that men may live together in ſociety, thoſe who make feathers to put into their maſters hats, are as uſeful in the republick, for the maintenance of themſelves and families, and for the good of the community, as thoſe who ſell beef and mutton; for the tendency of the whole is to live by aiding one another, without wronging or offending any body. As for a managed horſe, which they call dancer and prauncer; if thoſe gentlemen were to fight a duel, or go to the wars, they would find their error; for theſe horſes perform a journey, as well as they do the high airs; and the long marches occaſionally make them ſoon forget thoſe airs, which are calculated merely for pleaſure; moreover, they are much fitter for galloping, trotting, wheeling, or any thing elſe which is neceſſary.

I preſume thoſe great wits (the *ſneering gentlemen)* will give Kings, Princes, and perſons of quality leave to love pleaſure-horſes, as being an exerciſe that is very noble, and that which makes them appear moſt graceful when they ſhew themſelves to their ſubjects, or at the head of an army, to animate it; ſo that the pleaſure in this caſe is as uſeful as any thing elſe, beſides the glory and ſatisfaction that attends it.

THE

THE

NEW METHOD

OF

DRESSING HORSES.

BOOK I.

CHAP. I.

Certain queſtions anſwered, of which the firſt is, In what time a Horſe may be dreſſed? The ſecond, Why a Horſe, that goes well upon a March, ſhould not perform the Terre-à-terre, Curvets, Demi-airs, Balotades, Croupades, and Caprioles?

S to the firſt queſtion, it is abſurd, for it is very difficult to ſay in what time a horſe may be dreſſed, becauſe that depends upon his age, ſtrength, ſpirit and diſpoſition; his agility, memory, ſagacity, good or bad temper; for there are horſes naturally as ſtupid or as obſtinate as men; and it is a difficult taſk to make a learned man of a fool. One can't form a judgment of theſe horſes, but by repeated trials; and it is impoſſible even for the beſt horſeman to make a ſolid judgment concerning them, becauſe a young horſe alters his diſpoſition as he grows older. It is therefore as impoſſible to

CHAP. I.

D answer

anſwer this queſtion, as it would be for the ableſt maſter in the world to ſay, that all the ſcholars in the univerſity will become learned at a certain time. There are ſome ſcholars, that have ſuch a diſpoſition to ſtudy, that they will learn more in a year, than others in all their life: ſome are eminent doctors, others are but ordinary ſcholars; and others are ſo dull, as not to be capable of underſtanding Latin. Wherefore I wiſh people would not require more capacity of a horſe than of a man, whom they ſtile rational.

As to the other queſtion, whereby it is demanded, Why ſhould not a horſe go Terre-à-terre, in Curvets, Demi-airs, Balotades, Croupades, and Capriols, ſince he goes a Travelling-pace well? I'd fain know, whether all thoſe, who make learning their profeſſion, be themſelves perfect in every ſcience. Some are excellent preachers, and not very learned; others are very learned, and but indifferent preachers: ſome good orators, others good logicians: ſome good hiſtorians, others good philoſophers: ſome good poets, others are profound in morality and claſſical learning: ſome in church-hiſtory and controverſy, others in law: ſome in phyſick, and others in mathematicks. Among the mathematicians, ſome are good aſtronomers or aſtrologers, or geometricians, or geographers; others arithmeticians; notwithſtanding which they are all learned men, and excellent in their different profeſſions. Moreover, there are different degrees: among divines, one is capable of being a biſhop; another is hardly fit to be a reader, or ſchool-maſter in a country pariſh-church. In like manner, ſome are good aſtronomers, and others are not capable of making an almanack or ſun-dial: ſome underſtand algebra perfectly, and others know nothing of addition and ſubſtraction. Some are very learned in the law, whilſt others are not fit to be clerks to a country-attorney; and yet they would have horſes excell in every branch of the Manege, which is certainly a very unreaſonable expectation.

But to give an example likewiſe among muſicians, who all profeſs the ſame art: Perhaps it may be aſked of one who plays perfectly on the fiddle, or the viol, if he can play as well on the lute? (By the by, ſome are admirable players upon the fiddle, while others can hardly thrum a reel at a country-wake) or the harp, the organ, or on all other muſical inſtruments, or if he be a good ſinger? Would not this be very abſurd, ſince it requires a man's whole lifetime to make himſelf perfect in any one of thoſe branches? Once more then, do not require more of a horſe than of a man. Again, for example among painters, ſome draw to the life in oil-colours, and at full length; others draw to the life in water-colours and in miniature. Some have a genius for hiſtory-painting, others for beaſts, others for birds; ſome for painting the dead, others the living; ſome flowers, others fruit; ſome battles, ſome naked figures, others figures with drapery; ſome ſea-pieces and ſhips, others landſkips; and there are ſome who can unite all theſe pieces into a landſkip. Notwithſtanding, all theſe painters may be excellent in their different branches, and famous to poſterity. There are painters likewiſe, who can paint nothing elſe but doors and windows, or coach-wheels. It is juſt the ſame with horſes; and tho' a horſe may go a very good Travelling-pace, he is not fit for the army unleſs he knows more. If another goes a good Terre-à-terre, it's ſufficient; and ſo it is if he goes well in Curvets, or Demi-airs, or Balotades, Croupades, or Capriols. When he goes well in any one of the three laſt airs, he is eſteemed

a good

a good horſe, and bears a great price, and ought to be as much valued in his kind, as a learned man in his particular ſcience, or as a muſician for the inſtrument he excells in, or for his voice, or as any painter in his kind: wherefore whoever requires more of a horſe than of a man, thereby expoſes his own ignorance. All thoſe that go to a ball-room, don't dance equally well: ſome dance high, others low; ſome nimbly and gracefully, others heavily and aukwardly. In like manner, horſes perform according to their different genius and diſpoſition. As every particular man makes a part of mankind, ſo every horſe compoſes a part of his ſpecies; and truly, every particular air among horſes may be compared to every particular trade among men. Would it not be ridiculous, if one ſhould ſay, that man is a good taylor, and another ſhould reply, Yes, but he cannot make ſhoes, nor dance the ropes? The ſame may be ſaid of horſes airs, for they are as ſo many particular trades amongſt men. Altho' a horſe may perform two ſorts of airs pretty well, he poſſibly may not perform a third. Thus a man may profeſs to be of two or three different trades, but not ſo as to excell in every one; beſides, a horſe can never be put to any thing, unleſs nature has deſign'd him for it, any more than a man can undertake to be maſter of a trade for which he is not naturally qualified. Thoſe gentlemen, who aſk theſe fooliſh queſtions, are ſometimes led to it by ignorance, but for the moſt part it proceeds from a jealouſy, and envy they bear to the horſeman, and to the horſe for the rider's ſake, whom they would leſſen and bring into contempt; for having but little merit themſelves, they are not able to eclipſe by their actions the reputation of a man of worth, and ſo they have reſource to detraction, and by their malicious inſinuations endeavour to tarniſh the brighteſt virtues. But we have ſaid enough on this head with too much truth, tho' with little eloquence.

Many horſes, naturally good, fall into the hands of bad maſters, who ruin them; and many bad horſes are improved by good maſters, from whom ſome benefit will always ariſe. Tho' art ſhould always follow the dictates of nature, and never thwart her, ſince ſhe is miſtreſs of the world, and ought to be obey'd. I ſpeak with regard to the Manege, and ſuch like, without concerning myſelf with theological myſteries, but only with horſemanſhip. To proceed: there are ſome who ſay, this is a good horſe, and that is a jade; in which they are much miſtaken, for there is no ſuch thing in the world like to what they call a jade: it is altogether the ignorance of the horſeman that makes jades, and not nature; wherefore if the horſeman ſtudies nature, and the diſpoſitions of his horſes, he would know better how to appropriate them to the uſes for which they were created, and conſequently they would become good horſes. For example, to begin with the Manege:

If the horſe is fit to go a Travelling-pace, let him do it; if he is naturally inclined to make Curvets, he muſt be put to it; and ſo of the Demi-airs, Paſſadoes, Terra-à-terre, Croupades, Balotades, and Capriols. If he be not fit for any of theſe, put him to run the ring: if he be not cut out for that, uſe him as a drudge to go of errands. If none of theſe ſuit him, he will perhaps be good for racing, hunting, or travelling, or for the portmanteau, for burdens, or for coach or cart; or, in ſhort, he may be fit to turn the mill, or ſome ſuch uſe as that: ſo that it is the fault of the horſeman, and not of the horſe, if he paſſes for a jade; for really there is no horſe but what is fit for ſome

ſome uſe or other. If princes were as induſtrious to know the capacities of men for the different truſts they put in them, as good horſemen are to employ each horſe in that which nature deſign'd him for, kings would be better ſerv'd than they are; and we ſhould not ſee ſuch confuſion, as ſurpaſſes that of Babel, happen in ſtates through the incapacity of perſons entruſted. He that is qualified to be a biſhop, is not fit to command an army; nor he that is fit to be a ſecretary of ſtate, to be keeper of the ſeals; becauſe the conſcience of a ſecretary of ſtate might be ſomewhat too large for a keeper of the ſeals, who is entruſted with the conſcience of the king, and the commonwealth. Which ſhews what diſorder there is in all things when they are miſplaced. Would it not be abſurd to require of a taylor to make boots, or of a ſhoe-maker to make breeches? But leaving kings to chuſe their officers as they pleaſe, let us follow nature in what concerns horſes.

If a horſe be tractable, and has ſpirits and vigour, a quick diſpoſition, judgment, and memory, and without faults, he may be dreſs'd in three months: the practice muſt make him perfect, even as it does mankind in every thing. One thing I can venture to affirm, that in what time ſoever another dreſſes a horſe, and renders him perfect by all his care, whether tractable or vicious, the method I here propoſe will perfect him in leſs than half the time; nay, he ſhall go better, and more juſt and perfect, which is what I have ſeen few horſes do, that have been dreſſed by others.

CHAP. II.

A reproof to maſters who continually beat and abuſe their ſcholars, and always make uſe of the whip.

SOME maſters are ſo paſſionate, or at leaſt ſeem to be ſo, that they are always beating their ſcholars with the ſwitch or long ſtaff. I have even heard ſay, that ſome fill their pockets full of ſtones to throw at them. If they forbear thoſe vile practices, they abuſe their ſcholars all the while they are on horſe-back with moſt unbecoming language, ſuch as--*Poor fellow!--Your humble ſervant, ſir!---Ah the blockhead! he ſits his horſe like a portmanteau-----Simpleton!--turn your hand---help with your legs----Spur----Hold up----Ah the the devil--what a beaſt there is!*---Some make uſe of much worſe language than this, and that in a haughty and imperious manner, thinking to paſs for great and able maſters, by thus ſhewing their authority; whereas they expoſe their own indiſcretion and folly by giving themſelves ſuch inſolent airs. Such behaviour is very unbecoming gentlemen, who are ſuch by their profeſſion; beſides, it alienates the affections of their ſcholars, and tends to bring the maſter into contempt, by inſpiring them with ſentiments of revenge rather than confidence. Now without confidence there can be neither pleaſure nor profit in ſuch a ſchool: moreover, it confounds both the horſe and the rider; for it is impoſſible even for a good horſeman, though mounted on a well-managed horſe, to keep time with as much exactneſs and quickneſs as the maſter's tongue requires. What then can be expected of ſcholars? It may likewiſe happen, that the horſe is not thoroughly taught, and if the maſter himſelf were upon his back, perhaps he might not make a better figure; wherefore the maſter

maſter, in honour to his profeſſion, ſhould (gentleman-like) be courteous, and behave with gravity and modeſty, but yet with authority; and inſtruct his ſcholar what he ſhould do before he moves his horſe. After he has wrought him ſufficiently, order him to ſtop, and then tell him in private the faults he has committed, without reproaching him openly before the company; afterwards making him try again, repeating frequently what he has ſaid to him: for a ſcholar can't be a maſter in one day, no more than a colt can be a complete horſe within the ſame time. Firſt of all then teach your ſcholar what he ſhould do, repeating it often to him in a mild manner, or he will never learn. As to the whip, it is often-times of ſervice, but I wiſh it were more ſparingly uſed. For the too frequent uſe of it is the cauſe why a horſe will not go without it: beſides, it is a very diſagreeable ſight, to ſee two men about a horſe when he is a riding, and that a riding-maſter (like a carr-man) ſhould continually have the trouble of driving his horſe. I ſay then, I would have it uſed only in caſe of neceſſity, and never otherwiſe; for it is an unbecoming thing, that a man ſhould not be able to mount his horſe unleſs another helps him with his whip; beſides, the thing is ſcandalous, unleſs it be to make him go in a cart; but in that caſe it is proper for a carter.

When a man is in the wars, or obliged to fight on horſeback, muſt he have another to whip his horſe? No ſure, that would be ridiculous. I ſay then, I am for making uſe of it in caſes of neceſſity only, otherwiſe I would have it baniſh'd out of the Manege; the rather, becauſe a horſe that requires continual whipping is unfit for that exerciſe. If the hand and heels be not ſufficient, it is either the horſeman's fault, or elſe the horſe is not fit for that purpoſe; in which caſe condemn both horſe and whip to the cart. I muſt farther add, the whip is become now-a-days very odious in the Manege and the Academies, becauſe the maſter does not think himſelf ſuch if he has it not continually in his hand; and when any Prince or Nobleman comes to ſee his Manege, he is ſure to find him *Whip in hand*, which, as he fancies, is the moſt becoming air he can aſſume, whereas it is the moſt ridiculous; wherefore never uſe it when it can be avoided. It is very proper ſometimes behind a horſe, when he is between the pillars, provided you quit it afterwards; or when a horſe retains his ſtrength and is lazy; but when he is brought into ſubjection, leave it off, and take a ſwitch, which is the moſt becoming thing a horſeman can hold in his hand, whether on foot or horſeback.

CHAP. III.

Of the different Colour and Marks of Horſes.

SEveral horſemen have blotted more paper to demonſtrate their Natural Philoſophy, than their art in Horſemanſhip, endeavouring to diſcover the conſtitution and particular diſpoſition of horſes by their marks and colour, and which of the four elements enters chiefly into their compoſition, whether it be earth, water, air, or fire. Some philoſophers deny the exiſtence of elementary fire in this ſublunary globe, in which caſe there will be only three elements remaining: others ſay, that the whole world is only matter put into motion, therefore motion performs all. Antient philoſophers maintain, that we are preferved alive by means of the four elements compounded together; but as to my own part, I believe we fubfift by eating and drinking. Chymifts fay, that all matter is compofed of falt, fulphur and mercury; but my bufinefs is to treat only of Horfes, and not of Natural Philofophy; for I find by long experience, that their rules are as falfe as the predictions of the weather in an almanack, which in one year's revolution is difcover'd to be as falfe as true. But fuppofe I fhould take the oppofite fide of the queftion, one will prove as true as the other. Therefore thefe are only trifling and chimerical conjectures. From whence I conclude, that a horfeman ought to mount a horfe often, by which means he will be able to form a better judgment, than any of thofe who philofophize upon his colour, or by the elements, fince that is only a piece of empiricifm or quackery.

The marks of horfes, let them be in what manner you pleafe, are only fo many abfurdities, there being only four good marks and feven bad ones in a horfe that has white feet. The firft is, that of his having the off-foot before white and found; the fecond good mark is, his having his near hind-leg white, &c. But all this feems to be a kind of conjuration or forcery to me. For fhould thefe marks happen to be accidentally true, the caufe does not fo much proceed from the colour of the foot, as from the quantity of fpirits in the horfe's nature. Therefore the beft method to judge of a horfe is to ride and prove him often, before a proper opinion can be given of his perfections; fince the beft horfeman in the world may be deceiv'd when another perfon mounts a horfe, and he may be deceived even when he mounts a horfe himfelf, particularly when he is young, fince his fpirits are liable to alter in proportion to his age, as it happens in the human fpecies, only with this exception, that a horfe fooner arrives to perfection, with regard to his fize, than a mare.

But let us confider a little wherein the beft marks confift, or at leaft the greateft variety of the colours. For we ought to be careful of the colour of the ftallion's hair, if we aim at conveying a good one to thofe of the ftud. Men have different opinions with regard to the colour of horfes, yet fome are more agreeable to the generality of mankind; for example, the light bay, provided the horfe has a black mane and tail, a lift upon his back, black legg'd, with a ftar upon his forehead; others are white legged, but this fhould not be too high. The black ought to be marked like the bay; the chefnut with white upon the legs, and a ftar. A dark grey is the moft durable colour; tho' I have feen a mare with a forrel mane and tail, well marked in every other refpect, that has appear'd perfectly genteel; another with a forrel mane and white tail, and both equally good; but a pied horfe, which is properly black and white, is contrary to my tafte. I have feen many beautiful white horfes, with black eyes and noftrils. An afh-colour'd grey is not a bad colour. A grey of the colour of a fly is very beautiful, but few attain to it till they begin to be advanced in years. There are even fome iron-greys exceeding fine, tho' the colour is not extraordinary. The fallow is not a bad colour, provided the horfe's mane, tail, and feet are black. The colour of a horfe pleafes according to a gentleman's fancy, fince there are good and bad horfes of all marks and colours; therefore the only way of knowing them is by trial. Some have been pleafed to fay, that an ill colour'd horfe is never good; but, with fubmiffion to their judgment, it is very poffible to have a good horfe of a

bad

bad colour. But tho' it be indifferent as to the colour of a horſe's ſkin, I ſhould ever prefer one of the five firſt ſorts for a ſtallion, for which I gave you a reaſon before. And theſe are all the remarks I ſhall make with reſpect to the colour and marks of horſes.

CHAP. IV.

Of the Shape of a Horſe, and particularly of thoſe in Foreign Countries.

SOME authors, who have treated of the ſhape of horſes, have deſcribed them in ſuch a manner, as nature has not hitherto produced; becauſe they take and add together the moſt beautiful parts of horſes belonging to different nations, and by means of this compoſition frame a horſe according to their own fancies, and not according to nature. For Barbary, Turkiſh, Neapolitans, &c. are differently ſhaped; yet a horſe from each of theſe nations may be completely ſhaped, according to his kind; we may, however, diſtinguiſh from what country they come. I have been often aſk'd the queſtion, What nation produces the moſt beautiful horſe? To which I anſwer'd, that I could not decide it, till I knew for what purpoſe the horſe was intended, each breed being good and beautiful in its kind. Let us therefore examine into the qualities of horſes belonging to each nation, and enquire in particular what they excell in. I am not throughly acquainted with Turkiſh horſes; but they are of different breeds from the extent of the country, are generally tall, and exceeding beautiful, ſwift, ſtrong, and good winded, but ſeldom have a good mouth. I have often heard Neapolitan horſes commended, which I think they juſtly deſerve; but thoſe I have ſeen were ill ſhaped, though ſtrong and vigorous. I have ſeen Spaniſh horſes, and have had them in my own poſſeſſion, which were proper to be painted after, or fit for a king to mount on a publick occaſion; for they are not ſo tender as the Barbs, nor ſo ill-ſhaped as the Neapolitans, but between both. Genets have a lofty fine air, trot and gallop well, &c. but are ſeldom ſtrong; though, when they are well choſen, they bear a very good character. Fame ſtill adds ſomething more ſurpriſing, relating to the courage of theſe horſes, which is, that they have carried an officer ſafe from the field of battle, after their guts have been hanging on the ground, with the ſame courage and vigour as when he firſt mounted him. The beſt breed of horſes is in Andalouſia, eſpecially that of the king of Spain's at Cordova. With regard to Barbary horſes, I freely confeſs they are my favourites; which may proceed from my having ſeen more of thoſe, than of any other kind, and I allow 'em the preference as to ſhape, ſtrength, a natural genteel air and docility. Barbary horſes are ſaid never to grow old, becauſe they always retain their original natural ſtrength and vigour. I confeſs, that they have not ſo genteel a trot or gallop as the Genets; but no horſes in the world have a better movement in general, when they are well choſen and inſtructed. Tho' I have been informed in France, by an old officer of the army in Henry the fourth's time, that he had often ſeen a Barb beat down by the ſuperior ſtrength of a large Flanders horſe. I have experienced this difference between the bone of the leg of a Barbary horſe and one from Flanders, *viz.* that the cavity of the bone in one ſhall hardly admit of a ſtraw, whilſt you

may

may thruſt your finger into that of the other. Barbs, for the generality, are ſinewy, ſtrong, ſwift, and good winded; tho' we meet with one ſometimes that is dull and heavy. Mountain-Barbs are horſes of the beſt courage, and many of them wear the marks of wounds they have received from lions.

With reſpect to the Northren horſes, I have ſeen ſome beautiful in their kind, genteel in all ſorts of paces, and have excelled all others in leaping. Moreover they have a peculiar excellency in the motion of their fore-legs, which is the principal grace in the action of a horſe; but they differ from a Barb in one thing, which is, that they ſooner come to decay; and you will always find among them more horſes fit for the cart than the Manege.

Hence it appears how ridiculous it is to attempt the deſcription of a complete horſe. For provided a horſe carries his head well, has his neck well-proportioned, and is well ſhaped according to the country where he was bred, it is ſufficient; but a particular regard ought to be had to the ſoundneſs of his feet, otherwiſe the reſt of his beauties are of no value. If the paſterns of a horſe are ſtiff and long, he can never be active; if, on the contrary, they are lax and weak, he will, generally ſpeaking, be inactive; therefore his paſterns ought to be ſhort and flexible, ſince they are generally more active and ſtrong when formed in ſuch a manner.

It would be an endleſs work, to attempt the deſcription of horſes of a mix'd breed, ſince the reſult of ſuch mixture may produce both good and bad.

A ſhort horſe ſeems to be the moſt proper for the Manege, as we can compell him by art to contract himſelf, ſtop, or go backwards; whence it is evident, that a ſhort horſe is ſooner inſtructed in his paces than a longer: tho' I muſt take the liberty of obſerving, that I have ſeen ſome long horſes perform their exerciſe as well as the ſhort.

Many perſons have remarked, that a horſe heavy before, that is to ſay, one who is large-headed, thick-necked and ſhoulder'd, bears heavy upon the hand, eſpecially when he has not a large ſhare of ſpirits. But this is not the reaſon; for let him have the leaſt defect in his feet, legs, or ſhoulders, he muſt conſequently be heavy upon the hand, let his ſhape be ever ſo excellent.

Hence it appears, that an expert horſeman in ſuch a caſe cannot be ſo uſeful as a good farrier. Others ſay, that ſuch a horſe, tho' very ſound, muſt naturally be heavy upon the hand, and that a horſe differently framed will be light upon it; wherein I think they are much miſtaken, ſince I have ſeen horſes ſhaped like a bull before, that have been as eaſy upon the hand as thoſe of a more delicate ſhape. Whence it ſeems evident, that this does not proceed ſo much from the different make of the fore-part of the horſe, as from the inequality of ſtrength in his back and reins. For the principal art in horſemanſhip is to place a horſe well upon his haunches; and he that is ſtrong in his loins is the moſt capable of enduring the exerciſe of the academy; but a horſe with weak loins bears forward in order to relieve them. From whence I may conclude, that a horſe is heavy or light in hand, in proportion to the ſtrength of his loins. Methinks I hear ſome ignorant horſeman ſay, that the ſtronger a horſe is in his loins, the difficulty is ſo much the greater to place him properly upon his haunches. This may be really difficult to an unexpert rider, tho' not ſo to another more knowing than himſelf; ſince, in ſome horſes nature furniſhes us with a proper ſubject to work upon, and denies us the ſame aſſiſtance in others. Therefore, when you have a proper ſubject in hand to manage, the fault of the horſe entirely proceeds from the ignorance of the riding-maſter and his want of ſkill. Some horſes indeed are naturally apt to leap continually, in which caſe the rider ought to follow his natural diſpoſition; but he ought to put him upon his haunches notwithſtanding, otherwiſe he will never have a genteel and graceful air. Others conceit, that a horſe with a thick mane and tail is generally heavy and dull; but I have been maſter of ſome with ſuch marks, who were exceeding vigorous and active; whence I conclude, that a judgment cannot be ſooner formed from the ſhape of a horſe, than from his colour.

CHAP. V.

Fig. 6, 7, 8, 9, 10.

CHAP. V.

What kind of horſe is beſt for a Stallion, and in what manner he ought to be uſed. What Mares are the moſt proper, with the method of proceeding to procure a good breed.

THE beſt Stallion is a well-choſen Barb, or a beautiful Spaniſh horſe, well marked, that the ſame may remain in the breed. He had better have too much courage than too little, ſince the colt he produces will be apt to inherit the ſame imperfections in a greater degree. Therefore I ſhould think it abſolutely neceſſary to chooſe a ſtallion naturally well-diſpoſed in every reſpect, otherwiſe the breed will be the ſame, which I have often found by experience. A ſtallion of this kind is beſt both to produce a breed proper for ſervice or pleaſure. Some people pretend, that a Barb or a Genet produce too ſmall a breed, and give this reaſon for it, that nature is always in a declining ſtate. There is no fear of having too ſmall horſes in England, ſince the coolneſs and moiſture of the climate, and fatneſs of the land, rather produces horſes too large.

As to what is ſaid relating to the declining ſtate of a horſe, I take it to be falſe, ſince the ſame heat remains in the ſun at preſent, as when it was firſt created, and the earth is equally fruitful. If nature had been in a conſtant decay ever ſince the creation, we ſhould by this time have been no larger than ants. For which reaſon the Barbary and Spaniſh horſes are the beſt for ſtallions.

In the choice of Breeding-Mares, I would adviſe you to take either a well-ſhaped Spaniſh one, or a Neapolitan. But when theſe are not eaſily obtain'd, chooſe a beautiful Engliſh mare, which is as good as any, provided ſhe be of a good colour, and well marked, both which qualifications are neceſſary to produce a handſome breed. With regard to covering the mare, I diſapprove of its being in hand, or by confining the creature, ſince it is then rather a compulſion than a natural inclination; for every natural action of this kind ought to be perform'd with freedom and love, and not by violence or conſtraint. Moreover, I am no friend to aſtrological remarks in this caſe. The moon's aſpect, or that of any other celeſtial body, are equally abſurd in affairs of this kind; and it matters not whether the moon is increaſing or decreaſing, or whether any of the other planets are in conjunction or oppoſition; for horſes are not begot by aſtronomy, or by the almanack. Such obſervations are as ridiculous, as thoſe relating to the point from whence the wind blows, to produce a male or female colt; or that ridiculous practice of tying the left testicle to generate a male, and the right a female; or another of the same nature, which is, that of placing a cloth before the mare's face, of what colour you please, that she may conceive a colt of the same. This doctrine seems calculated only to amuse the credulous, and common sort of people, by endeavouring to make them believe there is some secret mystery couched under such remarks. Nature is exactly uniform in her operations, but particularly in that of generation; and we always find her so very circumspect in this action, that altho' she admits of copulation between two animals of a different species, yet the product is incapable of producing a creature of the same species. Therefore let us follow the laws of nature in the act of generation, since it is originally derived from her, and not from art.

Your stallion being well prepared and fed with good oats, beans, coarse bread, a little hay, and a large quantity of wheat straw, water him twice in a day, and breathe him gently to preserve his wind, but he must not be sweated; for should he not be in wind when he covers, he may chance to break it entirely. The reason why I advise that a horse should be well fed at this time, is, that altho' this action is pleasant in itself, it is laborious notwithstanding; and if he is not well nourished, he will deceive your mares, and generate none but weak colts; since, according to the old proverb, *Without meat and drink love grows cold.* Therefore feed him as well as you can, he will still be sufficiently lean. If he serves many mares, he will not last long, and his mane and tail will fall off to such a degree, that it will be difficult to restore him to his former strength the year following: he should therefore cover only a certain number of mares in proportion to his strength, but never exceed twenty in a season. The proper time in England is in the month of June, that your mares may foal the May following, when there is plenty of grass, for which reason they yield most milk at that time. You ought therefore at this season to put all your mares together into an inclosure well fenced, where there is plenty of grass during the time the stallion is with them, and they are hot: then let your stallion run with them, first taking off his hind-shoes, that he may not hurt the mares by a kick, leaving his fore-shoes on. Let him cover one mare twice in hand at first, to render him more gentle; then take off his bridle, and let him have the liberty of running among the rest, which will make him so familiar with them by degrees, that they will be fond of his caresses, so that no mare will be cover'd before she is inclined. When he has served them all, he will try them again one after the other, and cover all those that are willing to receive him. The horse is sensible that he has finished his performance, by the mare's refusal of his caresses, and then begins to kick against the fence that he may be gone: therefore it is proper to remove him at this time, and send your mares into a fresh pasture.

These are the prudent laws observ'd by nature; and I dare venture to affirm, that not one mare in twenty will fail, whilst half of those cover'd in hand will not prove with foal. A stallion will stay six or seven weeks with the mares, during which time he ought to be provided with a proper place to defend him from the heat of the sun, wherein there should be a manger stored with oats, pease, split beans and bread. Your stallion ought not to be under five, or more than fifteen years old; but this may be regulated according to his

his ſtrength, obſerving that your mares be not cover'd before they are three years old, nor after fifteen. The goodneſs of the mares and colts they produce will ſerve you for a guide in this caſe. A horſe may cover a mare of his own begetting, without hurting your ſtud; for there is no inceſt amongſt horſes, this being a privilege allowed them by nature. Moreover, they will produce finer colts when cover'd by a beautiful ſtallion, eſpecially by a good Barb. But you muſt never make uſe of a ſtallion of your breed, ſince he will be widely different from a real Barb; and if you continue to uſe them ſucceſſively, they will at length degenerate, and reſemble the horſes of the country where they are bred. The ſame thing may be ſaid of all other creatures in the world, and even of mankind; the climate, air, and land producing the ſame effect in all other animals. Therefore I would adviſe you not to make choice of a ſtallion of your own breed, but rather of a young Barb, or Spaniſh horſe, by which means you will be always maſter of a ſtud of fine horſes; but you muſt always take care to chooſe the moſt beautiful mares in your ſtud to breed from. By this means your ſtallion will be as jealous in his Seraglio as the Grand Seignor, and always furniſh you with a fine breed of horſes. It will be abſolutely neceſſary, whilſt the ſtallion runs amongſt the mares, that a man ſhould watch them night and day, to ſee how they are ſerved, and leſt another horſe ſhould be with them, or other mares with him, and to acquaint you with any accident that may happen. This is what I have to ſay relating to ſtallions and mares.

Fig. 11.

CHAP. VI.

What is the proper time to take a Colt from his Dam, and how he ſhould be managed afterwards.

YOU ought to build a lodge in the paſture-ground into which you remove your mares, as well as in all others where they feed, to defend them from the inclemencies of the weather; for there is no creature to which cold is more injurious than to horſes, neither will they endure much heat. Good ſtore of hay ought likewiſe to be provided for them againſt the winter. Several people recommend ſuckling of colts till they are one or two years old; but herein they are much miſtaken, ſince they become tender and ill-ſhaped by this method, and you loſe the fertility of your mares during that time. You ought therefore to take up your colts from their dams at the beginning of winter, when the weather begins to be cold, that is, between Michaelmas and Chriſtmas, putting both males and females into a clean warm ſtable provided with low racks and mangers. Always take care to keep your ſtable clean, and your colts well litter'd, leaving them looſe. They ought to be ſeldom handled, for fear of hurting them, or preventing their growth. They ought to be plentifully fed with good hay and bran, which, by making them drink freely, will render their bodies fat and plump. Feed them likewiſe with oats; for it is ridiculous to imagine, that oats will make them blind, or their teeth crooked. In fine weather walk them in the ſun-ſhine about your court, that it may comfort and cheriſh their ſpirits. Turn them to graſs towards the latter end of May into ſome paſture that will contain all your yearling colts, firſt providing a hovel or lodge to defend them from the heat of the ſun; the ſhape of it

you

BOOK I.

you ſhall ſee in the ſequel, it being left open on one ſide, that you may the better ſee how it is contrived; for it ought to be ſhut up by a large door, leſt they ſhould hurt themſelves. At the ſame ſeaſon next year take up your colts that are a year and half old, dreſs them, tie them up, and uſe them in the ſame manner as other horſes, to make them gentle and quiet. The ſummer following, when they are two years old, you may turn them out again into ſome good paſture, that is provided with a proper lodge, or otherwiſe keep them in the ſtable to make them fit to be mounted, which ought never to be done till they are above three years old; for by this practice they will be more able to endure fatigue. It matters not in what paſture they run, provided it be dry, and has a pond of water belonging to it. If they fill their bellies once in twenty four hours, it is ſufficient; and there is no neceſſity for a great variety of paſture, as rocky ground, mountainous, meadow, or fine graſs, provided you ſeparate the yearling colts from thoſe that are two years old, and thoſe of three from the reſt. I could feed a horſe very well in my own court; for what is the reaſon that the Barbs, Neapolitans, Turks, and Genets, are ſo ſleek and ſtrong, and of ſo delicate a ſhape, unleſs it proceeds from the dryneſs of their nouriſhment?

Therefore the ſecret of feeding horſes, in a cold climate, conſiſts only in keeping them warm during the winter, nouriſhing them with dry meat in that ſeaſon, and dry paſture in the ſummer. Take two colts equally beautiful, and deſcended from the ſame lineage; keep the one warm in the winter, and feed him with dry meat till he is three years old, and ſuffer the other to remain at graſs till he is of the ſame age, and I dare venture to affirm, that the legs of the former will be as beautiful, nervous, and pliant, as any Barb, or Spaniſh colt's whatſoever, whilſt the other ſhall have a coarſe head and neck, and be as ill ſhaped as a cart-horſe. Hence you may ſee the efficacy of a dry food and warm houſes for your ſtud.

As to your mare-colts, you may let them run abroad till they are three years old, becauſe they are not ſo ſubject to grow poor, eſpecially in the fore parts, as horſes are; but if you can in winter put your young mares into ſtables, as well as your horſes, it will be ſo much the better. I am afraid the charge will be too great for a private perſon, at leaſt if his ſtud be any thing conſiderable. I well know by my own experience, that this method of breeding horſes is the beſt; for I have tried all ways both with the males and females of every country. It is proper I ſhould adviſe you to back your young mares a year or two before you have them cover'd, or elſe they will grow ſo wild, they will be in danger of ſpoiling themſelves and their colts; but by this method they become ſo gentle, that neither the one nor the other will be afterwards in danger. This is the manner of managing your foals, your young horſes, and mares.

Fig. 12.

CHAP. VII.

Of the Saddle, Stirrups, Spurs, and Bridle.

THE ſaddle I uſe is ſo well made, that a man muſt ſit upon it with a good grace, whether he will or no; you have the faſhion and figure of it here, and alſo that of the ſtirrup and the ſpur. As to bridles, there are none like the ſimple canon for a young horſe; and for a horſe that you ride, a bridle

bridle *à la Pignatelle*, (made full and free, with reins *à la Conetable*) is the most proper. You have the figure of that alſo here annext.

It is neither a good ſaddle, nor good ſtirrups that make a complete horſe, any more than a good pair of ſpurs put upon the heels of an ignorant perſon. Neither is it a good bridle that breaks the horſe well. For if they were made tractable by this piece of iron put in their mouths, the bit-makers would be the beſt horſemen in the world. Thus if a book put into the hand of a boy would teach him to read without inſtructions, we ſhould have nothing to do but give give him a good and numerous library, to make him in a moment the moſt learned perſon in the univerſe. But it is in good leſſons, well applied to the nature, ſpirits, and ſtrength of every horſe, that the great and ſubtile ſcience of Horſemanſhip conſiſts, that ſcience that can manage a horſe with only a bit of wood in his mouth. The bridle, I confeſs, is of ſome uſe, tho' but little; art avails much more, as all your excellent riders well know; for I have managed a horſe with a halter only, and he went as well as with the bridle, of which I have many witneſſes in this city of Antwerp, who have ſeen the thing: I have alſo managed an Engliſh one with a ſcarf, and made him curvet and vault very juſtly; ſo that it is not the bridle, but the art of the rider, that renders the horſe tractable.

CHAP. VIII.

Of the Method of Breaking Colts.

IF the method I formerly preſcribed is made uſe of from the beginning, which is, to put him into the ſtable, and tie him up for two or three winters ſucceſſively, in order to make him tractable as other horſes, it will then not be difficult to back him; for by this means he will not be wanton, apt to lie down, or be guilty of any extravagant actions common to young horſes, and thereby endanger the rider. By this method you will avoid the trouble of working him upon ploughed lands, moraſſes, &c. before you mount him; by which exerciſe he is in danger of breaking his wind, or at leaſt of ſpoiling his genteel air. When you have made him tractable by theſe means, the firſt ſaddle you put upon him ſhould be quilted, or one made of chaff or ſtraw, well faſtened by a ſurcingle, that it may not hurt his back, but leave his ſhoulders liberty that he may trot freely, as every colt ſhould do. He ought not to be ſhod at all; but if he wear any ſhoes, they ought to be only *lunettes*, or half ſhoes upon his fore-feet, left he ſhould hurt himſelf by trotting briſkly. Nothing more ſhould be put upon his head than a halter, or caveſon, with reins to it of the ſame kind. Moreover, he ought to have nothing in his mouth; ſhould there be any thing in it, it ought only to be a ſmall piece of whip-cord, with a head-ſtall without reins, as this is an improper time to put a bit into his mouth. When he has been thus managed, the rider ought to mount himſelf upon a gentle horſe, and lead the colt behind him three or four days, till he follows the horſe freely. Then the maſter ought to mount him for two or three days ſucceſſively, and afterwards ſuffer him to go alone. But the rider muſt at this time take care to manage his head by degrees; and although he proves ſtubborn either as to his mouth or head, he

BOOK I. should by no means give way to it, but restrain him, and gradually gain his point, till he has placed his head in a proper posture, which he ought to keep thus, by working it downwards with his hand. Trot him upon large circles at first, holding the inward rein of the caveson tight, that he may not only keep within the circle, but have his haunches rather without than within it. In order to perform this, spur him gently with the leg on the inside the circle, which will not only render his shoulders pliant and easy, but make him a compleat horse, which requires some labour and pains. But above all things let me recommend this, not to stop him on a sudden, since such practice may occasion a violent pain in the reins of a young horse; therefore let him be gently stopped about five or six lengths, beginning with a trot, and stop him upon his walk. When you have backed and trotted him a small time, leave him at last as vigorous as you found him. When he has been a month exercised in this manner, then put a bit into his mouth, which should be a single curb with the branches *à la Conetable*. The first day you bridle him, let him be rubbed with a little honey, to make him the more quiet; then use him for a few days as you did before he wore the bridle. After this put the *gourmette* or curb upon him, which ought to be rather too long than too short, using him continually in the same manner, managing him with the caveson, and not with the bridle, so that he may be only just sensible of it: use him likewise sometimes to move gently backwards, and, when he seems to comply, caress him. During this time, which will require a month, or more, you must keep him trotting. After the expiration of two months, put his saddle on, and a caveson made according to my own invention, which I shall describe in its proper place. The main point is to manage a horse's head, and to give him a proper weight upon the hand; for it is very easy to manage his haunches. I have therefore been often surprized, that some horsemen should begin by managing the crouper or tail. If the head of a horse is well regulated, you may afterwards manage him as you please, provided his nature and strength will admit of it; for should you not secure his head, it is impossible ever to make him a compleat horse, since you have only your hands and heels to manage him, otherwise the most essential parts will fail you.

Fig. 13.

Hitherto I have succinctly and clearly shown my new method of breaking a colt, hoping you readily comprehend what I have said upon this subject; but the peculiar management of horses shall follow hereafter.

But before I begin the second book, I am willing to acquaint you, that there are a few other figures in this volume than those of my own, that of Captain MAZIN and my groom's. As to Captain MAZIN, I bred him from an infant, and he thoroughly understood the manner of dressing horses according to my new method, which he has imbibed from my instruction, as well as his own industry and long experience in the art of managing horses. From whence I may venture to affirm, there is not a more understanding horseman than himself. Tho' I have been always happy with regard to my servants, yet I must still confess, that I never found so much love, fidelity and honesty in any other: he constantly attended me in my adversity, both in the time of peace and war, and always with the same affection as if I had been in the greatest prosperity, notwithstanding the largeness of his family; which obliges me in gratitude to remember him.

THE

THE

NEW METHOD OF DRESSING HORSES.

BOOK II.

CHAP. I.

Of the true Seat and the necessary Actions of a good Horseman.

BEFORE a horseman mounts, he ought first to take care that all his horse's furniture be in order, which is soon done, without prying into every minute circumstance, to shew himself an affected connoisseur in the art. When he is once seated (for I take it for granted that every one knows how to mount a horse) he ought to sit upright upon the twist, and not upon the buttocks; though most people think they were made by nature to sit upon; however, it is not to be so on horseback. When he is thus placed upon his twist in the middle of the saddle, he ought to advance, as much as he can, towards the pommel, leaving a hand's breadth between his backside and the arch of the saddle, holding his legs perpendicular, as when he stands upon the ground, and his knees and thighs turned inwards towards the saddle, keeping

CHAP. I.

BOOK II.

keeping them as clofe as if they were glued to the faddle: for a horfeman has nothing elfe but this, together with the balance of his body, to keep himfelf on horfe-back. He ought to fix himfelf firm upon his ftirrups, with his heels a little lower than his toes, fo that the ends of his toes may pafs about half an inch beyond the ftirrup, or fomewhat more. He fhould keep his hams ftiff, having his legs neither too near, nor too far diftant from the horfe; that is to fay, they fhould not touch the horfe's fides, becaufe of the aids which fhall afterwards be explained. He ought to hold the reins in his left hand, feparating them with his little finger, holding the reft faft in his hand, having the thumb upon the reins, and his arm bent and clofe to his body, but in an eafy pofture. The bridle-hand ought to be held three inches above the pommel of the faddle, and two inches before it, that it may not hinder the working of the reins, which fhould be held ftrait over the horfe's neck. He fhould have a flender fwitch in his right hand, not too long, like a fifhing rod, nor too fhort, like a bodkin; but rather fhort than long, becaufe there are many ufeful aids with a fhort one, that a long one won't admit of. The handle of it ought to be a little beyond the hand, not only for the fake of careffing the horfe with it, but likewife to hold it the fafter. The right hand, that holds the fwitch, ought to advance a little before the bridle-hand, with the fmall end of the fwitch pointing towards the infide. The rider's breaft ought to be in fome meafure advanced, his countenance pleafant and gay, but without a laugh, pointing directly between the horfe's ears as he moves forward. I don't mean, that he fhould fix himfelf ftiff like a poft, or that he fhould fit upon a horfe like a ftatue; but, on the contrary, that he fhould be in a free and eafy pofition, as it is expreffed in dancing with a free air. Therefore I would have a Gentleman appear on horfeback without ftiffnefs or formality, which rather favours of the fcholar than the mafter; and I could never obferve fuch a formality, without conceiting the rider to look aukward and filly. A good feat is of fuch importance, as you will fee hereafter, that the regular movement of a horfe entirely depends upon it, which is preferable to any other affiftance; therefore let it not be defpifed. Moreover I dare venture to affirm, that he who does not fit genteely upon a horfe, will never be a good horfeman. As to the management of the bridle-reins and cavefon, I will teach you more concerning them in the following difcourfe than has been hitherto known.

Fig. 14.

CHAP. II.

Of the Movements of a Horfe in all his Natural Paces.

1. A Horfe, in Walking, has two of his feet in the air, and two upon the ground, which move otherways at the fame time, one fore and one hind-foot, which is the movement of a gentle trot.

2. The Trot; the action of his legs in this movement is two feet in the air, and two upon the ground, which he moves crofs-ways at the fame time; one fore and one hind-foot acrofs, which is the movement of the walk: for the movement of a horfe's legs is the fame in walking as in trotting, where he moves them crofs-ways, two in the air acrofs, and two upon the ground at the fame time; fo that thofe which were acrofs in the air at one time, are afterwards

afterwards in the ſame ſituation upon the ground, and ſo *vice verſa*. This is the real movement of a horſe's legs in trotting.

3. The Amble. A horſe in this action moves both legs on the ſame ſide; for example, he moves his two off-legs both before and behind at the ſame time, while thoſe of the near ſide are at a ſtand; and when thoſe two which were in motion before touch the ground, he moves the other ſide, *viz.* the fore and hind leg on the near ſide, and the off-legs are then at reſt. Hence a pacing horſe moves both legs on one ſide, and changes the ſide at each motion, having both legs on the ſame ſide in the air, and thoſe of the other ſide upon the ground at the ſame time, which motion is the perfect amble.

4. Galloping is a different movement; for in this pace a horſe can lead with which leg the rider pleaſes, but the leg on the ſame ſide muſt follow it; I mean when he gallops directly forward, and then this is a true gallop. But that the leading of the fore-leg may be rightly underſtood, which ought to be followed by the hind-leg of the ſame ſide, the leg moves in the following manner: for example, if the fore off-leg leads, it conſequently follows by ſuch leading, that the ſame fore-leg ought to be before the other fore-leg, and the hind-leg on the ſame ſide ought to follow, which hind-leg ought to be before the other hind-leg, which is the right gallop.

But in order to underſtand it the better, the motion in galloping is in this manner: the horſe raiſes his two-fore legs at the ſame time in the action I have deſcribed, which is one leg before the other, and when his fore-legs come down, before they touch the ground, they are immediately followed by thoſe behind; ſo that, as I have ſaid before, they are all in the air at the ſame time: for his hind-legs begin to move when the fore-legs begin to fall, by which the whole horſe is entirely in the air. How would it otherwiſe be poſſible, that a horſe in running ſhould leap twice his length, if the motion of the gallop was not a leap forwards? This deſcription is very juſt both with reſpect to the motion and poſture of a horſe's legs in galloping, which, though it be true, is not eaſily perceived in a gentle gallop, but very viſible in a ſwift one, where the motion is violent: I ſay, his four legs may then plainly appear to be in the air at the ſame time, running being no more than a quick gallop, the motion and poſture of a horſe's legs being entirely the ſame. It is however neceſſary to obſerve, that a horſe in a circular gallop ought to lead with his two legs within the volte, *viz.* his fore-leg and hind-leg within the circle.

5. Running. The motion of a horſe and the action of his legs are the ſame in running as in galloping, the different velocity of the motion only excepted; ſo that running may be properly called a ſwift gallop, and a gallop a ſlow running. This is the true movement in running. The trot is the foundation of a gallop; and the reaſon is, becauſe the trot being croſs-ways, and a gallop both legs on the ſame ſide, if you put a horſe upon a trot beyond the ſpeed of that pace, he is obliged when his off fore-leg is lifted up, to ſet down his near hind-leg ſo quickly, that it makes the hind-leg follow the fore-leg of the ſame ſide, which is a real gallop; and for this reaſon a trot is the foundation of a gallop.

A Gallop is the foundation of the Terre-à-terre, the motion of the horſe's legs being the ſame. He leads with the fore-leg within the volte, and the hind-leg on the ſame ſide follows. You keep him only a little more in hand in Terre-à-terre, that he may keep his time more regularly.

I could wiſh that Pacing was excluded the Manege, that action being only mixed and confuſed, by which a horſe moves both legs on the ſame ſide, and ſhifts them each movement; and this is as directly contrary to the Manege as is poſſible, if, from an amble, you would put a horſe to the gallop; for when he is upon a trot you may puſh him to a gallop, but being upon the amble you muſt ſtop him upon the hand before he can gallop.

I muſt here acquaint you with what is commonly ſpoken of, tho' little underſtood. It is ſaid that a horſe may gallop with the wrong leg before, which is impoſſible; for if the hind-leg follows the fore-leg on the ſame ſide, it is a real gallop; therefore it is rather the wrong leg behind. But let us explain what is meant by the wrong leg foremoſt. In the true gallop, the fore-leg that moves firſt ought to be followed by the hind one on the ſame ſide; and when a horſe puts down his two fore-legs, they are follow'd by the hind ones before they touch the ground; ſo that all four legs are in the air at the ſame time, and the horſe ſprings forward. What is therefore called the wrong leg foremoſt happens in this manner: when a horſe is in motion upon the quickneſs of the gallop, he ſhifts his legs croſs-ways, which is the action of a trot, and which is ſo contrary, that it is ready to make the horſe fall. This is one ſort of what is termed the wrong leg before: this the other. When a horſe is galloping, as I ſaid before, he ought in a gallop to keep both legs on the ſame ſide always foremoſt, inſtead whereof he changes the ſide every time, both fore and hind-leg on the ſame ſide, and changes ſides each time, being the action of an amble, which is performed by having both feet on one ſide in the air, and thoſe on the other ſide upon the ground at the ſame time. This action of ambling upon the ſwiftneſs of a gallop ſo far differs from the action of a gallop, that it is ready to make the horſe fall. Theſe two actions, *viz.* that of trotting and that of ambling upon the ſwiftneſs of a gallop, is what they ignorantly call the wrong leg before. It is very certain however, that altho' a horſe gallops as he ought to do, and his hind-leg follows his fore-leg on the ſame ſide; nevertheleſs, if he is not uſed to that ſide, he will not gallop ſo briſkly, or ſo faſt, as he will on that ſide with which he is uſed to lead: for it is the ſame with a horſe as with a left-handed man, or one that uſes his right. Cuſtom is very prevalent both in men and beaſts, and in reality upon all things in general.

CHAP. III.

Of the artificial Movements of a Horſe's Legs.

FIRST of Terre-à-terre. Here the horſe always leads with the two legs within the volte; his two fore-legs are in the air, as in the gallop, and his two hind-legs follow when he begins to put down thoſe before, in ſuch manner that the horſe has all his legs in the air at the ſame time, making a leap forwards. His action in the Demivolte is altogether like that of Terre-à-terre.

2. Secondly,

2. Secondly, he makes only a leap upwards in Curvets, Demi-airs, Groupades, Balotades, and Capriols: for he has all four legs in the air at the ſame time, as well when he brings down, as when he raiſes his fore-part. There are only theſe two artificial movements, *viz.* Terre-à-terre and the Airs I have juſt mentioned.

Some imagine that the croupe of the horſe is his center, and that his fore-part makes the circumference, which is impoſſible. For a horſe by no means reſembles a pair of compaſſes, that has only two legs, but an animal with four; ſo that the center is never in the horſe, but in the pillar, or in an imaginary center of the circle in which the horſe works: you ſhall ſee the true movements of his legs about the centre in all the artificial airs. It is neceſſary for you to know, that let a horſe be either on the right or left hand, he ought always to be a part of that circle in which he moves; and therefore he ought always to be bent on the inſide, and not on the outſide of it. For ſuppoſe him on the right hand, he ought to be bent to that ſide as the circle is. Should he be plied outward, he would be for the left hand, and not for the right, to which he is going; ſo that he would go falſe, not only with his body, but his legs. The nearer a horſe goes to the centre, the more ought he to be bent, or plied. If he goes Terre-à-terre large, altho' he ſeems near the center by a ſtrait line drawn, nevertheleſs, becauſe of the largeneſs of the circle, his ply will not be ſo great, and by it he will be more at his eaſe. Notwithſtanding a large circle may be more irkſome to him than a ſmaller, the bent or ply of his body will be leſs in the former than the latter. It is moreover neceſſary to obſerve, that let a horſe go to either hand, he ought to have the center or pillar on his inſide: for inſtance, ſuppoſe him to the right, the pillar ought to be on that ſide towards the volte, altho' he is very near it. For by this means the horſe will be always aſlaunt, let him do what he will, and the half of his ſhoulders will go before the half of his haunches, which is as he ought to be. Was he on the other ſide of the pillar, half his haunches would go before the half of his ſhoulders, which would be falſe. Beſides, were he ſo, half his croupe would go before half of his ſhoulders, which would be falſe as he is to the right hand, but as it ſhould be if he went to the left. Theſe things ought to be well conſider'd, becauſe they are the very foundation of horſemanſhip.

Let us therefore firſt conſider the natural poſture in which a horſe ſtands, and then what art can do to him; for art ought never to be contrary to nature, but to follow and perfect it. I have here given you the natural poſture in which a horſe ſtands, having his fore and hind-legs equidiſtant and parallel to each other, as you ſee in the figure. The artificial lines in which I make them move are thus; that is, to place his hind-feet in their natural poſition, as you ſee in the ſecond figure. By this means half the ſhoulders of the horſe will go before the half of his haunches on the inſide of the volte, and the other half of his haunches on the outſide of it will be in their natural poſture; ſo that his two hind-legs are brought by art within the lines of nature of his fore-legs, by which method a horſe will always move well, that is, with the half of his ſhoulders within that of his haunches on the ſide of the circle, and never become *entier*; and this alſo puts him upon his haunches,

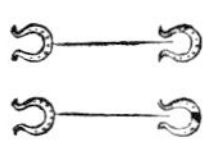

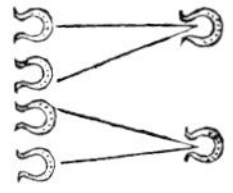

haunches, which is the quinteſſence of horſemanſhip. If a horſe puts himſelf upon his croupe by parting his legs, he will be indeed upon his croupe, but not upon his haunches, unleſs his hind-feet are in their natural direction, as you may ſee by the ſecond figure. Many riders work the croupe of a horſe, as if he had only one hind-leg, whereas he has two; and each of them ought to be conſider'd in all the actions he makes, otherwiſe he works ignorantly or by chance, as you will perceive by the following figure marked 3.

3.

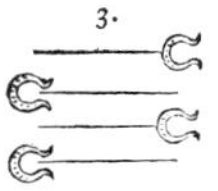

Moſt riders turn the bridle-hand when they go upon the voltes; for example, if they go to the right, they turn the bridle-hand to the ſame ſide, which muſt naturally throw out the horſe's croupe; which the rider perceiving, he ſpurs him briſkly with the left leg; he ſpurs him, I ſay, at the ſame time, ſo that he throws out the croupe of the horſe by one aid, and would bring it in at the ſame time by another, which is impoſſible; for the ſame thing cannot have two contrary motions at the ſame time. Some horſemen notwithſtanding are ſo ſtupidly ignorant, that they are continually whipping and ſpurring the poor beaſt till they have forc'd his hind-leg from its natural direction, which was before in a line with his fore-leg without the volte, as you may perceive by fig. 3. Thus the half of his croupe will be within the half of his ſhoulders, which is falſe, and very liable to make the horſe fall; all this proceeds from the ignorance of the rider.

4.

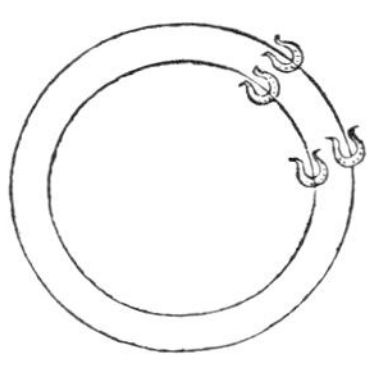

This volte or circle is by moſt horſemen ſuppoſed to be only of one piſte, which is abſolutely falſe; for as a horſe has by nature four legs, they muſt conſequently deſcribe two circles, or piſtes. A horſe in this figure goes according to the lines of nature, which in a Manege ought never to be done, as you ſhall ſee hereafter.

Your great philoſophers in horſemanſhip deſcribe theſe two circles for the Terre-à-terre, placing the horſe's two fore-feet in the larger and his hind-feet in the leſſer; ſuppoſing, that Terre-à-terre is the ſame action as Walking a horſe upon the voltes with his croupe in, by which they are much miſtaken. It is very true, that in Walking a horſe with his croupe within the volte, only two circles are deſcribed; but in the Terre-à-terre a horſe deſcribes four compleat circles with his four feet, as you may eaſily ſee in fig. 5.

5.

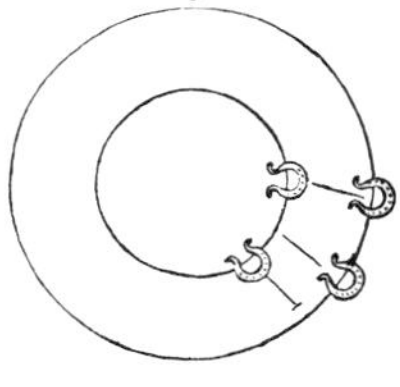

Another grand error is committed in this circle, which is, when you make the half of a horſe's croupe go before the half of his ſhoulders, as you may ſee in figure 5. which is both falſe and dangerous; becauſe in the Manege, the ſhoulders ought always to go before the haunches. Nobody travels with his horſe's croupe before his head, and this is equally as ridiculous with reſpect to a managed horſe. You therefore plainly ſee, by theſe two figures, the faults in the common way of working; the true one ſhall follow hereafter.

CHAP.

CHAP. IV.

My Method in faſtening the Reins of the Caveſon.

TAKE a long rein, with a ſmall ring faſten'd to one end of it, and paſs the other end of the rein thro' this ring, which bring over the pommel of the ſaddle, and fix it there in ſuch a manner that it cannot move; then draw the rein downwards, and paſs it under the fore-bolſter of the ſaddle, and then put the remainder of the rein through the ring of the caveſon directly before, bringing the ſame end of the rein into your hand; then do the ſame by the other rein, fixing both ends well to the pommel of the ſaddle, carrying it directly downwards, as above, under the fore-bolſter of the ſaddle, paſſing it thro' the other ring of the caveſon, and by this means bring the rein into your hand. This ſort of caveſon is exceeding uſeful, both to ſettle a horſe's head, to make him ſteady in hand, to give his body a proper bent, to preſerve his mouth, to ſtop him, make him go backwards, or to turn him eaſily to either hand; moreover, I have a greater command over him with two fingers in this manner, than with both hands by the common method. I may venture to ſay farther, that the old faſhion has not near ſo much effect as this; I therefore adviſe you to make uſe of it. The figure of it may be ſeen in the firſt part of this book.

CHAP. V.

The firſt Diviſion of LESSONS *for making the Shoulders of a Horſe free and eaſy.*

How a raw Horſe ought to be treated at firſt to make him trot to the Right Hand in a large Circle, with a Caveſon made according to my Faſhion.

FIRST, let the rider be ſeated as I have directed before, and let him pull the rein of the caveſon within the volte upwards, towards the left ſhoulder, the nails of the right hand upwards, and the little finger towards the ſhoulder. The reins of the caveſon ought neither to be too long nor too ſhort, for by both theſe faults the power of the rider will be diminiſhed. He ſhould therefore adjuſt the length himſelf, ſince he alone is the proper judge of it. Then drawing the rein of the caveſon inward, he ſhould touch his horſe gently with the right leg, which will force his croupe outward, and work his ſhoulders at the ſame time, but only the half of his croupe, the other being loſt, the rider having no feeling of it. Let him remember, that leg and rein of a ſide works always both the ſhoulders, and but one half of the croupe. The better to work his ſhoulders, the rider ſhould turn inward the contrary ſhoulder to the hand he is working the horſe upon. For example, in trotting him to the right hand, the rider ſhould place his left ſhoulder within, having his bridle-hand a little out of the volte, working all the time with the caveſon, and very little with the bridle. The rider's leg out of the volte ought to be a little more advanced than the other, becauſe the aid is with the inward, and not the outward leg. Both the horſe's ſhoulders being work'd in this manner, both with the rein of the cavefon and the rider's leg on the fame fide as the volte (his croupe being outwards) which always works the fhoulders, they muft therefore be more wrought than his hind-part; for the croupe is put out, and the fhoulders neareft the center, and the part neareft thereto will always be more reftrained, more laboured and confined, than that which is farther off, whether it be in walking, trotting, or galloping, as appears by the figure following.

The firft Leffon for a Colt or young Horfe trotting on the Right Hand.

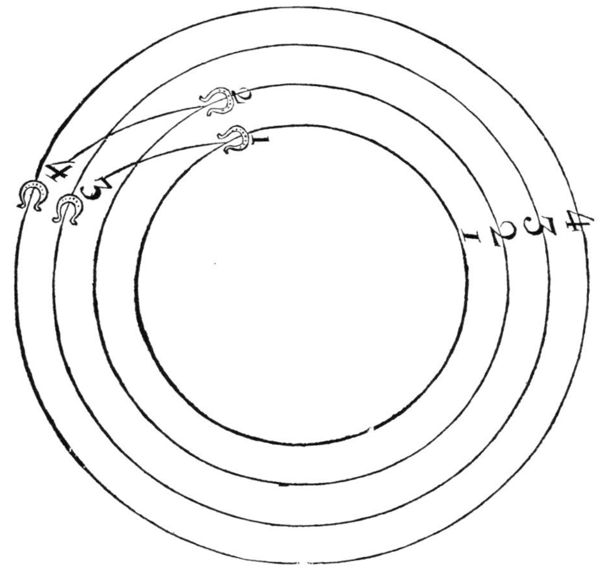

By this figure it appears, that the feet of a horfe defcribe four diftinct circles on the right hand. The fore-foot, marked 1. defcribes the fmalleft; the other marked 2. defcribes the fecond; the hind-foot marked 3. defcribes the third; and the other hind-foot the fourth. Thus you fee, that he keeps his fhoulders within his hind-legs, which prevents him from being *entier*, (that is, to refufe to turn) and renders his fhoulders fupple and pliant; and this is the beft leffon for a young horfe in the beginning, it being more difficult to work the fhoulders than the croupe. You ought moreover to ftop him in this pofture, and make him advance and retire at a proper time, fince there is no fear of making him throw out his croupe at the beginning, or even for fome time after; but it is much to be feared, that he may be apt to throw it in, this being abfolutely wrong, and may chance to make him *entier*, (viz. refufe to turn) and render his fhoulders ftiff, fo that he may never turn eafily afterwards, which is the greateft fault belonging to a horfe. It is not fufficient to keep the head and neck of a horfe within the volte, but give an entire ply or bent to his whole body from the nofe to the tail. I have already

already demonſtrated, in what manner it ſhould be done. For altho' ſome object that his neck will be weaken'd by this method, I can anſwer that objection in no other manner, than by ſaying, that ſuch horſemen do not underſtand the art they pretend to profeſs, who would make a horſe ſtiff-necked by their management, and not able to turn or wheel about. As to my own part, I confeſs, when I have uſed my utmoſt endeavours, I find them hardly ſufficient to make the ſhoulders of a horſe eaſy; and therefore would adviſe you to follow the inſtructions I have laid down. And thus I finiſh my diſcourſe upon trotting a horſe on the right hand.

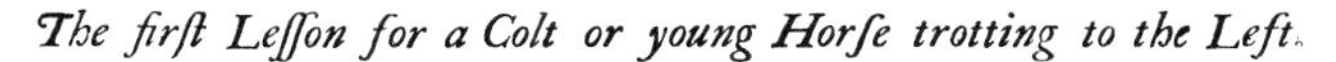

The firſt Leſſon for a Colt or young Horſe trotting to the Left.

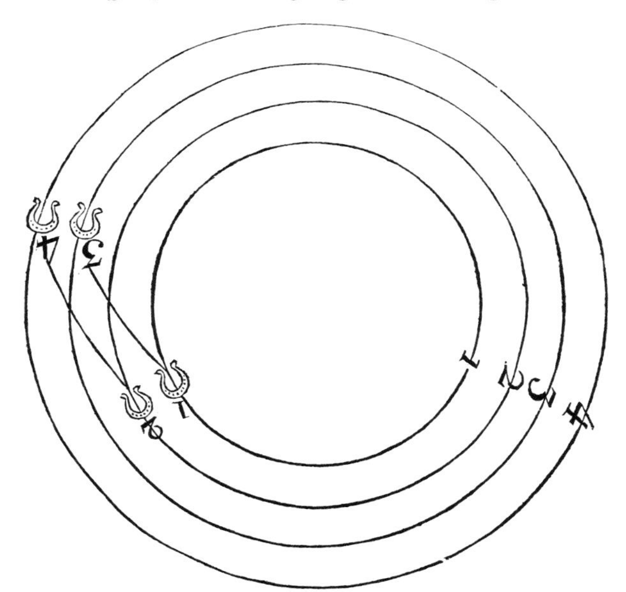

The feet of a horſe in this motion deſcribe four diſtinct circles on the left hand. The fore-foot mark'd 1. deſcribes the leaſt, and the other fore-foot mark'd 2. the ſecond; the hind-foot marked 3. the third, and the other hind-foot marked 4. deſcribes the fourth. From whence you may perceive the excellency of this leſſon in making a horſe's ſhoulders free and eaſy. But it will be here unneceſſary to repeat what I have ſaid before, and therefore I ſhall only ſhow you the aids neceſſary for the left hand, which are theſe. Now the rider ought to take the bridle-reins in his right hand, and thoſe of the caveſon in his left, and the ſwitch in which hand he pleaſes. The reins of the caveſon being thus held in the left hand, that is, toward the volte, they muſt be drawn, having the nails turned towards his right ſhoulder, aiding with the left leg, ſo that you may work both his ſhoulders, and only the half of his croupe. This leſſon ought to be continued till the horſe is very light, and ſo light that he offers to gallop of himſelf, for till then he ſhould not to be be put to it. I muſt however remark one thing, which is, that in working the ſhoulders of a horſe, he muſt neceſſarily be put a little upon his ſhoulders; for it is plain, when his croupe is loſt, it is impoſſible to place him upon his haunches; but the ſhoulders is the moſt difficult taſk, it being an eaſy matter to ſettle the croupe, as you ſhall ſee hereafter. Whilſt you are working the ſhoulders of a horſe, he ought to feel very little of the bridle, which may ſerve to put him gently upon his haunches, ſince he has little for his fore-part to lean upon: the rein of the caveſon ought moreover to be held lightly, and as eaſy as poſſible, which will aſſiſt him likewiſe in placing himſelf upon his haunches. He ought to be ſtopt very gently at firſt, and more ſtrongly by degrees. You ought to conſider beſides, that as the rein of the caveſon and the leg, both working upon the ſame ſide, work both the horſe's ſhoulders and only half of his croupe, that by this means his croupe is entirely loſt to the rider, ſince he feels nothing of it: a ſhort trot will likewiſe put him upon his haunches. Thus I have finiſhed my diſcourſe upon the method of trotting a horſe to the left hand.

CHAP. VI.

When and in what manner a Horſe ſhould be Galloped.

WHEN a horſe is perfect in his trot, and ſo eaſy that he begins to gallop of himſelf, then gallop him upon the ſame large circles in the following manner.

For the Gallop to the Right Hand.

The rider ought to be ſeated in the ſame manner as when the horſe was upon the trot, drawing the right rein of the caveſon towards the volte, putting the bridle-hand a little out of the turn, and aiding the horſe with the right leg, ſince it is always rein and leg of a ſide that works the ſhoulders, and only half of the croupe; but the croupe is actually loſt, ſince the rider has no feeling of it. A horſe's ſhoulders are more worked than his croupe, as they are nearer the center, and conſequently more preſſed than the croupe, which is large and at liberty. The left ſhoulder of the rider ought to be turned towards the volte or circle, that he may better manage the horſe's ſhoulders, having his left leg a little more advanced than the other, becauſe no aid is to be given with that but with the right, that is within the volte. It ought to be obſerved in this place, that nature has framed a horſe's legs of equal length; this being granted, and the rider working with the rein within the volte, and with his leg on the ſame ſide, the horſe's fore-leg next the volte will be longer than the other, and more advanced, and thus he will begin his gallop, the hind-leg on the ſame ſide ought to follow, being more at liberty, which is the true gallop to the right; for the fore-leg within the volte ought always to move firſt, and the hind-leg on the ſame ſide ſhould follow. By this means he is obliged to gallop right, which is not eaſily performed by any other method. You may ſee this in the preceding figures for this leſſon upon the trot: for the horſe's legs in the gallop deſcribe here the ſame circles; the fore-foot mark'd 1. makes the little circle, the other fore-foot mark'd 2. makes the ſecond circle, the hind-foot mark'd 3. makes the third circle, and the other foot mark'd 4. makes the fourth circle. This is the beſt leſſon that can be given to a young raw horſe, becauſe there is more difficulty in working the ſhoulders than the croupe. He ought to be ſtopped in that poſture, without raiſing him, for the reaſons given before, and ſhould be made after his ſtop to rein gently back. This is the method of galloping a horſe to the right. Remember, that the Gallop ſettles a horſe's head, and gives him a good *appuy*, or feeling of the bit. Moreover, as a Trot is the foundation of a Gallop, ſo a Gallop is the foundation of Terre-à-terre, as has been ſhewn in its proper place.

For the Gallop to the Left.

The rider ought to be ſeated as was ſhewn before in the gallop to the right, only with this difference, that he ought to hold his bridle in the right hand, the caveſon in the left, and the ſwitch in which hand he pleaſes. The reins of the caveſon being held in the left hand, that is, next the volte, he muſt draw them, having the nails of his hand turn'd up towards the right ſhoulder, and bringing that ſhoulder in, muſt help his horſe with the left leg, that he may work both his ſhoulders, and only half of the croupe. It appears plainly by the foregoing circles, that a horſe by this method cannot gallop falſe. His fore-leg next the volte ſhould move firſt, ſince it is the longeſt on account of the bent of the horſe's body, as I have ſaid before, and the hind-leg on the ſame ſide ought to follow, becauſe it is moſt at liberty. This is the true gallop to the left, as you may ſee by the preceding figures for this leſſon upon the trot; for the horſe's legs in the gallop here deſcribe the ſame circles, by which it appears, that the feet of a horſe deſcribe four compleat circles when he gallops to the left. The fore-foot marked 1. deſcribes the inward circle, the other fore-foot marked 2. the ſecond circle; the hind-foot marked 3. deſcribes the third, and the other foot marked 4. the fourth circle. Thus you may ſee how this excellent leſſon renders the ſhoulders of a horſe ſupple and eaſy, wherein the difficulty of the work conſiſts; if theſe are made ſupple at firſt, the reſt will be no hard taſk. You muſt ſtop, and rein him back in the ſame poſture; but don't make him riſe before, till he is very perfect in this leſſon, and ſome others to be ſhewn hereafter. This only makes the ſhoulders of a horſe free and ſupple, for the croupe is entirely out of the queſtion, tho' he obeys the rider's leg next the volte. This gives a proper ply to his body, which is not eaſily done by any other method, and is the principal thing in the dreſſing of a horſe. Thus I conclude the method of working a young raw horſe's ſhoulders at firſt both upon the trot and gallop, which is the perfection of the beginning of the work. You ought ſometimes to walk your horſe upon theſe large circles in the ſame manner as you trotted and galloped him before, in order to work his ſhoulders. This gentle walk will pleaſe him, divert him in his exerciſe, and make him love the Manege.

CHAP. VII.

Of the Method of ſtopping a Horſe.

WHEN a horſe is trotting, the rider ought to preſs him a little faſter before he ſtops, and ſtop him immediately after, by drawing the inward rein of the caveſon a little ſtronger than the other, and more towards his body, putting his body a little back, that he may be obliged by the weight to

BOOK II. put himſelf upon his haunches; but particular care ought to be taken, that he does not advance, by which I mean that he ſhould not riſe before, but only ſtop without riſing; for a ſure way to ſpoil a horſe, is to teach him to riſe before he trots and gallops freely, for he would be apt to riſe and be reſtif, inſtead of advancing. Particular care ought therefore to be taken never to make him riſe, till he anſwers freely the ſpurs both in trotting and galloping; but the ſpurs in the beginning ſhould be given with great care, and but ſeldom, and then gently. He ſhould be ſtopped without ſuffering him to riſe, as this figure and my inſtructions direct.

The bridle ought to be ſlack, when the horſe firſt begins to rein back, drawing both reins of the caveſon, as if you was ſawing a piece of wood, the rider leaning a little back, when the horſe goes back, according to the deſcription in the following figure.

Trotting and ſtopping a horſe is the foundation of all airs, they ſettle his head and croupe, put him well upon his haunches, and make him light before.

Reining back ſettles the horſe's head, puts him upon his haunches, and makes him light before.

I muſt in this place ſhew you, that it is a bad practice to make a horſe go more turns to the right hand than the left. Notwithſtanding their philoſophical argument, that a foal lies upon the left ſide in the womb of the dam, ſucks on the ſame ſide; that he is always ſaddled, turned about, and led ſo; many horſes being however eaſier to the right hand than the left; therefore the moſt difficult ought always to be the moſt worked; for what can you deſire more, than to have your horſe equally ſupple to both ſides? In the old way of fighting on horſeback, they always turned to the right to get the advantage of the croupe. But Monſieur FURGO, who was an excellent horſeman, and the beſt in the world for the ſingle combat, by a new invention of his own, never took that method. You muſt obſerve, that the motion of a horſe's legs in trotting is croſs-ways; that thoſe legs in the air are always the moſt advanced, and thus they change alternately; for inſtance, when the near fore-leg is in the air, the off hind-leg is from the ground at the ſame time, and thus *vice verſa* he changes them in every motion. When a horſe has been thus well worked to both hands upon theſe large circles, you may walk him gently and in his length, in the ſame manner you had worked him before. Work him both with rein and leg on the ſame ſide, which will render his ſhoulders ſupple and eaſy; and the narrower the circle, the more pliant will it make them; but let him be ſoftly worked in this manner, firſt on the right hand, and then on the left.

Upon the Right Hand in a Walk in the Horſe's Length.

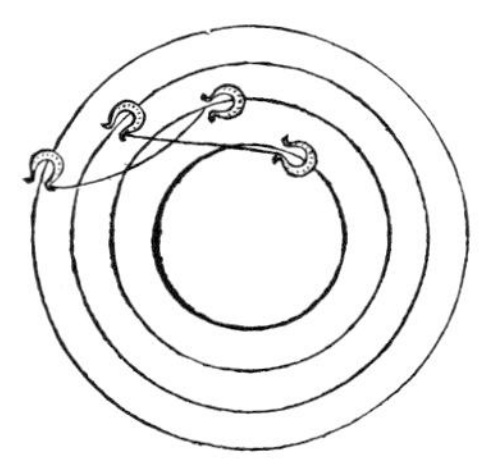

Upon

Upon the Left Hand the ſame Leſſon.

CHAP. VIII.

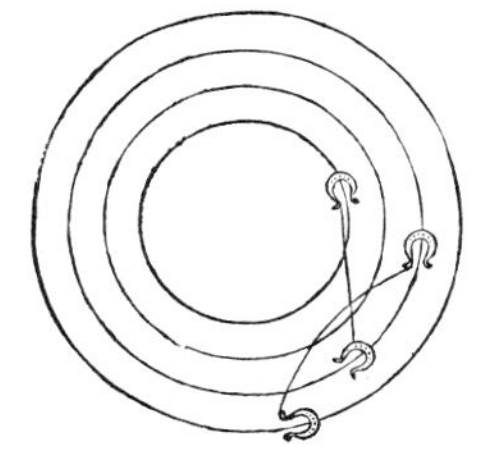

An End of the firſt Diviſion of LESSONS *which were to render the Shoulders of a Horſe free and eaſy.*

Vide Fig. 15, 16.

CHAP. VIII.

The ſecond Diviſion of LESSONS.

A new Method of working a Horſe's Croupe to the Right Hand.

I SHALL now begin to inſtruct you firſt how to make a horſe obey the ſpur. Place his head towards the wall, for the right hand, drawing the inward rein of the caveſon, with the nails of your hand directed upwards to the left ſhoulder, and the bridle-hand a little outward, and the left ſhoulder a little within, aiding him gently with the left leg, to advance his ſhoulder within the volte; by which means his body will have a right turn, and he will look into the volte. It ſhould be here obſerved, that the rein within the volte, and the rider's leg without, uſed at the ſame time, work always his croupe; for I plainly perceive, that the rein towards the volte works the hind-leg on the ſame ſide. It is neceſſary to be obſerved beſides, that the wall is a ſort of center or pillar, when the horſe's head fronts it; therefore when his head is placed towards the wall, upon a trot, his fore-legs are nearer together than the hind-ones: therefore the lines of his fore-legs are within thoſe of his hind, becauſe his fore-part is placed againſt the wall, which ought to be looked upon as the center. I find however, that I work his croupe, ſince leg and rein contrary always does. In this leſſon, when a horſe trots, he deſcribes only two lines; one where his fore-legs move near together, and the other where the hind-ones move at a greater diſtance from each other. A horſe in this action paſſages, which is, to lap one leg over another; but becauſe he is upon the action of the trot, in which he moves his legs croſsways, he places or croſſes the outward fore-leg over the inward, and at the ſame time he advances the inward hind-leg; the next ſtep he advances the inward fore-leg, and croſſes the outward hind-leg over the inward, ſo that it is impoſſible for him in this action to croſs both his near-legs at the ſame inſtant over his off-ones; but he croſſes them one over the other every ſecond movement. When you are near the end of the wall, aid your horſe more briſkly with the left leg than the other, in order to command more of his croupe, and if he yeilds to it, careſs him. Thus I have ſhewn you the manner of working a horſe's croupe to the right hand.

CHAP. IX.

The Method of working a Horſe's Croupe to the Left Hand.

I MAKE the horſe obey the heel in the following manner: Since it is on the left, you muſt ſhift your bridle-rein into the right hand, and hold thoſe of the caveſon with the left, turning the horſe's head towards the wall, for the left, and drawing the inward rein of the caveſon with the nails of your hand directed to the right ſhoulder, and that ſhoulder a little in, the bridle-hand a little outward, aiding him gently with the right leg, to advance his ſhoulder within the the volte, by which means his body will have a right turn. It ſhould be here obſerved, that the rein within the volte, and the rider's leg without, working at the ſame time, always work a horſe's croupe; for I plainly perceive, that the rein towards the volte works the hind-leg on the ſame ſide, and my own leg that on the other ſide. The wall being a ſort of center confines his fore-legs, whilſt the others are at liberty. The head to the wall, the fore-part muſt be the moſt preſſed, which I have no occaſion to repeat in this place, ſince I ſhewed it you in the preceding chapter. I ſhall only obſerve one thing more, which is, that when you come near the end of the wall, you muſt aid your horſe briſkly with the right leg, in order to have more command of the croupe before you ſtop, and work him upon this leſſon till he is perfect at it.

CHAP. X.

A new and true way to work the Croupe of a Horſe upon a Walk, which is the Action of the Trot, the Croupe to the Center, which is the Pillar.

WHEN the croupe of a horſe is near the center or pillar, you muſt draw the rein of the caveſon within the volte, having the nails upwards, and the little finger towards the left ſhoulder, aiding him with your leg out of the volte, which is the left, and by this means the horſe's hind-legs will be brought nearer together. The rein of the caveſon within the volte preſſes the hind-leg on the ſame ſide outward, whilſt the rider's leg on the outſide preſſes the other hind-leg inward; ſo that they are put both under his belly. By this method therefore both the horſe's hind-legs are in ſubjection, and only the half of his ſhoulders preſſing his croupe, and leaving his fore-part at liberty, that he may the better embrace the volte. If both his ſhoulders ſhould come in, one of his haunches muſt conſequently be without, which would be falſe. This being to the right, your left ſhoulder ought neceſſarily to come in, not only to keep yourſelf upright in the ſaddle, but to facilitate the motion of the horſe's ſhoulders, and you muſt turn your head to look into the volte. In this paſſage, which is the action of the trot, a horſe croſſes his legs without the volte, only every other time; for example, when he croſſes the outward fore-leg over the inward fore-leg, the inward hind-leg advances at the ſame time; in the next motion the horſe croſſes his outward hind-leg over the inward hind-leg, and he advances at the ſame time the inward fore-leg. He cannot poſſibly croſs his legs but every other time, ſince the movement of them upon the trot is always

always acroſs. The pillar, which is the center, ought always to be within the croupe, by which the fore-part of the horſe will always go before his croupe, and he will go ſideways, as he ought to do, when his croupe is to the pillar or center. Working a horſe this way upon a walk, which is the action of the trot, he deſcribes only two circles; his hind-feet, as being next the center, deſcribe the leſſer, and his fore-feet the larger, ſince they are at a greater diſtance from it, as you may ſee by the following figure.

For the Right Hand.

A horſe deſcribes but two circles, becauſe he is upon the trot, which is croſsways, and he croſſes his legs only every other time.

The ſtrait line within the leſſer circle de-

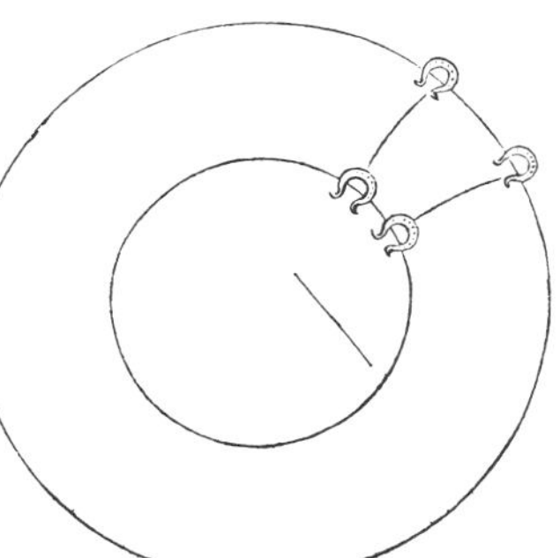

monſtrates, that the center is within the horſe's croupe, and that though the center was farther diſtant, he will never become reſtive, as long as it remains within the croupe.

CHAP. XI.

To work a Horſe upon his Paſſage upon a Walk, which is the Action of a Trot, to the Left Hand.

HERE it is proper to change the bridle from the left hand to the right, and hold the reins of the caveſon with the left, having your little finger towards the right ſhoulder, aiding the horſe at the ſame time with your outward leg, *viz.* the right, which brings his hind-legs together. The rein of the caveſon within the volte puts the horſe's hind-leg next to it out, and the rider's leg out of the volte puts his other hind-leg in, ſo that they come under his belly, and put him upon his haunches. By this method therefore a horſe's hind-legs are both worked, and only the half of his ſhoulders, by forcing his croupe, and leaving his ſhoulders at liberty, that he may the better embrace the volte. In this paſſage, which is a trot, a horſe only croſſes his legs without the volte over thoſe within it, every other movement, for the reaſons I explained in the former chapter. But one conſtant rule ought always to be obſerved, which is, to keep the center or pillar always within the horſe's croupe, though he ſhould be never ſo near it; by which means his ſhoulders will neceſſarily move before his croupe, and ſideways, as they ought to do. By working a horſe upon the trot in this manner, he deſcribes only two circles with his legs; thoſe neareſt the center deſcribe the leſſer, and the moſt remote the larger, as you may ſee by the figure following.

For the Left Hand.

A horſe deſcribes but two circles when he is upon the trot, becauſe he only croſſes his legs alternately.

The ſtrait line within the leſſer circle, ſhews, that the center

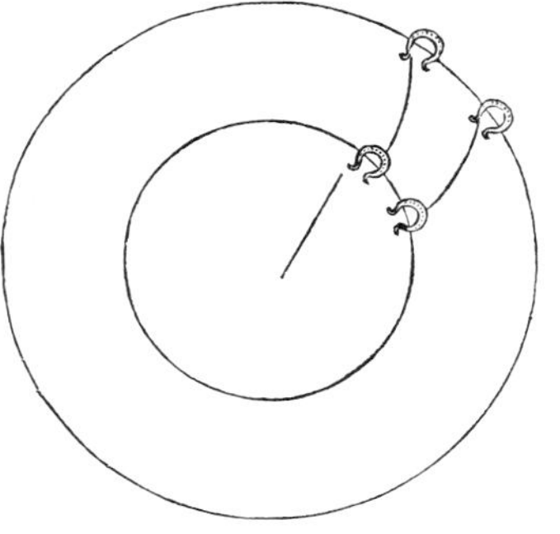

is within the horſe's croupe; and, though the center was farther diſtant, he will never become *entier*, which is, to refuſe to turn, as long as it remains within his croupe.

CHAP. XII.

To work to the Right Hand, the Horſe's Croupe out.

HERE the horſe's head ought to be towards the pillar, for the right hand. I have laid it down as a maxim before, that when a horſe's croupe is worked towards the pillar, it ought to be always within his croupe; but when his head is towards it, and his croupe from it, the pillar ought to be quite contrary. For inſtance, in the preſent caſe, the horſe ought to have the pillar on the outſide of his head; whereas in the other he had it on the inſide of his croupe, when it was turned to it. The reaſon why the horſe's head ought to be within the pillar, is, that by this means his ſhoulders are ſo worked, that he cannot bring his croupe too much within, nor become *entier*. The horſe's croupe ſhould be worked as much as poſſible, always obſerving to keep the pillar without his head; for by this means his croupe cannot be thrown too much in, but will make him move perfectly well ſideways: the fore-part of the horſe, which is neareſt the center, is more conſtrained than his croupe, that is more diſtant from it. Here follows the method of working a horſe's head on the right hand, having the pillar without it, which is on the left.

The rider ought to pull the inner rein of the caveſon, having the nails of his hand turned upwards, and his little finger towards the left ſhoulder, the bridle-hand a little without, and the left ſhoulder ſomewhat in, turning his face towards the volte, touching him gently at the ſame time with the left leg. The horſe's ſhoulder next the volte ought to advance a little, that he may have a proper turn with his body, and may look towards it. It is neceſſary to obſerve in this place, that the inward rein and the outward leg of the rider, moving at the ſame time, conſtantly work the horſe's croupe, as they are oppoſite to each other. For I am perfectly ſenſible, that the inward rein of the caveſon works the hind-leg on that ſide, and that my own leg works the other without the volte. It ought moreover to be obſerved, that when a horſe's head is toward the pillar or center in this action, his fore-part is more conſtrained than his croupe, ſince it is nearer the center, by which means his fore-legs are within his hind-ones; but ſtill I perceive that I work the horſe's croupe.

croupe. A horſe deſcribes but two circles when he is upon the trot, one where his fore-legs go narrow, and the other where his hind-legs go larger. The horſe goes upon his paſſage, which is when he laps one leg over the other; but as he is upon the action of the trot, and moves his legs acroſs, he only does it at every other motion, which I have ſufficiently ſhewn already; and for this reaſon he deſcribes only two circles. When you think you have walked your horſe ſufficiently, preſs him very much with the left leg, to put his croupe towards the pillar, and let him take breath in that poſture. Here is the figure, to ſhew how a horſe's head is to be worked when it is towards the pillar, and his croupe from it.

For the Right Hand.

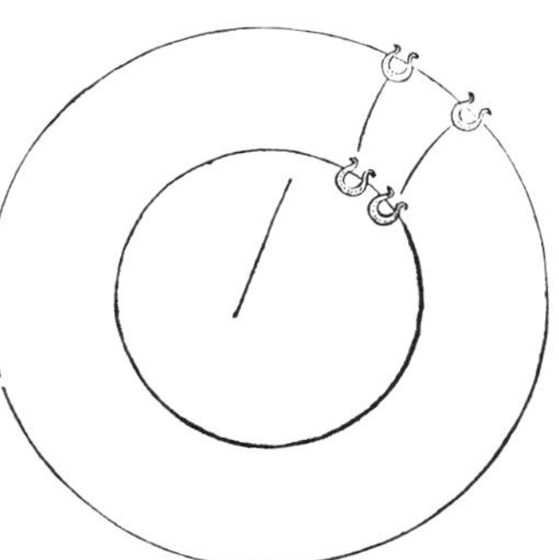

The ſtrait line within the leſſer circle ſhews, that the horſe's head ought to be within the pillar or center. The reaſon why he deſcribes but two circles, proceeds from his head being towards the pillar, and that when he trots, he croſſes his legs one over the other only every other time.

CHAP. XIII.

To work to the Left, the Horſe's Croupe out.

THE horſe's head, for the left-hand, ought to be to the pillar. I gave it to you before as a maxim, that when the croupe is worked to the pillar, it ſhould always be within the croupe; but in the preſent caſe, the horſe ought to have the pillar without his head, his croupe being out, which is quite contrary, for he has it within his croupe, when that is towards the center. The reaſon why a horſe ſhould have the pillar without his head is, that he then works better with his ſhoulders, which prevents his bringing his croupe too much in, or becoming *entier*. One may work the horſe's croupe as much as poſſible, provided the pillar is without his head, for ſo he can't put it too much in, but will go perfectly ſideways; the fore-part of the horſe next the center, being narrower than his croupe, which is more diſtant from it. This is the method of working a horſe's head towards the pillar or center on the left hand, his head being on the inſide of it: The bridle ought to be put into the right hand, drawing the inward rein of the caveſon with the left, having the nails of the hand turned upwards, and your little finger towards the right ſhoulder, holding the bridle-hand a little out, and your right ſhoulder a little in, with your head turned to look into the volte, touching him gently with the right leg, to make him advance his ſhoulder within the volte. It is neceſſary

BOOK II.

neceſſary to obſerve in this place, that the inward rein and the outward leg of the rider, moving at the ſame time, always work the croupe, as they are oppoſite one to the other. I am perfectly ſenſible, that the rein within the volte works the hind-leg on the ſame ſide, and that my own leg without the volte works the other hind-leg. It is moreover neceſſary to obſerve, that when a horſe's head is towards the pillar or center upon a trot, that his fore-part is more confined than his croupe, and therefore his fore-legs will conſequently be within the lines of the hind-ones. Nevertheleſs, I perceive that I work his croupe, ſince the rein of the caveſon and my own leg, that are oppoſite, always work the croupe. The horſe being upon the action of the trot, deſcribes but two circles, one where his fore-legs go narrow, the other where his hind-legs go larger. The horſe goes upon his paſſage, which is, when he laps one leg over the other; but as he is upon the action of the trot, in which his legs move croſsways, he only does it at every other motion, which I have ſufficiently ſhewn already. When you imagine that your horſe has been walked enough, preſs him ſtrongly with the right leg to place his croupe towards the pillar, and let him take breath in that poſture. Here I give you the figure of working a horſe's head to the left-hand, with his head to the pillar and his croupe from it.

For the Left Hand.

The ſtrait line drawn within the leſſer circle ſhews, that the horſe's head ought to be on the inſide the pillar or center.

The horſe's head to the pillar, upon the action of the trot, he can only deſcribe two circles, by reaſon that he croſſes his legs one over the other only every other movement.

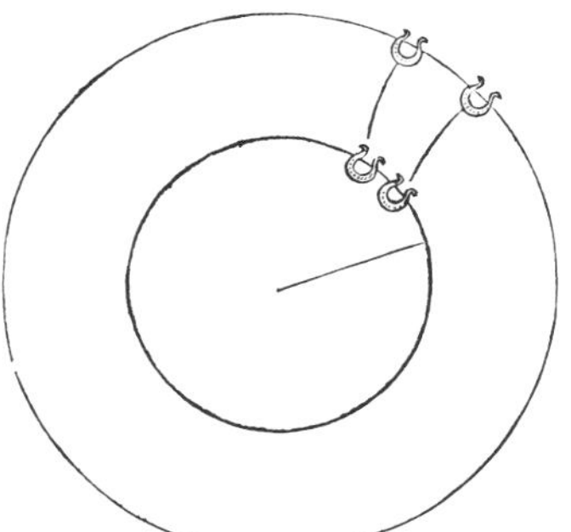

CHAP. XIV.

To work a Horſe to the Right in his own Length upon a Walk or Paſſage, which is the Action of the Trot.

WHEN a horſe is rode to the right upon a walk, in ſo ſmall a compaſs as his own length, it ought not to be performed round a pillar, ſince he ſhould move in leſs compaſs than the pillar will admit of; ſo that the beſt method will be to perform it in a corner of a covered Manege, where two walls meet. Here are the aids for the right hand: Firſt draw the reins of the caveſon within the volte with your right hand, the nails being turned upward, and your little finger pointing towards the left ſhoulder; then touch him gently with the contrary leg, which will keep his ſhoulders free, and command his croupe. If his ſhoulders ſhould go too much in, take care to keep them a little out; and when they are not ſufficiently within, you may touch him gently

gently with your outward leg, and ſometimes with the other, to keep him even, putting it back afterwards in its proper place to be ready upon occaſion. This is the beſt leſſon in the world, for if a horſe is perfectly obedient to me upon a walk in his own length, and anſwers both hand and heel, I can make him perform all that his ſtrength will permit. This method far exceeds that of the quarters, halfs and three quarters of voltes; ſince you have an entire volte by this, wherein thoſe diviſions and ſubdiviſions are all included, and one quarter more added: But this can be performed only by a maſter, as it requires the greateſt exactneſs and nicety. You muſt always change as you ſee occaſion, not forgetting, that though the ſhoulders go more ground than the croupe, the latter is the moſt conſtrained notwithſtanding, ſince it is the leaſt at liberty. Here follows the figure.

For the Right Hand.

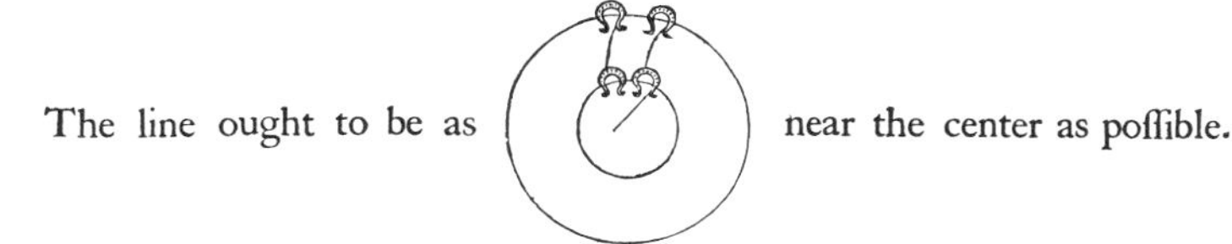

The line ought to be as near the center as poſſible.

CHAP. XV.

To work a Horſe to the Left in his own Length upon a Walk or Paſſage, which is the Action of the Trot.

WHEN a horſe is rode to the left upon a walk, in ſo ſmall a compaſs as his own length, it ought not to be performed round a pillar, ſince he ſhould move in leſs compaſs than the pillar will admit; ſo that the beſt method will be to perform it in the corner of a covered *Manege*, where two walls meet. Here are the aids for the left hand. The bridle muſt be changed from the left hand to the right; then draw the reins of the caveſon within the volte with your left-hand, the nails of it being turned upward, and your little finger pointing towards the right ſhoulder; then touch him gently with the contrary leg, which will keep his ſhoulders free, and command his croupe. If his ſhoulders ſhould go too much in, take care to keep them a little out; and when they are not ſufficiently within, you muſt touch him gently with the outward leg, and ſometimes with the other, to keep him even, putting it back afterwards in its proper place, to be ready upon occaſion. This is the beſt leſſon in the world; for if a horſe is perfectly obedient to me upon a walk in his own length, and he anſwers both hand and heel, I can make him perform all that his ſtrength will permit. This method far exceeds that of quarters, halfs and three quarters of voltes, ſince you have an entire volte by it, and one quarter more added, wherein thoſe diviſions and ſubdiviſions are all included. But this can be perform'd only by a maſter, as it requires the greateſt exactneſs and nicety. You muſt always change as you ſee occaſion, not forgetting, that though the ſhoulders go more ground than the croupe, the latter is the moſt conſtrained notwithſtanding, ſince it is the leaſt at liberty.

For the Left Hand.

The line ought to be as 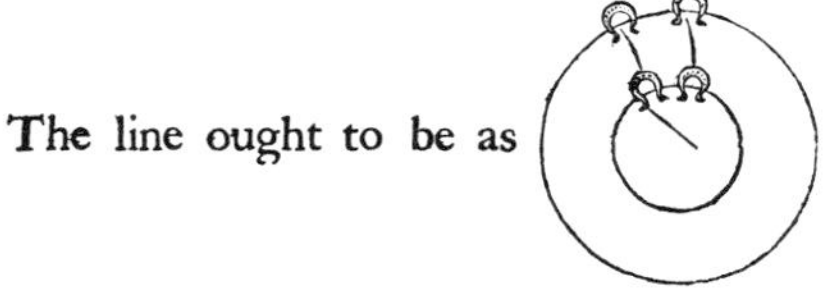 near the center as poſſible.

CHAP. XVI.

A new and exact Method of making a Horſe go Terre-à-terre, *with Obſervations never made before. This Practice was a kind of* Terra à Terra Incognita, *till I had attained it by ſtudying the Art of Horſemanſhip; and I have found a Treaſure of Knowledge, which I offer to all Honourable and worthy Horſemen.*

THE motion of a horſe's legs in Terre-à-terre, is a gallop in time. To the right, draw the rein of the caveſon within the volte, the nails of your hand turned upwards, and your little finger towards the left ſhoulder, aiding him gently with your leg out of the volte. Work the horſe in this manner acroſs, with the rein of the caveſon on one ſide, and your leg on the other, and they will always work his croupe, ſince his hind-legs are by this means kept cloſe together. The rein of the caveſon puts out the horſe's hind-leg within the volte, and the horſeman's leg without the volte puts in the other hind-leg ſo, that it goes under his belly, and puts him upon his haunches. Conſequently, by this correct method, both the horſe's hind-legs are worked, and only the half of his ſhoulders; and it conſtrains his hind-legs, leaving the others at liberty, that he may the better embrace the volte. If both the ſhoulders of the horſe come in, the outward hind-leg muſt go out, which is falſe. By this method a horſe deſcribes four circles with his four feet, as he ought to do when he goes Terre-à-terre; that is to ſay, his fore-leg next the volte deſcribes the largeſt, his other fore-leg the ſecond, his hind-leg next the volte deſcribes the third, and his other hind-leg the fourth or ſmalleſt circle. The legs of a horſe, being of an equal length, he muſt conſequently be upon his haunches, when his hind-legs are within the lines of nature; I mean, within the lines of his fore-legs. For the ſame reaſon, when you pull the inward rein of the caveſon, and make the body of the horſe deſcribe a ſemicircle, the fore-leg within the volte muſt of neceſſity be longer than that without; which is as it ought to be, that the hind-leg on the ſame ſide may go foremoſt. By drawing the inward rein, the hind-leg within the volte is forced outward, and affords him the greater liberty of tracing the ſtep of the foremoſt on the ſame ſide, which is right; aiding the horſe with the outward leg conſtrains and ſubjects his hind-leg on that ſide, and of neceſſity puts it behind his other hind-leg, which is as it ſhould be. You may obſerve from what I have ſaid, that a horſe ought always to fly the pillar or center with his hind-leg within the volte, which makes the half of his ſhoulders go foremoſt, as they ſhould. But here the danger is, that the horſe ſhould not bring his hind-legs cloſe enough together: If he anſwers the outward leg of the rider, it will do; if he does not, it won't: I ſhall explain how to make him do it hereafter.

The

The rider ought to be ſeated upon his twiſt according to the inſtructions I have given before, in the chapter relating to the proper ſeat of a horſeman. When a horſe goes Terre-à-terre on the right hand, he ſhould pull the inward rein of the caveſon, having the nails of his hand turned upward, the little finger directed towards the left ſhoulder, looking into the volte, aiding him with the outward leg, to make him convex like a bow in the middle, and concave at each end, bending towards the circle; for every horſe ought to form a part of the circle in which he moves; from whence it naturally follows, that every horſeman muſt deſcribe a part of the circle of his horſe. He ought therefore to incline his body on the ſame ſide, which, on the right hand, is to place his left ſhoulder within, then, his right ſhoulder being behind, he makes room for the horſe's legs to advance within the volte, which are the longeſt, on account of the bent of his body. The right ſhoulder of the rider being thus without, and his left within, the horſe's legs out of the volte are by this means ſo confin'd, that they are the ſhorteſt, and don't alter his Terre-à-terre, which is only a gallop in time, termed *Relevé*; not becauſe it is high, but becauſe he beats time with his feet, whilſt he is upon his haunches. Since a horſe therefore is bent like a bow, convex in the middle, and concave at both extremities within, it may be plainly perceiv'd, that the inſide of this arch is more at liberty at each end, than it is in the middle, one part being more ſtretched than the other. Whence that part of the horſe within the volte may be compared to the concave part of the bow, and that without to the convex part of the ſame. A horſe going in this manner, can never move irregularly with his feet, for reaſons I have given before. Being without convex, it is impoſſible he ſhould go back or lean; ſince the inward rein of the caveſon forces his hind-leg within the volte out, and the rider's manner of ſitting upon him gives him liberty within, and ſtops him there; becauſe his left ſhoulder can only advance to a certain degree, which gives him a juſt ply and no more, which is as it ought to be.

As to the horſeman's helps, he ought to be ſeated upon his twiſt, leaning more upon the ſtirrup without the volte, than upon that within it, having his leg within the volte more advanced than the other. If he bears hard upon the ſtirrup within the volte, his weight will be on the ſame ſide, which would be abſolutely wrong. Nobody will pretend to deny, that the weight does not bear in this manner; for example, only look at the ſtirrup, and you will plainly perceive that within the volte to be four inches longer than that without. This is to be weighed as with a pair of ſcales. But one queſtion may be accidentally aſked, What is there to ſupport the horſe? You have nothing to do, but to help him with the rein of the caveſon, as I ſaid before; that is, by drawing it to a certain degree, which not only forces the horſe's hind-leg next the volte out to ſupport him, but keeps it there, which is a farther ſupport; from whence he has room to move the half of his ſhoulders before the half of his croupe within the volte, which affords him a natural and eaſy ſupport. Hence you may perceive, that it is the inward rein of the caveſon that ſupports him, and not the rider's leg within the volte, extended like that of St. GEORGE's when he ſlew the dragon, and I am ſurpriſed this thought ſhould have eſcaped mankind. My way is to have the rider bear upon the ſtirrup within the volte, with his toes turned a little outwards, and ſomewhat more advanced than the outward

outward leg. The old method of a horſeman's leaning back for a Terre-à-terre, in order to put his horſe upon the haunches, is falſe, ſince it rather puts him upon his ſhoulders; for the rider, who is only one piece, cannot lean back, without placing himſelf upon his buttocks, which is very falſe, as he then is no longer upon his twiſt. Moreover, when he is ſeated firm upon his ſtirrups, and leans backward, his legs muſt neceſſarily come forward, which is not their proper ſituation; ſo that the rider, in order to keep a juſt ſeat, and have his heels at command, ſhould bend his body gently forward, by which means his legs will go back, and be in their right poſition; for by the motion of the body backward, the legs will come forward, and ſo *vice verſa*, if he leans firm upon his ſtirrups. By ſaying, that I would have the rider advance his body, I don't mean that he ſhould bend his back; but, on the contrary, that he ſhould keep it ſtrait, and advance his cheſt, and have a general inclination of his whole body from head to foot, and that however ſo little, as in many riders, it can hardly be perceived: by this means, he will always be fixed upon his twiſt, and his legs properly placed, to be ready for any aid that may be wanted. I am now going to tell you how to help the horſe with the leg. If the rider extends his ſinews till he is ſtiff in the ham, this preſſes the horſe with the calf of the leg; but the thigh, by the particular mechaniſm of the body, goes from him; ſo that by the extenſion of the ſinews, that is to ſay, by keeping a ſtiff ham, the thigh becomes concave on the inſide next the ſaddle, whilſt the calf of the leg preſſes againſt the horſe: if you bear much harder upon the out ſtirrup, than the other, and bend the outward knee, that cavity will be filled, and become convex in that part where it was concave before; at this time the horſe is preſſed by the thigh, and the calf of the leg goes from him. From hence you may perceive, that bending in the ham is the leaſt help, being the help with the thigh; and being ſtiff in the ham is a ſtronger help, as it is the help of the calf of the leg; and pinching the horſe with the ſpurs is the ſtrongeſt help, which is done in the following manner: The rider's legs being very near the horſe, and placed a little backward, he ſhould touch him gently with his heels, bending his hams a little upon each motion he makes. Thus you ſee there are three degrees of helps; one with the thigh, which is the moſt gentle; a ſecond with the calf of the leg, that is ſtronger; and a third with the ſpurs, which is the ſtrongeſt of all: any one of theſe are to be uſed as you ſee occaſion.

It is a conſtant maxim, that the pillar ought always to be within the horſe's croupe, when it is towards the center, by which means a horſe can never become *entier*, becauſe the half of his ſhoulders go before his hind-leg within the volte, ſo that he is obliged to go ſideways, as he ought. I muſt adviſe you likewiſe, not to lean too hard upon the out-ſtirrup; for, ſhould you do ſo, your horſe will be apt to lean on the ſame ſide, which is not only ungraceful, but is abſolutely falſe; a horſe in ſuch a poſture may be compared to a wooden bench with four legs; when the inward legs are held up, they become ſhorter than the others that are not held up. The horſe is in the ſame poſture, if you lean your body too much on the outſide, for he will lean on that ſide too; from whence it will neceſſarily follow, that his legs within the volte will be ſhorter than thoſe without, which is entirely falſe, ſince his legs within the volte ought to be longeſt when he advances Terre-à-terre. Take

particular

particular care therefore not to incline too much on that ſide, but ſit as ſtrait as you can, for the reaſons I have given you. I have already ſaid, that when a horſe goes Terre-à-terre, he deſcribes four diſtinct circles with his four feet; his fore-foot within the volte deſcribes the largeſt, the other fore-foot the ſecond, his hind-leg next the volte deſcribes the third, and the other without the volte deſcribes the fourth and ſmalleſt circle, as will appear by the following figure.

CHAP. XVI.

Terre-à-terre towards the Right Hand.

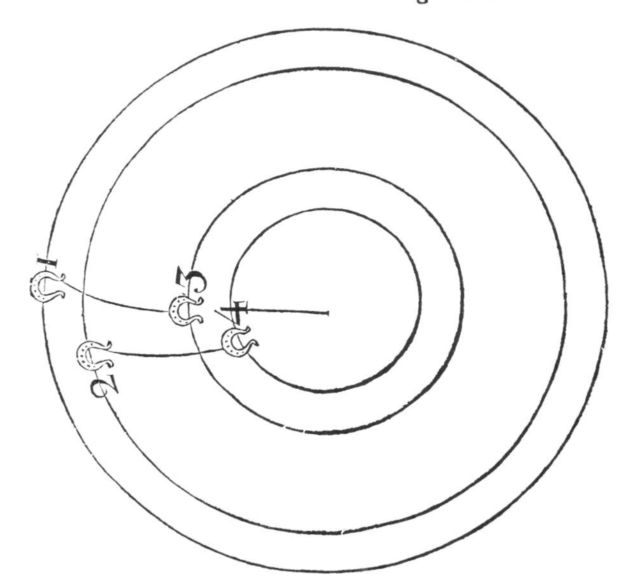

Here you have a true deſcription of a horſe's movement Terre-à-terre, as I have expreſſed it. The line drawn towards the center ought always to be within the horſe's croupe.

CHAP. XVII.

Terre-à-terre to the Left Hand.

NOW the rider ought to change his bridle, and take it in his right hand, drawing the reins of the caveſon with the left, having the nails of his hand upwards, and the little finger pointing toward the right ſhoulder, turning his face within the volte, and bringing his right ſhoulder within it likewiſe, helping the horſe with the contrary leg, which is the right. I gave you the reaſons for this in the former chapter, and therefore ſhall avoid troubling you with a repetition of them.

Terre-à-terre towards the Left Hand.

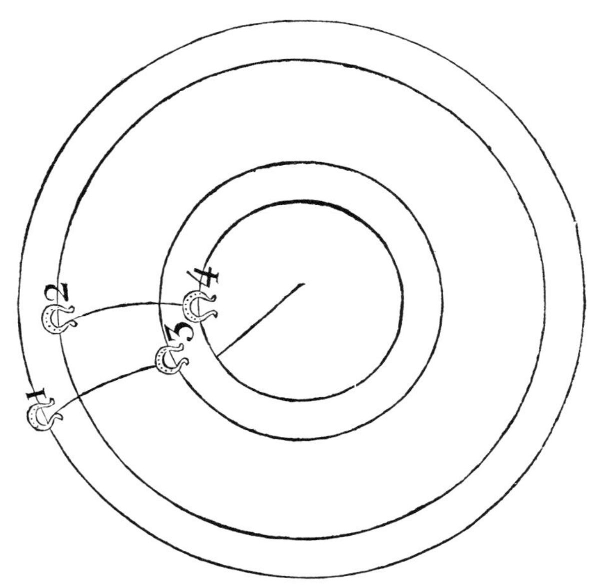

The line drawn towards the center ſhews, that the pillar ought always to be within the horſe's croupe.

People may be ſurpriſed, that I don't make uſe of the *longe* or long rope about the pillar in this leſſon. To ſpeak truth, I have entirely baniſhed it my Manege, becauſe my only aim is to make a horſe obey the hand and heel. Thoſe who imagine that a horſe goes Terre-à-terre with the *longe* about a pillar, are miſtaken, ſince he is not then at all in the hand and heel, but obeys only the rope and *chambriere*, going quite by rote: without the rope he don't mind the hand, nor without the *chambriere* does he mind the heel: he can do but ſo, for the rope keeps him in, and the *chambriere* makes him go forwards. For which reaſon I never make uſe of the ſingle pillar, neither in the walk, trot, or gallop, nor in Terre-à-terre. The pillar, according to my method, only ſerves me for a mark, that I may diſtinguiſh the center, and mark the circle round it the better, whether it be large or ſmall. But as to the caveſon, I conſtantly uſe it both to horſes and colts, to thoſe half dreſſed or quite dreſſed, young or old; in ſhort, to all horſes; it gives them a right ply, and preſerves their mouths, ſo that, when I take it off, they go ſurpriſingly well with the bridle only. For by preſerving the mouth, they are ſo ſenſible upon the bars and to the curb, that you have them under command by the leaſt motion; whereas when you always make uſe of the bridle, it makes them hard-mouth'd; and nothing is more requiſite in the dreſſing of a horſe, than to keep his mouth and ſides as tender as poſſible, becauſe he goes only by the hand and heel. Beſides other advantages ariſing from the uſe of the caveſon, it preſerves the mouth, as I mentioned before; but the preſervation of his ſides depends wholly upon the

diſcretion

discretion of the rider. With regard to Curvettes and Demi-airs, altho' I don't make use of a rope about the pillar, I use the caveson after a new and odd method, as you shall see hereafter, which produces an admirable effect. This is the true method of dressing a horse Terre-à-terre.

CHAP. XVIII.

The Method of putting a Horse between two Pillars after the old Fashion.

WHEN a horse knows to trot, stop, and gallop, and is in the least obedient to the hand and heel in his walk, and begins to move a little Terre-à-terre, I then put him between two pillars, and make him move his croupe from side to side with the switch; then I make him raise himself gently with the button of the reins down; afterwards I mount him, and oblige him to do the same when I am upon his back; and when I have once taught him to make two or three Curvettes, or rather Pesades, so that he bears the hand, I never use this after, for I have a new method, which you will find produces a wonderful effect. The pillars make a horse very impatient; you ought therefore to have yourself as much patience as possible; the moment he shews the least mark of obedience, you must put him into the stable, to endeavour to please him. Thus far as to the old method, which I shall soon leave for a much better, as you shall see hereafter.

CHAP. XIX.

An excellent Lesson for all Horses, as well those that are heavy upon the Hand as those that are light.

IF you follow my lessons, most of the horses you ride will be light upon your hand, and have a good *appuy*. The lesson I am going to recommend is this: You must put the head of your horse to the wall in the cover'd Manege, and walk him thus the length of the four walls, or, at least, of three: and to the right hand, draw the inward rein of the caveson, and help him with the outward leg, which is the left. Just the contrary helps must be for the left; for rein on one side and leg on the other always works a horse's croupe. I have mentioned before, that when a horse is upon a walk with his head to the wall, that the wall is a kind of center; so that his fore-part will be pressed, and his croupe at liberty; I say, when he is upon the walk, which is the movement of a trot: but when he goes Terre-à-terre with his head to the wall, his action is very different to that of a trot, which is cross-ways, in which the fore-part is pressed, and the croupe at liberty, when his head is to the wall or center; but in Terre-à-terre, which is the action of the gallop, the two legs on the same side advance together, and continue so; the near-leg leads, and the hind-leg on the same side immediately follows, let the horse go to either hand. So that in this action, the horse's head being to the wall, his croupe is pressed and his shoulders at liberty, although his head is to the wall, which is as a center: it is the action of a horse's legs Terre-à-terre that occasions this difference. The head of the horse being thus placed towards three or four of the walls,

walls, any horſe may this way be brought to obey both the hand and the heel. Let him be to either hand, he muſt always be worked with leg and rein contrary. This leſſon has the ſame effect both for the Curvette and Peſade; but you ought at firſt, both for the Curvette and Peſade, to make him do three or four in one place; then make him advance, and make three or four more; by which means he will move at length freely in Curvettes ſide-ways, as well as Terre-à-terre, his head to the wall. I would have you know, that the doctrine is falſe, which concludes, that the hand commands a horſe from the muzzle to the ſhoulders, and the heel from the ſhoulders backwards; for the inward rein of the caveſon not only commands half the ſhoulders, but puts out likewiſe the hind-leg within the volte, ſo that that is govern'd by it too. Thus the caveſon-rein helps half the croupe, and the rider's outward leg helps the horſe's hind-leg of the ſame ſide, putting it in. You may perceive from hence, that the rein of the caveſon helps half the croupe, and the leg of the rider the other half. And thus I conclude this uſeful leſſon.

End of the Second Diviſion of LESSONS.

CHAP. XX.

The Third Diviſion of LESSONS, *Which is to ſhew how to make a Horſe obey the Bridle.*

How to make him obey the Bridle.

WHEN you have made a horſe's ſhoulders ſupple by the firſt diviſion of leſſons, and taught him by the ſecond to obey the heel, this third diviſion is intended to make him know the bridle, which is to be done in the following manner.

Let the rider put the rein of the caveſon, fixed my way, which he holds in his right hand under the burr of the ſaddle, that is, under his thigh, and faſten it well to the pommel; and ſo ſhort, as to bend the horſe's ſhoulders to ſuch a degree, as to force his hind-leg within the volte out, but not ſo much as to force out the outward leg too; for that is a ſoleciſm in horſemanſhip, as you will ſee hereafter. When the horſe's head is thus faſtened to the pommel of the ſaddle, the caveſon gives him the proper ply, and the rider ſhould work him with the bridle upon a large circle. When he goes to the right, you muſt place your hand without the volte a little towards the left ſhoulder, helping him at the ſame time with the leg within, which is leg and rein of a ſide, and that always works both the ſhoulders, and not his croupe. This leſſon is the ſame as the firſt, excepting only, that in this you work more with the bridle. This is the figure both for the right and left hand.

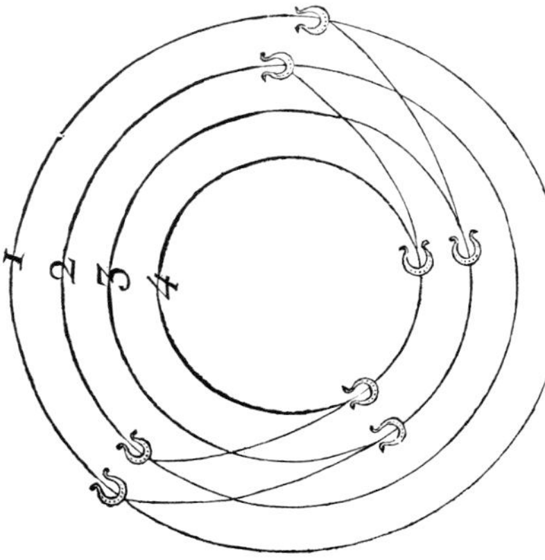

For

For the left, you muſt faſten the left rein of the caveſon to the pommel of the ſaddle. The rein and leg on the ſame ſide, work always the ſhoulders, and not in the leaſt the croupe.

A horſe deſcribes only two circles in a walk to the right hand, when his croup is to the center.

A horſe deſcribes only two circles in a walk to the left hand, when his croup is to the center.

A horſe deſcribes two circles, when his head is to the center, and his croupe out.

When one paſſages a horſe after this manner upon a walk, the rein of the caveſon ought to be faſtened according to the ſide on which he is to go. If he is to go to the right, you muſt turn your bridle-hand toward the left, on the outſide of the neck of the horſe, the nails of your hand turned upwards towards your left ſhoulder, which pulls the inward rein of the bridle, for reaſons I have given you before, helping him at the ſame time with the contrary leg, which will work his croupe and the half of his ſhoulders. For the left hand, the rein of the caveſon being fixed to the pommel of the ſaddle, you muſt turn your bridle-hand towards the outſide of the horſe's neck, which is the right ſide, having the nails of your hand turned upwards to the right ſhoulder, by which means you work the inward rein of the bridle, helping him at the ſame time with your out-leg, that is, leg and rein contrary, which always work the croupe. Thus a horſe ought to be work'd in his walk, the rein fixed to the pommel of the ſaddle, with the croupe either in or out.

CHAP. XXI.

For Terre-à-terre *to the Right Hand, the Caveſon being faſten'd to the Pommel of the Saddle, and the Bridle in the Left Hand.*

THE right rein of the caveſon being fixed to the pommel of the ſaddle, you muſt put the horſe's croupe within the volte, having the pillar on the inſide of it, with the left hand turned towards the outſide of the horſe's neck, which draws the inward rein, and makes it work in the manner I have deſcribed before. At the ſame time you work the horſe thus with the hand, you muſt help him with the contrary leg, which is that without the volte, or the left. Here I give you the figure for Terre-à-terre both for the right and left hand.

BOOK II.

The inward rein of the caveſon fix'd to the pommel of the ſaddle is wrong for Terre-à-terre.

For the left hand, the left rein being faſten'd to the pommel of the ſaddle, in order to give the horſe a good ply, place your bridle-hand on the right ſide of the horſe's neck without the volte, having the nails of your hand turn'd upwards towards the right ſhoulder, helping him at the ſame time with the contrary leg. As to any farther obſervations, I refer you to what I have ſaid before, which you ought to ſtudy well, leſt I ſhould offend you by many repetitions.

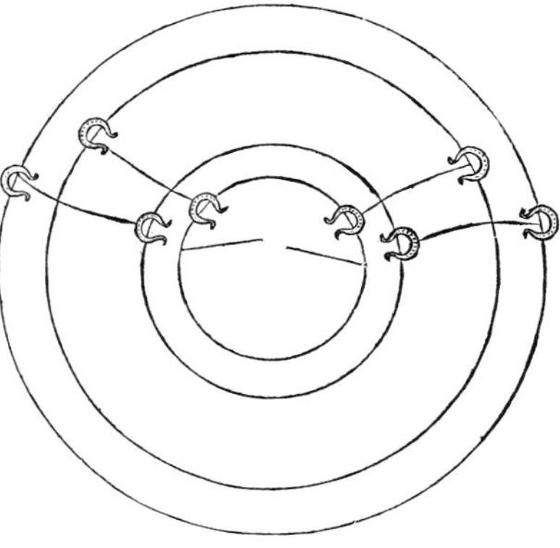

End of the Third Diviſion of Leſſons.

CHAP. XXII.

The fourth Diviſion of Leſſons.

To work a Horſe with falſe Reins.

THE ſame reins of the caveſon you uſed before, will ſerve you for falſe ones, and muſt be faſtened in the ſame manner; excepting only, that you muſt put them through the banquet of the bridle, and bring them back to your hand.

In my firſt diviſion of leſſons I ſhewed you how to ſupple a horſe's ſhoulders with the caveſon my way, which is very efficacious, tho' the taſk is difficult.

In the ſecond, I have ſhewed you how to work a horſe's croupe with the half of his ſhoulders when he goes Terre-à-terre, and to obey both the hand and heel.

In the third, you have faſtened the reins of the caveſon to the pommel of the ſaddle, and have begun to work a little more upon the barrs and reſting-place of the curb, ſince you had nothing in your hand but the bridle, and the reins of the caveſon were faſtened to help the horſe's ply.

Now in this fourth diviſion of leſſons you have the falſe reins to help the *appuy* upon the barrs, but they make the curb looſe, and thereby eaſe the place where it ſhould reſt, ſo that it don't work at all; for the more the falſe reins are drawn, the looſer is the curb, tho' the barrs are preſſed.

The advantage ariſing from theſe falſe reins, is, that they are ſerviceable to all kinds of horſes; they help the *appuy* of thoſe that want it; they *appuy* their barrs more freely upon the bit, having no apprehenſion of the curb; they are uſeful beſides to thoſe that have too much: Provided you work them with their heads to a wall, you may put them then ſo much upon the haunches, as to make them light upon the hand; and when they are upon the haunches, they are much lighter and more at their eaſe, by not being pinched by the curb.

After

After the laſt diviſion of my leſſons, I dare venture to ſay, there is none better, or more efficacious in the working of a horſe than this; for it gives him the ply, and that by the barrs, makes him obey the inward rein of the bridle, and anſwers our intention; therefore this leſſon is excellent, was it only upon that account. The horſe ſhould be worked in the ſame manner with falſe reins as he is with the caveſon, and with the ſame helps, both as to ſhoulders and croupe, aiding him with your leg in the ſame manner; give him the ſame leſſons upon walk, trot, gallop, and Terre-à-terre, faſtening them to the pommel of the ſaddle, as thoſe of the caveſon. You ſhould get by heart your firſt leſſons, and therefore I ſhall not trouble you with repetitions.

End of the fourth Diviſion of Leſſons.

CHAP. XXIII.

The fifth Diviſion of Leſſons.

To work a Horſe with the Bit only, the Reins ſeparated in both Hands.

IF you work the ſhoulders of the horſe with the two reins of the bridle held ſeparate in each hand, you ought to uſe the inward rein, and the leg on the ſame ſide, which work upon both ſhoulders, and not upon the croupe. You may ride him thus to both hands upon walk, trot, or gallop, either in large circles, or in his own length; but this works only the ſhoulders. If you deſign to work the croupe, either head or croupe to the pillar or wall, it muſt e leg and rein contrary. If the horſe is to the right, draw the inward rein, with the nails of your hand upwards, and your little finger to the left ſhoulder, helping the horſe at the ſame time with the contrary leg, as I ſaid before. This ought to be done upon a walk, which is the action of the trot. If you go to the left, you muſt draw the left rein, the nails upward towards the right ſhoulder, and help the horſe with the contrary leg. When you would go Terre-à-terre, you muſt always pull the inward rein towards your oppoſite ſhoulder, put that ſhoulder in, and look into the volte. He ſhould be put ſometimes upon a gentle gallop, with his croupe in, working conſtantly with the inward rein and the oppoſite leg, as I ſaid before. When he goes upon a gentle gallop, make him take two or three times of Terre-à-terre, and put him again upon his gentle gallop. This ſhould be done either with the reins of the caveſon fixed to the pommel of the ſaddle, or when you hold them in your hand. When you are upon a gentle gallop, the helps you give him both with hand and heel ought to be moderate, but ſtronger when you make him go two or three cadences Terre-à-terre, and gentle again when you put him to the gallop. This is an excellent leſſon; for the gentle gallop pleaſes the horſe, and the times of Terre-à-terre make him obey the hand and heel; and thus he is made perfectly obedient to both. It is an excellent leſſon to make a horſe go Terre-à-terre with his head to three walls, the two reins parted, one in each hand, working him at the ſame time with the inward rein and the oppoſite leg; by it any horſe may be brought to go perfectly well, and nothing reclaims like it a vicious one. You may work him in the ſame manner upon his Demi-voltes, with the reins parted, and by it you will be able to judge abſolutely whether he has been worked right upon his firſt leſſons, or not.

End of the fifth Diviſion of Leſſons.

BOOK II.

CHAP. XXIV.

The ſixth Diviſion of Leſſons.

To work a Horſe with the Reins of the Bridle only in the Left Hand, which is the Perfection of Horſemanſhip; for any Horſe that obeys that and the Heel, may be reckoned compleatly dreſſed.

THE rider is to be ſeated according to my former directions in a preceding chapter upon that. Whether a horſe walks, trots or gallops in large circles, the rider's hand ought to be a little without the volte, that he may work the inward rein; and his leg on the ſame ſide ought conſtantly to work the horſe's ſhoulders. If upon a walk you work the horſe's head to the pillar, and the croupe out, leg and rein contrary, you narrow him before and enlarge him behind; yet his croupe will be work'd notwithſtanding, for leg and rein contrary work always the croupe, which is at liberty, as it is farther from the center. Remember that I am ſpeaking of the walk, which is the action of the trot. In like manner if you put the head to the wall, the croupe is at liberty, and the fore-part preſſed, becauſe the wall is as the center; and what is neareſt the center muſt always be moſt preſſed, and what is the fartheſt from it the moſt at liberty; I ſay upon a walk, which is as the trot, for you will ſee that it is very different in other actions. Suppoſe now that we put a horſe's croupe upon a walk to the center, his hind-part will then be preſſed, and his fore-part at liberty, let him go to which hand you pleaſe. And becauſe his croupe is to the center, I ſuppoſe him ſtill upon a walk, the helps muſt be leg and rein contrary, by which means both his haunches will be worked, and only the half of his ſhoulders. When he goes to the right, the nails of the rider's bridle-hand ought to be turned upwards, his little finger to the left ſhoulder; and to the left, turn'd upwards to the right ſhoulder, helping always with the contrary leg. You muſt uſe the ſame helps when he goes in his own length. To work a horſe well upon his walk, is the foundation of all; for when he is upon a gentle walk, he is more patient, and ready to comprehend what one would teach him; beſides, his memory is ſo help'd by it, that he is not ſo apt to forget. If a horſe is perfectly obedient in the walk, that is to ſay, if he obeys the hand and heel, I can make him do all that his ſtrength will allow. Take care to remember, that you make your horſe in every thing he does, unleſs it be when you correct him for a fault, I ſay in every thing he does, both upon walk and trot, gallop, terre-à-terre, demi-voltes, or whatever elſe it is, to be obedient to the hand and heel, and upon his haunches, and to go forwards a little in every thing he does, though but a little, not only becauſe it makes him appear more graceful, but alſo becauſe it gives him ſtrength, and makes him go with truth and ſafety; otherwiſe he would be in danger of falling. Moreover, going backwards makes him ſeem reſty; for which reaſon he ought always to advance, unleſs when you rein him back. It is ungraceful to ſee a horſe go backwards in capriols, and looks like reſtineſs. Theſe are the helps for a horſe upon the walk, both reins of the bridle in the left hand.

CHAP.

CHAP. XXV.

To work a Horſe Terre-à-terre, with the Bridle only in the Left Hand.

AS the walk is the action of the trot, which is with the horſe's legs acroſs, ſo is Terre-à-terre the action of the gallop, in which both legs on the ſame ſide move; ſo that in a trot, that part neareſt the center is always moſt preſſed, and the other moſt at liberty, whether it be the ſhoulders or the croupe. But the action of Terre-à-terre is very different, being that of a gallop, in which both legs on the ſame ſide continue to advance, and you work with the inward rein and the contrary leg. Therefore he muſt be helped here as in the gallop, the horſe always having his croupe preſſed, and his ſhoulders at liberty, whether the one or the other be to the pillar. So that you may percieve, that being either nearer or farther from the center, his ſhoulders are neither more preſſed, nor more at liberty, nor does it make any alteration in his croupe; for in the trot, one works one way, and in the gallop, or Terre-à-terre quite another, as I mentioned before. But you muſt remember, that this muſt be always done by the inward rein and the oppoſite leg; for leg and rein of a ſide is quite another thing, ſince they work both ſhoulders, and not at all the croupe. So much for this in general.

I muſt now acquaint you of an old abſurd way, which is even practiſed at this time, relating to the bridle-hand; but what is moſt ſurpriſing, the very philoſophers in that art teach it in their writings. I'll explain to you, wherein their error conſiſts. When a horſe goes to the right, they turn the hand on the ſame ſide within his neck, by which they put both his ſhoulders in, and conſequently his croupe out, ſpurring him at the ſame time to keep it in, and thus they give him two contrary aids at one and the ſame time, which is impoſſible. For this reaſon I invented the method of working the inward rein, as you may perceive in all my leſſons, which is the moſt excellent invention that can be to make a horſe go true, and can't be done by any other method, and is certainly the quinteſſence of horſemanſhip for almoſt every thing, Terre-à-terre, and moſt Airs.

To work a Horſe Terre-à-terre when the Bridle is held only in the Left Hand.

The action of a horſe's legs Terre-à-terre is a gallop in time, which is term'd *Terre-à-terre relevé.* The rider ought to be ſeated upon his twiſt, his legs perpendicular down. To the right, he ſhould put the bridle on the outſide of the horſe's neck, which is to the left, turning the inſide of his hand upwards as much as poſſible, with his little finger as much above his thumb as he can, pointing to the left ſhoulder, and help the horſe with the leg out of the volte. By aiding him in this manner acroſs, with the rein within, and the leg without, his croupe is always worked, ſince by this means his hind-legs are put together; the drawing the inward rein puts out the inward hind-leg, and the rider's outward leg puts in the other hind-leg, ſo that they go under his belly, which puts him upon his haunches. By this true method, both the hind-legs are work'd, and only the half of his ſhoulders preſſes his hind-legs, leaving his fore-part at liberty to embrace the

volte

BOOK II.

volte the better; for ſhould both the ſhoulders come in, his haunch or leg without the volte would be out, which would be falſe. By this method a horſe deſcribes four circles with his legs, as he ought to do when he goes Terre-à-terre; that is to ſay, his fore-leg within the volte deſcribes the largeſt, the other fore-leg the ſecond, the hind-leg within the volte the third, and the other the fourth or ſmalleſt circle. The legs of a horſe being of equal length, he muſt of neceſſity be upon his haunches, when his hind-legs are in the line of nature, that is to ſay, within the line of the fore ones. For the ſame reaſon, when you draw the rein within the volte, and that the horſe is bent to be like a ſemicircle, the leg within the volte will be the longeſt, which is as it ought to be for him to advance the hind-leg on the ſame ſide; and by drawing the rein within the volte, as I ſaid before, the hind-leg within the volte is forced out, which gives it more liberty of following the fore-leg within the volte; and this is as it ſhould be. The rider's helping with his outward leg conſtrains the leg of that ſide, ſubjects it, and conſequently puts it behind the other hind-leg, which is entirely right. You ſee the neceſſity of a horſe's always avoiding the pillar or center with his hind-leg within the volte, which makes him move with half his ſhoulders firſt, which is as it ſhould be. You muſt remark here, that the outſide of the volte is open, and that you have no other way to ſhut it but with the heel: if the horſe obeys it, it is ſhut; if he does not, it is open. I'll ſhew you in its proper place how to ſhut it.

Terre-à-terre to the Right Hand.

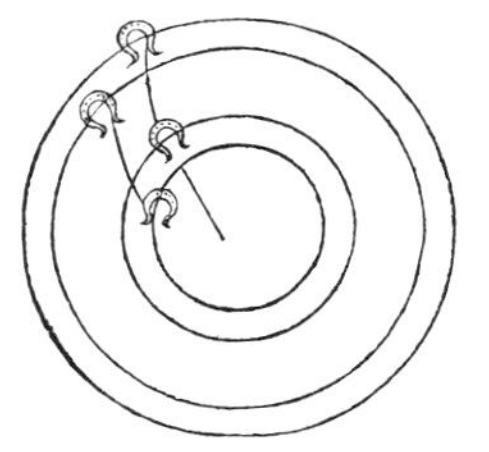

The line drawn towards the pillar ſhews in what manner a horſe's hind-leg ought to avoid the pillar.

Terre-à-terre to the Left Hand.

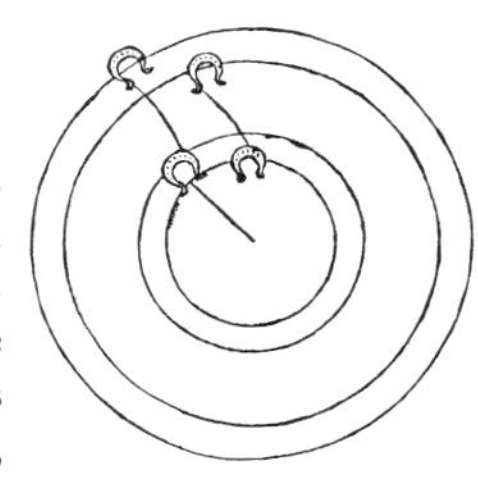

Here the bridle-hand ought to be on the contrary ſide, that is to ſay, on the right, with the nails of the rider's hand turned upwards, and his little finger pointing towards the left ſhoulder, having his face turned into the volte, and helping the horſe with his contrary leg, which is the right: I gave you my reaſons for it in the preceding chapter, and therefore ſhall avoid troubling you with a repetition. This is the figure for Terre-à-terre on the left hand.

Fig. 21.

The line drawn towards the pillar ſhews in what manner the horſe's hind-leg ſhould avoid it.

CHAP.

CHAP. XXVI

CHAP. XXVI.

For Passades along the Wall with the Bridle only, and many other Instructions.

YOU must begin first upon a walk, then do it upon a trot, then upon a gallop, and afterwards full speed, and make the demivolte with the same exactness as you did it in Terre-à-terre, only the volte here should not be more than the horse's length.

When the wall is on his left, he ought when he gallops, in order to prepare him for the demivolte, on the right hand, to be help'd in the following manner: You must draw the rein opposite to the wall, as I have taught you before, or streighten it a little, in order to force his hind-leg out on the same side, and put the half of his shoulders in, that he may upon his gentle gallop advance his inward fore-leg, which is the leg farthest from the wall, and that the hind-leg of the same side may follow. Thus he will be in a proper posture to make the demivolte Terre-à-terre; and if you draw the inward rein a little stronger at the same time, helping him with the opposite leg, he will make his volte as true as if he was fix'd in a frame; that is to say, that neither his shoulders nor croupe will be either too much in or too much out. But as soon as he has closed his demivolte to the right hand, the right rein must be left loose, and the left drawn, as the right rein was before, that he may be ready to make the demivolte to the left hand, since at that time he should change his legs, and alter his posture, by advancing his near leg, and making the other on the same side follow it; by this means he will take the demivolte as he ought. The rein and leg ought to be changed in this manner upon each Passade. Just before your horse makes the demivolte, I would advise you to stop him upon your hand, leaning back a little, so that he may make two or three *falcades* before he turns, or makes the demivolte, which will fix him more upon his haunches, and enable him to perform his demivoltes the better; besides, it will give him an additional grace. If the Passades are done at full speed, which is what the French call *Passades furieuses*, the same method ought to be observed, only the rider ought to have his legs closer to the horse. Nothing more strongly proves a horse to be thoroughly dressed, than Passades, since nothing can make a horse perfect but the hands and the heels, and he obeys both in Passades. He flies the heel upon strait lines, and obeys the hand in going slower and turning; the heels too in his demivoltes, and again the hand in stopping, which is all that can be required. I must hint to you, that when you go in Passades in the country, or in any open place, you are confined to nothing (as horsemen say) but may make your demivolte on which hand you please. They are in the right, since you are at liberty to begin on which hand you please, as there is no wall to confine you; but when you have once begun, you ought to make the demivolte upon that leg which advances in a direct line, and on the same side, otherwise your horse will cross his legs, be confused, and go false. So that you may begin on which side you please, but then you are afterwards confin'd to keep to that side, tho' in an open plain, as if there was a wall. Thus much for Passades: as to those called *relevé*, they are easily done if the horse goes in curvettes.

Fig. 22.

When

BOOK II.

When the croupe of a horſe is towards the center, you cannot work too much with the rein and oppoſite leg, as I ſhew'd before, ſince they throw out the hind-leg on the ſide of the volte, and give the ſhoulders liberty to come and go firſt, as they ought; inſomuch that the inward hind-leg is only in the line of nature, or in the line of the outward fore-leg; if it be ſo only one inch, or half inch, it is ſufficient. Thus he will go with ſpirit and eaſe, as if he deſpiſed the ground.

You cannot work the ſhoulders of a horſe too much, provided his outward hind-leg is in the line of the fore-leg on the ſame ſide; for example, you may perceive this by working a horſe in the quarter or demi-voltes; for though you draw the inward rein to work the ſhoulders, his hind-leg remains pretty near in the ſame place. You ſhould always take care to make a horſe advance, be it never ſo little, though not more than a ſtraw's breath. If he offers to riſe, or retain himſelf, looſe the reins of the bridle a little, and ſpur him to make him advance. Remember, that an eaſy hand is one of the principal aids we have; for it puts a horſe upon his haunches, when he finds nothing elſe to lean upon; beſides, it pleaſes him, and prevents his being reſty.

Obſerve always to alter your leſſons, although they have a tendency to the ſame end, otherwiſe a horſe will take ſuch a habit of it that he will go quite by rote, and not mind at all the hand and heel; ſo that when you imagine you have perform'd wonders, you are nothing advanced.

I make frequent uſe of this leſſon, to make a horſe obedient to the hand and heel, and find it a very good one. I make him go ſideways to one hand, and then forward a little; then ſideways to the other hand, and forward a little; and thus ſideways from hand to hand; which is an excellent method, ſince by this, a horſe expects the hand and heel, ſubmits himſelf to them, and don't go by rote. But this leſſon requires room, otherwiſe the horſe will be impatient, and knowing too well what he is to do, go by rote, eſpecially if you continue it long. It is the ſame in all other leſſons, and therefore they ought to be changed often; obſerving always, not to ſtop a horſe twice in the ſame place; for he may remember it, and ſtop there before company, to the diſgrace of the rider. Avoid therefore every thing that looks like going by rote, and make your horſe think of nothing but obeying the hand and heel.

I have invented another leſſon, which is this: When my horſe is ſtrait, I make him advance; if he is to the right, I preſs his ſhoulders as much out as I can with the inward rein of the bridle, and give him the contrary leg, in order to put his croupe as far as I can to the right, and oblige him to anſwer the hand and heel. Being thus ſideways, I make him advance a little upon his walk; I work him to the other hand in the ſame manner, and thus continue to change from one hand to the other as long as the ground permits. This leſſon is good to make a horſe anſwer both the hand and heel.

I invented this leſſon to work the croupe upon the quarter voltes, which is, when to the right he makes a ſtrait line; I draw the contrary rein, which is the outward one of the bridle, giving him the contrary leg, which forces his croupe out upon that quarter to the left hand, and puts him ſtrait upon the ſecond line, as if he went to the right. And I go on ſo to take the other quarter for the left, which works his croupe. The ſame to the other hand; though I am going to the left, I work his croupe for the right;

for

for by this means, the croupe is worked upon the quarters, and the ſhoulders aſſured near the center, according to the other old way, which is a very good one, in which one works within the lines, making the ſhoulders come round, and keeping the haunches or croupe at the ſame time.

A horſe that does not go well upon his haunches, can never do well in the Manege, ſo that our whole ſtudy is to put him upon them; but I would have you underſtand, when a horſe may properly be ſaid to be upon his haunches, and when not. Suppoſe a horſe to be almoſt ſitting upon his croupe, he is not upon his haunches notwithſtanding, if his hind-legs are diſtant from the lines of nature (which is to have them much aſunder,) altho' he was almoſt upon his croupe. But to be upon his haunches, his hind-legs ought to be in their natural poſition, with the haunch-bone pointing directly forward, and his hind-legs under his belly, bending his hocks as much as poſſible; and this is the juſt ſituation of a horſe upon his haunches. But we ought to conſider the natural form and ſhape of a horſe, that we may work him according to nature. You may obſerve in all my leſſons, that I tell you how the legs go, and thoſe who are unacquainted with that, are entirely ignorant and work in the dark. Here is then the form, in which nature has made a horſe's legs: his fore-legs are made like thoſe of a man, having his knee bending forward; and his hind-legs like a man's arm, having the ſinews of his ham bending backwards, which is diametrically oppoſite to the former. If the hind-legs of a horſe bent in the ſame manner as thoſe before, he would walk upright like a man; but his hind-legs bending contrary, they reſemble the arm of a man, and his fore-legs bend as ours, which makes him go upon all four; and there is no other reaſon for beaſts going upon all four, with their bellies to the ground. Horſes then ought to be worked according to their make, and that form which nature has given them.

You may perhaps ſay, that there is nothing in changing a horſe from one hand to the other; ſince, by this method, he arrives to the utmoſt perfection in obeying both the hand and the heel, becauſe he can change when you pleaſe. This is true, but you ought notwithſtanding to know what to do, otherwiſe you may chance to fall. Do then thus: changing one *piſte* (as it is call'd) upon a large circle to the right, put your bridle a little to the contrary ſide, aſſiſting your horſe gently at the ſame time with the leg within the volte, that he may have the greater liberty for ſhifting his ſhoulders; his croupe muſt not come too much in, leſt it ſhould make him *entier*. Every time you change, whether it be within or without the circle, make him go forwards, helping him with rein and leg contrary, feeling him a little more than uſual both in hand and heel. The time a horſe takes in changing is Terre-à-terre, and ſometimes that of the Demi-volte, according as his manner of changing is. After this quarter or demi-volte, he ſhould be put to his gallop as before, and do it as I told you. He ſhould be worked thus to both hands.

To change upon the Voltes Terre-à-terre.

You muſt work the horſe Terre-à-terre, as I taught you before, both with hand and heels; and before you change make him go in a leſſer circle, helping his ſhoulders ſomewhat more, which will put him more aſlaunt, and will fix his croupe the better to make his change. When he is in this poſture, make him go forwards, and at the ſame time change your hand and heel, and you will do well in changing to draw the inward rein of the bridle at the ſame time.

BOOK II.

In Terre-à-terre Relevé a Horſe ought to go according to this Figure.

The meaſure of the ground in Terre-à-terre is to allow ſomewhat more than a horſe's length; but you may take more or leſs compaſs, if you pleaſe.

The ſame aids muſt be uſed in Terre-à-terre determiné, and the horſe's poſture the ſame, excepting that Terre-à-terre determiné is lower, being much like the Carriere, only that the Carriere is not upon the volte.

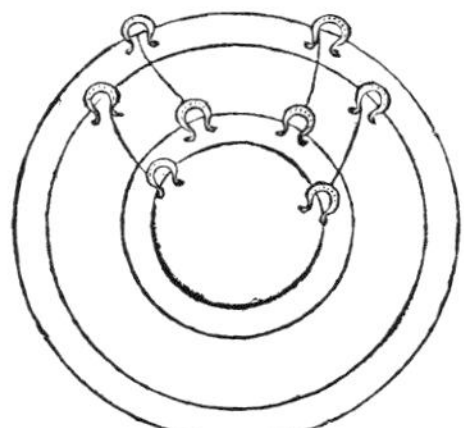

I give you here a univerſal map of horſemanſhip, containing the whole variety of the Manege, *viz.* the Gallop, Changes of all kinds within or without the circle, going upon Quarters to both hands, working the Shoulders or the Croupe either within or without, Demivoltes, Curvettes upon the voltes, or ſtrait forwards; to Serpentine, or to go in Caprioles, the horſe's head to the wall, going ſideways in an Oval, or in Quarters; in ſhort, I have omitted nothing.

CHAP.

CHAP. XXVII.

Three Leſſons to work, and I may ſay to perfectly finiſh a Horſe for the Manege.

THE caveſon my way held in the rider's hand gives the true ply to the horſe; and there is nothing like it, for it bends him from noſe to tail. When he has been compleatly worked in this manner, and is very ſupple, there is ſtill ſomething in the bridle or bit, with which he is not well acquainted. For which reaſon I would adviſe you to fix the caveſon my way to the pommel of the ſaddle, as I taught you before, and take the bridle-reins ſeparate in both hands, and help him (as I have told you before) with the inward rein and outward leg, which will make him know the bridle, whilſt the caveſon gives his body the ply it ſhould have.

After this, I would adviſe you to make uſe of falſe reins, and faſten them to the banquet of the bridle, as you did the caveſon before. This works the barrs, but leaves the curb looſe, ſo that he is under leſs apprehenſion of the bridle, and his *appuy* is helped; and when you come to work with the bridle, and conſequently with the curb, the bridle will make him light upon the hand. Thus the falſe reins give an *appuy*, and at the ſame time makes a horſe light in hand; ſo that it is good for thoſe that have too much, as well as thoſe that have too little, and they give the ply juſt as the caveſon does, excepting that the caveſon works upon the noſe, and the falſe reins upon the barrs, which makes his mouth ſenſible, as it ought to be, and on the ſame ſide of the barrs as the bridle would do; ſo that when he is rode with the bridle only, and that he has the help of the curb, he goes vaſtly well.

But take notice here, that when the falſe reins are faſtened to the banquet of the bit, they are two hands breadth nearer the rider than the caveſon, which is upon his noſe, and for that reaſon have leſs effect and leſs power, though the barrs are more ſenſible than the noſe, but the horſe's ply won't be ſo great, as you have not ſo much command.

But if you have ſuppled your horſe, and given him ply ſufficient with the caveſon, and afterwards with the falſe reins; the falſe reins will continue to keep his body ſupple, and will work vaſtly well upon his barrs to uſe him to the bridle only; ſeparate your reins in your hands, and work always with the inward rein, and you will find him very ſupple. This way of working is to make him ſenſible to the curb, which is finiſhing your work as to the hand. Obſerve here, that as the caveſon has more power when you pull, than any thing elſe, being upon the horſe's noſe, and the fartheſt from you; and the falſe reins have leſs, being nearer by two hands breadth, as they are faſtened to the banquet of the bridle: ſo now working with the bit only, you bend him leſs, for this is ſtill two hands breadth nearer than the falſe reins; for the caveſon is upon the noſe, the falſe reins faſtened to the banquet of the bit, and the bridle-reins to the end of the branches, which makes them leſs efficacious, as they are nearer the rider.

This way of working a horſe is the quinteſſence of horſemanſhip, ſince by theſe three different degrees, firſt the caveſon, then the falſe reins, and afterwards the bridle, you make a horſe ſo perfect, that it is wonderful, provided they

they are regularly uſed, and by a maſterly hand, otherwiſe neither this, or aught elſe can do any thing in this noble art.

The helps of the hand, of the thighs, of the calfs of the legs, pinching with the ſpurs, in ſhort, all ſorts of aids ought to be more gentle upon a walk when one paſſages a horſe, than when one makes him go in his air; or elſe, if there is no difference, there is nothing left to make him go in his air. The gentle Paſſage requires gentle aids, and ſtronger Airs require ſtronger aids, which is agreeable to reaſon.

CHAP. XXVIII.

For Terre-a-terre.

THE figure of Terre-à-terre ſhews, that the horſe's croupe is preſſed, and his ſhoulders at liberty triangularly and circularly. He is moſt preſſed there, where his legs are confined to the narroweſt compaſs, and conſequently that part is more ſubjected and more worked. He deſcribes four circles with his legs, as is evident from the figure, the action of them being the ſame as when he is upon the gallop. Therefore, whether a horſe's head or his croupe is to the pillar in Terre-à-terre, his fore-part will be always at liberty, and his croupe confined; ſo that the center makes no alteration, but only the action of his legs.

When he goes to the right, the bridle ſhould be held upon the contrary ſide of the horſe's neck, the nails of your hand upwards pointing to the left ſhoulder, the left ſhoulder in, turning your body to the ſame ſide (the horſe's croupe being within) this makes him go with freedom the ſhoulders firſt: rein and leg contrary work the croupe, and let the ſhoulders go large, ſo that the horſe is bent as in a vice. The bridle-hand ought to help him to go forwards, by ſlackening the reins, and you muſt keep as regular as if he was in a frame.

For Terre-a-terre again.

Since drawing the inward rein brings the half of a horſe's ſhoulders within the volte, therefore it muſt conſequently throw his haunch on the ſame ſide out, and keeps it off from the pillar or center. This turn of the horſe's body makes his legs towards the volte, the more extended, to go firſt. Thus he has his croupe ſubjected, and his ſhoulders at large, is at liberty within the volte, and preſſed without; ſo that his outward legs may be ſaid to be kept back by the inward that are at liberty, rather than that they begin any action of themſelves.

So Terre-à-terre is being half at liberty on one ſide, and half preſſed on the other; that part of him within the volte is at liberty, the other is confined, and ſo his legs keep their four circles; thoſe that are at liberty advance, and thoſe that are confined follow. Here I give you the figure both for the right and left hand.

Some

CHAP. XXVIII.

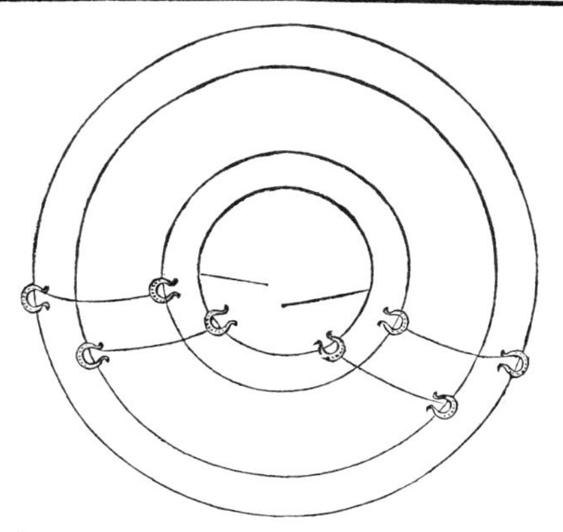

Some horſemen have had the vanity to imagine, that a horſe may be managed upon the firſt mounting him, or in the ſpace of a quarter of an hour. Theſe gentlemen will certainly think moſt of theſe leſſons of mine very tedious, and of little conſequence.

But they ought to underſtand and conſider, that it requires more paper to write theſe leſſons, and more time to read them, than to put them in practice: ſince they are ſo very methodical, and ſo wonderfully efficacious, being the truth of horſemanſhip, that I may venture to ſay, that a raw horſe of five years old, of a proper diſpoſition to undergo the fatigue of the Manege, will be perfectly dreſſed in leſs than three months, provided he is under the care of an expert horſeman. This is not only my opinion, but my certain knowledge, which is the acquiſition of a long experience. For ſince I have invented this new method, I have dreſſed under me myſelf, and under my *ecuyer* Captain MAZIN, very many horſes in very little time; and I have never perceived nor ſeen that Captain MAZIN, by uſing this method, ever failed with any horſes of any ſort, both the docile and thoſe that had a good diſpoſition for it, and the vicious of all kinds; the weak, the ſtrong, thoſe of moderate ſtrength, of all humours, all natures, and of all different diſpoſitions; Hungarian horſes, mares, great large horſes, middle-ſized ones, little ones, poneys, horſes of all countries, Spaniards, Polanders, Barbs, Turks, Neapolitans, Danes, all ſorts of Flanders horſes, and horſes of mix'd breeds that he has dreſſed are almoſt without number; he never failed with any, unleſs they fell ſick, lame, or died in his hands.

This I dare affirm from experience, and therefore recommend theſe leſſons to your ſerious peruſal. Underſtand them properly, make uſe of them, and you will reap a pleaſure in the practice, and all the advantage a good horſeman can require.

End of the ſixth Diviſion of Leſſons, and of the Second Book.

R. Parr Sculp.

THE

NEW METHOD

OF

DRESSING HORSES.

BOOK III.

Teaching how to Dreſs a Horſe in all ſorts of AIRS, by a New Method.

CHAP. I. *Of the ſeveral Sorts of Airs.*

YOU muſt in all Airs follow the ſtrength, ſpirit, and diſpoſition of the horſe, and do nothing againſt nature; for art is but to ſet nature in order, and nothing elſe: but to make a horſe Gallop and Change, and to go Terre-à-terre, is for the moſt part forced; and in Paſſadoes the like; for, if a horſe be impatient, he will hardly go well in Paſſadoes.

No other airs are to be forced, but every horſe is to chooſe his own air, unto which nature hath moſt fitted him, which you may eaſily ſee, when he is tied ſhort to the ſingle pillar my way.

For

For Curvets, a horſe ought to have a great deal of patience; and the air of Curvets gives a horſe patience with diſcreet riding, as they ſay. But I have ſeldom ſeen that diſcreet riding; I doubt there is a miſtake in it, which is this: Firſt the horſe hath patience, and then that horſe goes in Curvets; but ſeldom impatient horſes are made patient by Curvets: ſo ſeeing moſt horſes that go well in Curvets to have patience, they think Curvets give them patience, when it is patience that gives them Curvets. But there is no rule without an exception, yet I doubt I am in the right; for though ſome young horſes may by chance go in Curvets, yet I aſſure you, for the moſt part, horſes muſt have a great deal of time, with the cuſtom of often repetitions; to be in years, and to have gray hairs in their beard, before they will be ſettled, and firm'd, to go certainly in Curvets both forwards and upon their voltes; Therefore it is an error in thoſe that think they can force Curvets, if the horſe's inclination be not to go in that air; for I have known many horſes, that all the force in the world would never make go in Curvets, their diſpoſition being againſt it. Curvets is an air built only of art; for if the horſe be not perfectly in the hand and the heels, and upon the haunches, he will never go in Curvets: yet I muſt tell you, this new way of mine will make horſes go in Curvets, which by no other way would have been brought to it, and it ſeldom or never fails me.

For Leaping-horſes, there are four ſeveral airs, which are Croupades, Balotades, Capriols, and a Step and a Leap. The height of theſe may be all alike, but not the manner; though the horſe that goes the longeſt time muſt needs go the higheſt.

Croupades is a leap where the horſe pulls up his hinder legs, as if he drew or pull'd them up into his body.

Balotades is a leap where the horſe offers to ſtrike out with his hinder legs, but doth not, and makes only an offer or half ſtrokes; ſhewing only the ſhoes of his hinder legs, but doth not ſtrike, only makes an offer, and no more.

Capriols is a leap, that when the horſe is at the full height of his leap he yerks, or ſtrikes out his hinder legs, as near and as even together, and as far out as ever he can ſtretch them, which the French call *nouër l'aiguilette*, which is, to tie the point.

A Step and a Leap is as it were three airs; the Step Terre-à-terre, the raiſing of him a Curvet, and then a Leap. Theſe airs can never be forced to go well in them, in ſpite of their poinſons, but what nature ordains them; for they are called well-diſpoſed horſes.

What belongs to Leaping-horſes (according to the old opinion) are theſe things: A horſe of huge and vaſt ſtrength, an excellent mouth, perfect good feet; in which laſt they have not ſaid amiſs, for good feet are very requiſite, elſe the horſe dares never light on them for fear of hurting them (no more than a man that hath the gout dares leap) and ſo will never riſe.

I could wiſh a good mouth (which is a good *appuy*) neither too hard, nor too ſoft, but to ſuffer a good *appuy* upon the barrs, and ſo to ſuffer the curb, which is to be underſtood a good mouth: yet I muſt tell you, the rareſt leaping-horſe that ever I ſaw, or rid, went not at all upon the curb, but only upon the barrs of his mouth, which I do not commend; but it is better to have him leap ſo, being ſo rare a horſe, than to be ſo over-curious as not to have him leap at all, becauſe he went not upon the curb. That

BOOK III.

That they muſt be very ſtrong horſes to be leaping-horſes, is a very great error; for it is not the ſtrongeſt horſes that are fitteſt for the delight of the Manege, and eſpecially not for leaping-horſes; for I have ſeen many ſtrong horſes, that muſt be galloped very long before you could abate the ſtrength of their chines; and all that while they would do nothing but yerk, and fetch diſorder'd counter-times of falſe leaps, and the beſt horſemen in the world could never make them leaping-horſes: ſo it is not ſtrong, but well-diſpoſed horſes; for the beſt leaping-horſes that ever I knew, were the weakeſt horſes I have ſeen.

Take one of the guard, the ſtrongeſt fellow that is, and I will bring a little fellow that ſhall out-leap him many a foot; yet that ſtrong fellow would cruſh that little fellow to death in his arms: ſo 'tis not ſtrength, but diſpoſition fits horſes for leaping. But ſome will ſay, that a little man's ſtrength is above his weight, and the great man's weight is above his ſtrength; but that is not ſo; for the great man's ſtrength ſhall be more above his weight, than the little man's ſtrength above his, and yet the little man ſhall out-leap him. Nay, two little men of equal ſtrength, the one ſhall leap excellently, and the other not; and more, a weaker little man ſhall out-leap the ſtronger; and ſometimes a weak ſlender ſlim fellow will out-leap a knit ſtrong fellow; ſo that it is nothing but diſpoſition, which nature gives, and not art. Sometimes a ſtrong great fellow will out-leap a little man, but that is ſeldom, becauſe their ſpirits are more dilated, aſunder, and diffuſed, than in little men. The like I will aſſure you in horſes, as I have told you of men; there may be a ſtrong horſe diſpoſed for leaping, and that no doubt is an excellent horſe; but for the moſt part they are but weak horſes that are diſpoſed for leaping. Sometimes a horſe finds himſelf ſo pincht with curvets upon the haunches, being weak, that he finds eaſe in leaping.

Thus you ſee that leaping-horſes are diſpoſed by nature, and not art, being full of ſpirit, and light; ſo that a horſeman hath nothing to do in making leaping-horſes, but only to give them the time, which is all the art ought to be uſed to a leaping-horſe; and he that thinks to ſhew more art in a leaping-horſe, will but ſhew his ignorance and folly.

A Step and a Leap is an air, in which horſes commonly go when they have not a good *appuy*; for the Step puts him upon the hand, and gives him a riſe to leap, like one that runs before he leaps, and ſo may leap higher than he that goes every time a leap. Thus I have ſhewed you theſe Airs, Curvets, Croupades, Balotades, Capriols, and a Step and a Leap, which nature muſt do more than art: Two Steps, and three Steps and a Leap are not comely, and are indeed rather a Gallop Galliard, than can be called an Air.

The firſt Diviſion of Leſſons.

A new Method of Horſemanſhip to teach Horſes all kinds of Airs round a Pillar, wherein they are taught to go perfectly in Curvets without any body upon their Backs, de ferme à ferme, *which is, in one Place; upon the Voltes, and ſideways upon the Voltes, which is the moſt excellent and uſeful Invention to make a Horſe go regularly in all ſorts of Airs, that ever was found out, to fix him upon his Haunches, and make him obedient to the Hand and Heel. I adviſe you therefore carefully to follow theſe Directions, for more can't be taught a Horſe.*

CHAP.

CHAP. II.

The new Method of the Pillar for all Airs; and firſt, for the Right Hand.

THE pillar ought to have two rings on each ſide, fixed according to the uſual height; the horſe ſhould be bridled and ſaddled without any body upon his back, and the button of the bridle ſlip'd down; then the right rein of the caveſon is to be faſtened very ſhort (but it would be better was it held by a groom, for ſo a horſe may make as many voltes as you pleaſe) and take the other rein in your hand. Then the rider ſhould take a little *poinſon* in his hand, which is a ſhort ſtick with an iron point at the end of it, and ſtand on the ſide oppoſite to the ſhort rein; another rider ought to be placed on either ſide, which you pleaſe, with a ſwitch in his hand, to make the horſe riſe. When one has made him riſe, the other ought at the ſame time to prick him gently in the ſpurring-place with the *poinſon*, at the very inſtant he begins to riſe. Thus he ſhould make the croupe of the horſe move from him towards the pillar on the ſide where the rein is faſtened, for ſo the ſhort rein has the greater effect, and puts the horſe in the true poſture to bend the half of his ſhoulders, which makes him obey the hand, and the rider with his *poinſon* makes him obey the ſpurs. So that if the horſe yields to it, which he will, and ought to do in a ſhort time, he will not only go perfectly in Curvets forwards, but alſo upon the voltes, the firſt time you try him; which is ſomething extraordinary, and was never practiſed before. For as to the pillar the old way, it only makes a horſe advance, whereas this makes him go upon the voltes, tho' in the ſame place; for the ſhort rein on the right ſide, and the *poinſon* on the other, forces him to go in Curvets to the right hand upon the voltes, as you will learn hereafter. I ſhall ſhew you in its proper place the left rein faſten'd ſhort, when a horſe is to go to the left hand; but have ſomething more to ſhew you yet to the right. Some may perhaps ſay, To what purpoſe is all this, unleſs a horſe goes in Curvets? This is an abſurd queſtion. Only make him riſe, and help him as I have directed before, and altho' he never takes the proper cadence of a Curvet, or any other air, this method will put him upon his haunches notwithſtanding, and make him obey the hand and heel, which is every thing, and make him go Terre-à-terre perfectly. This method ſeldom fails of making any horſe go in Curvets, when he is tied thus, making him riſe with the ſwitch, one helping him gently at the ſame time on the contrary ſide with the *poinſon* inſtead of ſpurs, and another behind the horſe with a *chambriere* to animate him, this way you will make him go to perfection. If the *poinſon* is too ſharp, turn the end of the ſtick, and touch him with it in the ſpurring place, or with the handle of another ſwitch; for ſharp ſpurs ſometimes do more harm than good. Thus you give a right bent to the body of the horſe, and make his legs go true. This is the moſt eaſy and effectual method for airs. But let us go on with our right caveſon rein faſten'd to the pillar, which is for Curvets in one place *de ferme à ferme* to the right, as is ſhewn by this figure. The rein being thus fix'd ſhort, the horſe cannot eaſily riſe; therefore, to find eaſe, he puts himſelf upon the haunches.

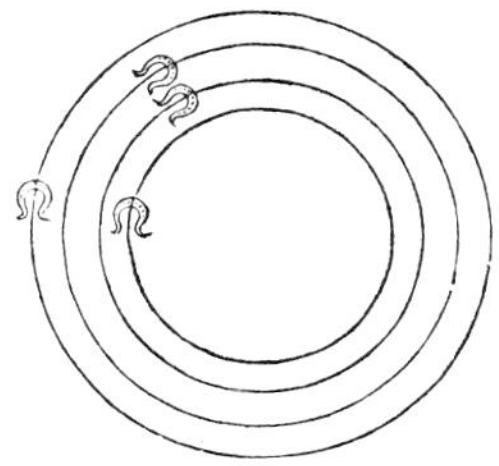

BOOK III.

CHAP. III.

For the Voltes to the Right Hand, the Horſe as he was before with the Right Rein of the Caveſon faſtened ſhort to the Pillar.

I FIRST make the horſe go backward as far as the ſhort rein will permit, placing a horſeman with a *poinſon* in his hand on the outſide of the volte, who is to help him in caſe of neceſſity; or rather, let him go before, and be placed as if he held him by the long rein of the caveſon; another ſhould follow him with a *chambriere* on the outſide the volte, whilſt a third touches him with a ſwitch upon the breaſt, to make him riſe upon his voltes; but this perſon ought to be within the volte. He who is to help him with the *chambriere* walks circularly forward, but rather before the horſe, as I have mentioned already; and the perſon who touches him before with the ſwitch ought to go circularly backward, if he is within the volte. You may perceive that a horſe thus performs almoſt a volte in Curvets upon his air, as far as the ſhort rein will permit him to turn, which is almoſt an entire volte. All this time that you are working with the right rein, the pillar is to be within the volte for the right hand. This ſhort rein works mightily the horſe's ſhoulders, and leaves his croupe at liberty, that he may make his volte perfect; and it alſo pulls his ſhoulders to that degree, as to make him go in a round, or, as it is commonly expreſs'd, of one *piſte*. But the horſe deſcribes four circles with his four feet; his fore-foot within the volte deſcribes the ſecond circle, the other fore-foot the third; the hind-foot within the volte deſcribes the leaſt, ſince it is neareſt the center; and the other hind-leg without the volte deſcribes the largeſt, being the fartheſt from it. The action of a horſe's legs in Curvets preſſes his fore-legs, and leaves the others at liberty, for which reaſon the fore-legs will be within the line of the hind ones: the fore-leg within the volte is a little before that on the outſide of it, and the hind-leg without the volte is a little before the other that is within it, otherwiſe he could not go in Curvets, ſo that all his four feet are off the ground at the ſame time, as in a little leap. A horſe being thus faſtened with the ſhort rein of the caveſon, his fore-part is ſo much confined, that he muſt neceſſarily throw out his croupe, otherwiſe he could not turn, and conſequently the action is as I have deſcribed it. This is an exceeding good invention, ſince it ſo far conſtrains his fore-part as to force him into this air whether he will or not, provided he is faſtened at a proper length, ſo that he can neither ſpring forwards, nor get from off his haunches.

CHAP.

CHAP. IV.

To work a Horſe in Curvets backwards upon the Voltes to the Right Hand, with the Rein of the Caveſon faſten'd ſhort as it was before.

SUppoſe at preſent, that a horſe has been upon the voltes to the right hand as much as the fixed rein will permit, you muſt then allow him a little time to take breath; then the rider muſt raiſe him with his ſwitch, following him round, and looking him a little in the face. Whilſt one makes him riſe with the ſwitch, another ought to help him a little firmer with the *poinſon*, moving circularly by his ſide. There is no occaſion for the third with the *chambriere*, ſince a horſe can not move backwards and forwards at the ſame time; but ſhould he go back too faſt, he muſt be kept up with the *chambriere*, and by this means he will go backwards perfectly in Curvets upon the voltes, which is ſomething uncommon, eſpecially when he has no body upon his back. You may make him go forwards and backwards in this manner, as much as you pleaſe; for when he has made the rein too ſtrait to which he is faſtened, by going back as far as he can, you may make him advance upon his voltes to untwiſt the rein, and when he is as far advanced as he can, you muſt make him go backwards to ſlacken it again; and thus you may work him as much as you pleaſe.

CHAP. V.

To work a Horſe ſideways with the Right Rein faſtened ſhort as it was before.

AS the pillar has been hitherto placed within the volte for the right hand, when a horſe was to go forward, and was likewiſe the ſame when he went backwards, which always worked him to the right hand, the rein being faſtened in the ſame manner as it was at firſt; ſo, at preſent, to work him ſideways, his head muſt be placed within the pillar, which will work him to the left. Going thus ſideways, the right rein being faſtened ſhort, helps the horſe on the outſide, which fixes his croupe the better, as his head is to the pillar. The rider muſt raiſe him with his ſwitch before, and help him upon his ſide with the hand-end of another. If the horſe goes too faſt, the perſon who holds the *poinſon* muſt be with the long rein in his hand on the contrary ſide, to help him only in caſe of neceſſity, his preſence alone being ſufficient to prevent his going too faſt, by which means the horſe will keep a juſt and exact time. The right rein faſtened in this manner to the pillar, works to the right *de ferme à ferme* (in one place) in Curvets, as you have ſeen before in chap. 2. The right rein ſtill in the ſame manner faſtened, works a horſe in Curvets upon the voltes to the right hand, as I have ſhewed before in chap. 3. Moreover, the ſame rein of the caveſon, as it was at firſt, works the horſe upon the voltes backwards, as you have ſeen in the ſame chapter. The rein of the caveſon thus, works a horſe ſideways upon the voltes, but to the left hand, and all the former were to the right, becauſe the pillar was on the inſide of the horſe, and his croupe was in: but now that he goes ſideways, the pillar or center is on his outſide, and his croupe is out, and diſtant from it. The right rein of the caveſon being tied ſhort to the pillar, the fore-part of the

the horſe is neareſt the center or pillar. Tho' the action of the Curvet confines the fore-part of a horſe, and leaves his croupe at liberty; nevertheleſs his hind-legs are within the lines of nature. He deſcribes four circles with his feet. The fore-foot within the volte deſcribes the leaſt, the other fore-foot the ſecond; the hind-leg within the volte the third, and the other hind-leg without it the largeſt. When a horſe's head is to the pillar in Curvets to the left, and the pillar without the horſe's head, his legs are off from the ground at the ſame time and acroſs. The hind-legs ought to follow the fore-ones exactly, neither more within nor more without; but the fore-legs are within the lines of the hind ones, becauſe they are nearer together. The pillar or center is without the horſe's head, when you work his croupe out, which makes his two fore-legs deſcribe the ſmalleſt circles, and the hind-legs the largeſt; the fore-leg within the volte deſcribes the leaſt of the two ſmaller circles, and the other fore-leg the ſecond, the hind-leg within the volte the third, and the other hind-leg the largeſt of the two greater. Therefore a horſe deſcribes four circles when he has his croupe without and to the left, and remains at the pillar with the right rein of the caveſon faſtened as at firſt. What can be more required for Curvets upon the ſame ſpot of ground, than to make him go forward, backward, and ſideways upon the voltes? I am of opinion, that nothing can be added to it; moreover, all this is performed about a pillar without any body upon the horſe's back: here is the figure.

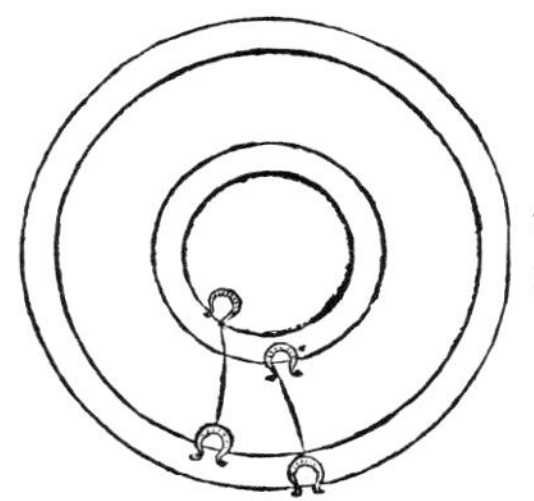

Sideways to the left, with the horſe's head towards the pillar, altho' the right rein is faſtened.

CHAP. VI.

The new Method of the Pillar for Airs to the Left Hand.

THE pillar ought to have two rings on each ſide fixed at the uſual height, and the horſe bridled and ſaddled without any body upon his back, and the button of the reins down: then faſten the left rein of the caveſon very ſhort, holding the other in your hand. The rider ought to have a little *poinſon* in his hand, which is a ſhort ſtick with an iron point at one end of it, and place himſelf on the oppoſite ſide to the ſhort rein, and another ſhould be placed on which ſide you pleaſe, with a ſwitch in his hand to make the horſe riſe: when one has made him riſe, the other ought at the ſame time to prick him gently with the *poinſon* in the ſpurring-place, at the very inſtant he begins to riſe, to make the croupe of the horſe go from him towards the pillar on that ſide where the rein is faſtened, becauſe ſo the ſhort rein works the more, and puts the horſe in a proper poſture to bend the half of his ſhoulders, which makes him obedient to the hand, and he with the *poinſon* makes him obey the

the ſpurs. So that if the horſe obeys, which he ought and muſt in a ſhort time, he will not only go perfectly in Curvets forwards, but alſo upon voltes, the firſt time you try him, which was never done before. For the pillar the old way only makes him advance, but this makes him go upon the voltes, tho' in the ſame place; for the ſhort rein on the left ſide, and the *poinſon* on the other, make him curvet to the left hand upon the voltes. He is certainly worked upon the voltes by this method, as you ſhall ſee hereafter; but we have not yet done with the left hand. Some may perhaps ſay, To what purpoſe is all this, unleſs a horſe goes in Curvets? One that aſks this queſtion ſhews his ignorance. Only make him riſe, and help him as I have directed before, and altho' he never takes the proper cadence of a Curvet, or any other air, it will put him upon his haunches notwithſtanding, and make him obey the hand and heel, which is all we want, and will make him go Terre-à-terre perfectly. This method ſeldom fails of making any horſe go in Curvets, when he is faſtened thus with a ſhort rein on the left ſide, making him riſe with the ſwitch, another perſon helping him gently at the ſame time on the contrary ſide with the *poinſon* inſtead of ſpurs, and a third behind the horſe with the *chambriere* to make him advance, this cannot fail making him go to perfection.

Chap. VII.

If the *poinſon* is too ſharp, turn the other end of it, and touch him with it in the ſpurring-place, or with the hand-end of another ſwitch; for ſharp ſpurs do much harm in a Manege. Thus you give a true ply to the body of the horſe, which makes his legs go true. But we muſt go on ſtill with the left rein of the caveſon faſtened to the pillar, which is for the left hand, as the figure here demonſtrates. One may work him on both ſides with one ſwitch, only one after the other, or with two, one on each ſide, or help him with one under the belly, to put him upon his haunches, and the other to help him before on which ſide you pleaſe.

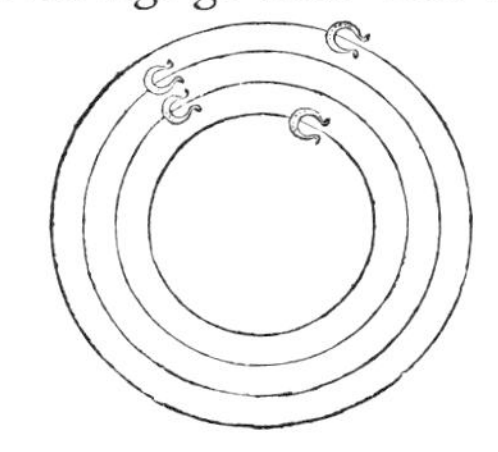

CHAP. VII.

For the Voltes to the Left Hand, the Horſe being faſtened to the Pillar with the left Rein, as he was before.

I FIRST make the horſe go backward as far as the ſhort rein will permit, placing a horſeman with a *poinſon* in his hand on the outſide of the volte, who helps only in caſe of neceſſity; or, being rather before him, he is as if he held him by the rein that is not faſtened; another ſhould follow him behind with the *chambriere* on the outſide the volte, whilſt a third aids him with a ſwitch upon the breaſt, to make him riſe upon the volte; but this perſon ought to be placed within it. He who has the *chambriere* walks circularly forward, and he who holds the *poinſon* and the long rein of the caveſon ſhould be over-againſt the ſpur-place, and move forward with the horſe, but rather before him, as if he led him, as I have ſaid before; and he that helps him with the ſwitch ſhould walk circularly backward, if he is placed within the volte. Thus you ſee the horſe makes a perfect volte in Curvets upon his air, and as far as the ſhort rein will permit him to turn, which is almoſt an entire volte,

Book III.

volte. All this time that you are working with the left rein, the pillar ought to be within the horſe, to work him to the left.

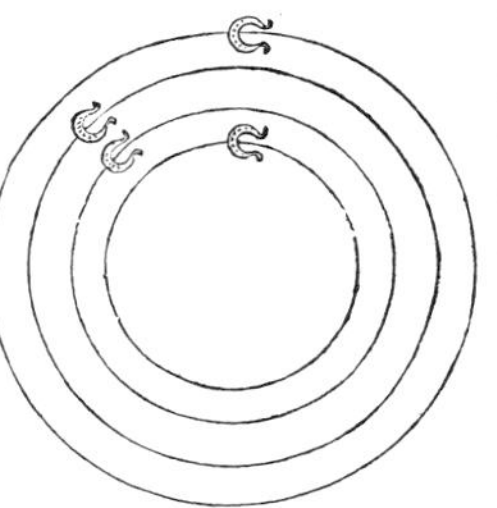

This ſhort rein bends mightily a horſe's ſhoulders, and leaves his croupe at liberty, that he may make the volte true.

CHAP. VIII.

To work a Horſe in Curvets upon the voltes backwards to the Left Hand, the Rein of the Caveſon being tied ſhort as it was before without any Alteration.

LET us now ſuppoſe a horſe to have gone upon the voltes to the left hand, as far as the ſhort rein would permit; let him repoſe for ſome time, then let the rider make him riſe with his ſwitch, and follow him round, looking him a little in the face; and whilſt one makes him riſe, let another help him a little ſtronger with the *poinſon*, walking ſideways in a circle. He who has the *chambriere*, ſince a horſe can not go backward and forward at the ſame time, ought not to help him unleſs he goes too faſt back. Thus he will go backwards perfectly in Curvets upon the voltes, which is ſomething uncommon, eſpecially as he has no body upon his back. You may make him go backwards and forwards in this manner, as much as you pleaſe; for when he has drawn the rein ſtrait to which he is faſtened, and can go no farther, you may make him advance upon the voltes to ſlacken the rein; and

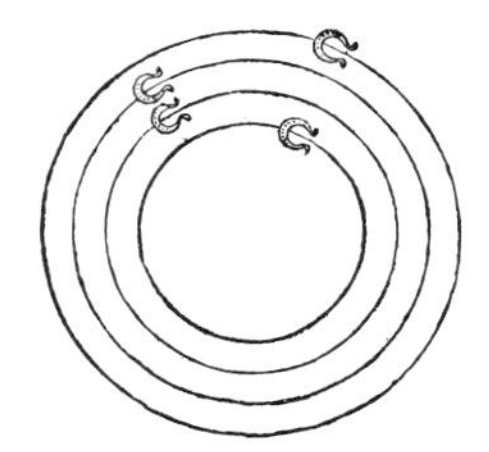

when he is as far advanced as he can, you may make him go backward again to ſlacken it; and thus you may work him as much as you pleaſe.

CHAP. IX.

To work a Horſe ſideways, the Rein being faſtened ſhort as it was before.

THE pillar has been placed within the horſe or the volte on the left hand in one place; when the horſe goes either forwards or backwards upon the voltes, the pillar is ſtill always within it to the left hand, and the rein faſtened as it was before. Now going ſideways, the horſe's head ought to be within the pillar, and conſequently the pillar will be on the outſide of the horſe, which will work him to the right hand. When he goes thus ſideways, the ſhort rein being faſtened on the left ſide, aids the horſe without the volte, which confines his croupe the more, ſince his head is to the pillar. The rider here muſt make his horſe riſe before with his ſwitch, and touch him with the hand-end of another upon his ſide or in the ſpurring-place. Should the horſe

go

go too faſt, he who has the *poinſon* ought to be on the contrary ſide, holding the looſe rein of the caveſon in his hand, not to aid him but in caſe of neceſſity; for his preſence alone is ſufficient to prevent his going too faſt, ſo that he will take a true and equal time. By this method a horſe will go perfectly ſideways upon the voltes to the right hand, becauſe the pillar is on his outſide, and his head in or to the center. Thus by fixing the left rein of the caveſon to the pillar, it works him to the right hand in Curvets *de ferme à ferme*, in one place, as you may ſee before in the ſixth chapter of airs. The left rein works in Curvets upon the voltes to the left hand, as appears in the ſeventh chapter. The left rein of the caveſon remaining thus faſtened as it was at firſt, works the horſe backwards upon the voltes, as you may ſee in chapter the eighth. The ſame rein of the caveſon works him ſideways upon the voltes, but for the right hand, whilſt all the former were for the left, as the pillar was then placed within the horſe's croupe, and his croupe in: now that the horſe goes ſideways, the pillar or center is without, and his croupe likewiſe out, and at a diſtance from it, therefore his feet are from the ground at the ſame time. The horſe's hind-legs that are out ought to follow the fore-legs that are in, neither more in nor more out; the fore-legs however are within the lines of the hind ones, ſince they go narrower. The pillar or center is without the head of the horſe when you work the croupe out, for which reaſon his fore-legs deſcribe the ſmalleſt circles, and thoſe behind the largeſt. The fore-leg within the volte deſcribes the leaſt of the two ſmaller, and the other fore-leg the largeſt of them. The hind-leg within the volte deſcribes the leaſt of the larger circles, and the other without the volte the greateſt. Therefore a horſe deſcribes four circles when his croupe is out for the right hand, and he remains faſtened to the pillar with the left rein of the caveſon. When you have uſed the *poinſon* a little time only, you will have no farther occaſion for it; two ſwitches, one in each hand, will be ſufficient, helping him with one upon the cheſt and the other under his belly, to put him upon his haunches. I recommend this method of mine, of the ſingle pillar, as the very quinteſſence of horſemanſhip, to dreſs horſes in all kinds of airs, and to make them obey both the hand and heel; I would therefore adviſe you to ſtudy it well, for I am ſure you will be pleaſed with the effect you will find from it.

This is my method of working a horſe at the ſingle pillar without any body upon his back. What more can be deſired in Curvets, than to make a horſe go forwards, backwards, and ſideways upon the voltes? unleſs you would have a horſe fly, or dance upon a rope. All this is about the pillar without any one upon the horſe's back. A horſe going ſideways with the left rein of the caveſon faſtened to the pillar is deſcribed in the following figure.

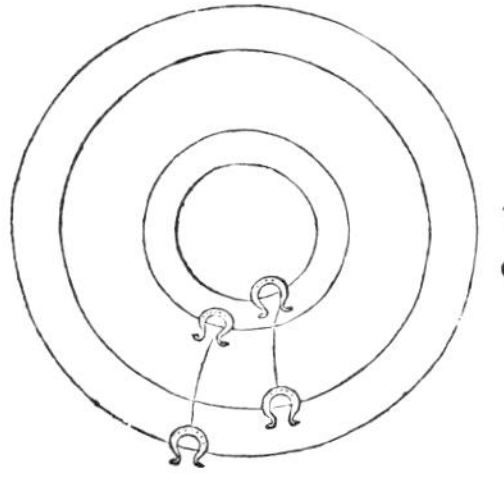

Sideways to the right hand, becauſe the rein of the caveſon is tied ſhort on the left. *Fig.* 24.

CHAP.

BOOK III.

CHAP. X.

To fasten the Horse to the Pillar with the right Rein short, holding the long one in Hand. He should now be mounted.

YOU must first make the horse go in his air *de ferme à ferme*, helping him gently with your hand, drawing the inward rein a little, as I have shewed you before, which is by placing your bridle-hand on the outside of the horse's neck, being seated as I have told you, and aiding him with the leg within the volte, which ought to be a little bent at the knee, that the help may be with the thigh, and oblige him to be upon his haunches. You should put your breast out, leaning your body a little forwards, that the horse's croupe may have the greater liberty. You may put him upon the voltes in the same manner, and with the same helps; excepting, that upon the voltes forwards you must aid him gently with the leg within it, otherwise he cannot advance, and the short rein would be too much strained; this puts the horse's croupe a little out, eases the rein, and gives him liberty to go in a circle, which works the shoulders. When he goes backwards upon the voltes, you must pull him back with your hand, turning it upwards, but always towards your body, leaning a little back at each time, your legs somewhat backwarder than upon any other action, helping him with your leg without the volte, which will press him back, and slacken the short rein. This method of making a horse go backward works his croupe more than his shoulders, provided you help him with your hand and body at each time. You must thus gain upon him gradually, till he has made a compleat volte backward, looking a little out of the volte, and your left shoulder a little out.

When a horse goes sideways, the rein of the caveson ought to be on the outside, to confine the croupe more; but then the right rein is for the left hand. The bridle-hand here should be on the outside, that it may draw the inward rein, helping him gently with the hand to support him, and with the outward leg, should there be occasion. Thus the horse will go under you *de ferme à ferme* (which is, in one place) upon his voltes, forward and backward to the right hand, and sideways to the left, the right rein of the caveson being fastened short as it was at first.

Fig. 25.

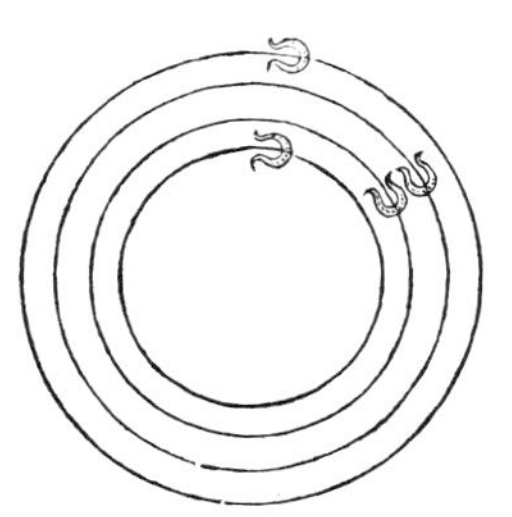

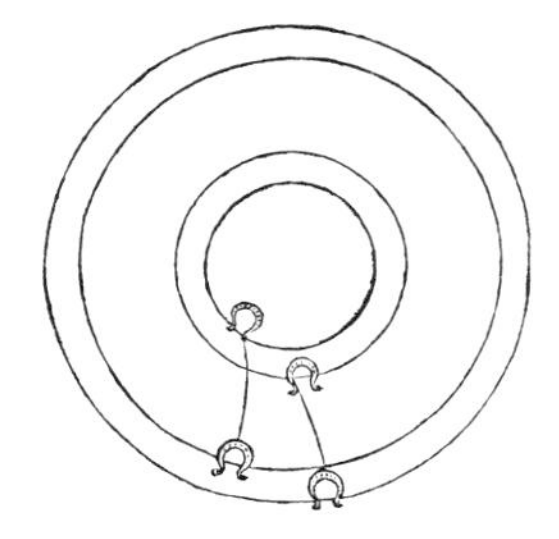

CHAP.

CHAP. XI.

CHAP. XI.

The Method of faſtening a Horſe ſhort to the Pillar with the left Rein, holding the long Rein in your Hand; and in this Caſe he ought to be mounted.

YOU muſt firſt make your horſe go in his air *de ferme à ferme*, helping him gently with your hand, drawing the inward rein a little, as I have ſhewed you before, which is, by placing your bridle-hand on the outſide of the horſe's neck, being ſeated as I have told you, and aiding him with the leg within the volte; but your legs ought to be a little bent at the knee, that the aid may be with the thighs, and force him to be upon his haunches. You ſhould put your breaſt out, leaning your body a little forwards, that the horſe's croupe may have the greater liberty. You may put him upon the voltes both forward and backward in the ſame manner, and with the ſame aids; excepting, that when he goes forwards upon the voltes, you muſt help him gently with the leg within the volte, otherwiſe he cannot advance, and the rein would be too much ſtrained; but thus you ſlacken the rein, and make it eaſier for the horſe to go in a circle. By putting thus the croupe of the horſe a little out, you work his ſhoulders.

When he goes backwards upon the voltes, you muſt pull him back with your hand, turning it upwards, but always towards your body, leaning a little back at each time, your legs a little backwarder than upon any other action, aſſiſting him with your leg without the volte, which will preſs him back and ſlacken the ſhort rein. This method of making a horſe go backward works his croupe more than his ſhoulders, provided you help him with your hand and with your body a little at each time. You thus gain upon him gradually, till he has made a compleat volte backward, looking a little out of the volte, and your left ſhoulder a little out.

When a horſe goes ſideways, the rein of the caveſon ought to be on the outſide, to confine the croupe the more, and the pillar without his head, but then it is for the right hand. The bridle-hand ſhould be on the outſide here, that it may draw the inward rein, helping him gently with the hand to ſupport him, and with the outward leg, ſhould there be occaſion. Thus the horſe will go under you *de ferme à ferme*, that is, in one place, upon his voltes forward and backward to the left hand, and ſideways to the right, the left rein of the caveſon being faſtened ſhort as it was at firſt.

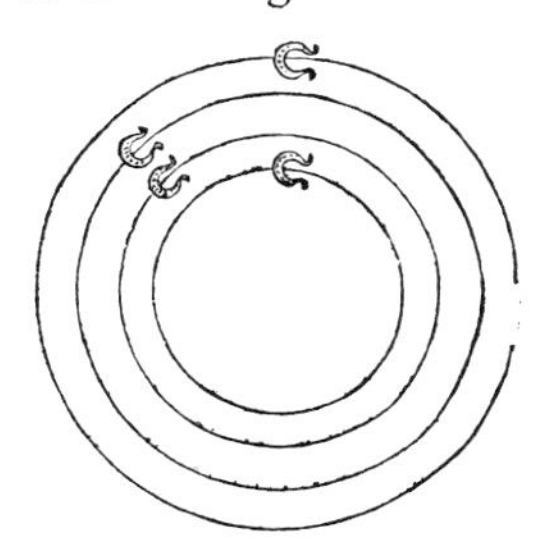

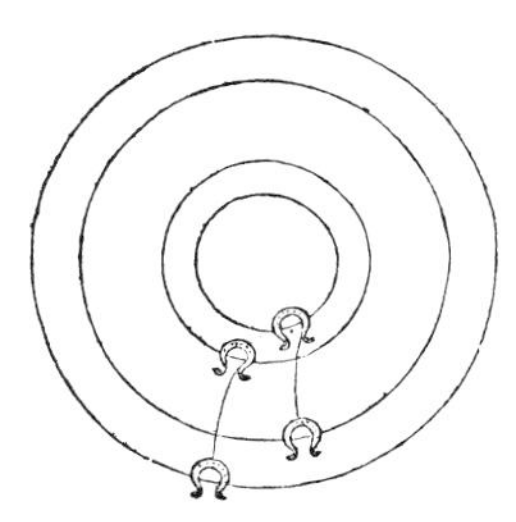

This new invention of mine, of faſtening a horſe ſhort, is a true method for airs, ſince it puts him upon his haunches, and preſſes him before, which is as all airs ſhould be. So that, you ſee, this new way conſtrains and obliges a horſe to go according to nature, which is, to go with his fore-legs nearer together, and his hind ones farther apart, and his hind-legs are in the lines of nature notwithſtanding.

This method forces the ſhoulders to turn, (as it conſtrains them, and the hind-legs are the more at liberty) otherwiſe they could not advance in the airs. The hind-legs ſhould follow the fore-legs with the greateſt exactneſs. A horſe going circularly in this manner, faſtened ſhort with the rein of the caveſon, deſcribes four circles with his feet; the fore-leg within the volte deſcribes the ſecond, his fore-leg without the volte deſcribes the third, his hind-leg within the volte deſcribes the leaſt, as it is neareſt the center, and the hind-leg without the volte deſcribes the largeſt, being moſt diſtant from the center He muſt of neceſſity deſcribe theſe four circles in going round, becauſe he is narrower before than behind, and muſt conſequently have his two fore-feet upon the middle circles; and his two hind-legs, that are farther diſtant from each other, muſt neceſſarily be placed in this manner: the hind-leg within the volte ought to deſcribe the ſmalleſt circle, and the hind-leg without the volte the largeſt; becauſe his fore-legs are within the lines of his hind ones, and becauſe the horſe goes in a round.

So it is with my new method of faſtening a horſe with a ſhort rein to the pillar, when he goes either forward or backward, but not when he goes ſideways, as I have demonſtrated before. Whether the ſhoulders are to the center in going ſideways with the croupe out, or with the croupe next the center, going ſideways upon curvets, the fore-legs are always narrower than the others; becauſe the action of this air is naturally ſo, which we ought to continue ſo by art.

End of the firſt Diviſion of Leſſons, which is for the new Way of working a Horſe in his Airs about a Pillar.

CHAP. XII.

The Second Diviſion of Leſſons, for CURVETS.

For Curvets upon the Voltes to the Right Hand, the Croupe to the Pillar.

FIRST faſten the right rein of the caveſon to the pommel of the ſaddle the way I ſhewed you before, but not too ſhort, only ſo as to give the true ply to the horſe; then help him with the rein within the volte, which is, by putting the bridle-hand on the outſide the neck; that is to ſay, draw the inward rein, which will bend half his ſhoulders, (*viz.* the ſhoulder within the volte) and ſtop it there; the fore-leg within the volte it puts a little before the other, and the hind-one on the ſame ſide a little backward; ſo that you ought only to help him with your hand, putting it a little on the contrary ſide, to draw the inward rein. Keep an eaſy ſeat, not too ſtiff; that is to ſay, you muſt bend your ham a little, and ſo your help will be with the thigh, and the horſe's air makes the aid of the thigh to be truer and better than any other aid you can

can give him. By helping him in this manner in Curvets, the horſe will go true with all his four legs in the air at the ſame time.

For Curvets to the right hand, with the croupe to the center, but the center

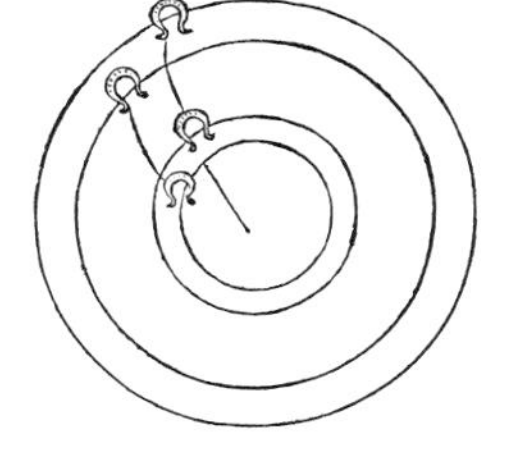

within the croupe notwithſtanding.

CHAP. XIII.

For Curvets upon the Voltes to the Left Hand, the Croupe to the Pillar.

FASTEN the left rein of the caveſon to the pommel of the ſaddle, the way I ſhewed you before, but not too ſhort, only ſo as to give the true ply to the horſe; then help him with the rein within the volte, which is, by putting the bridle-hand on the outſide the neck; that is to ſay, draw the inward rein, which will bend half the ſhoulders, (*viz.* the ſhoulder within the volte) and ſtop it there; the fore-leg within the volte it puts before the other, and puts the hind-leg on the ſame ſide a little backward; ſo that you ought only to help him a little with your hand, putting it a little on the contrary ſide to draw the inward rein. Keep an eaſy ſeat, not too ſtiff; that is to ſay, you muſt bend your ham a little, and ſo your help will be with the thigh, and the horſe's air makes the aid of the thigh to be truer and better than any other aid you can give.

By aiding him in this manner in Curvets, the horſe will go true with all his four legs in the air at the ſame time.

For Curvets to the left hand, with the croupe to the center, but the center

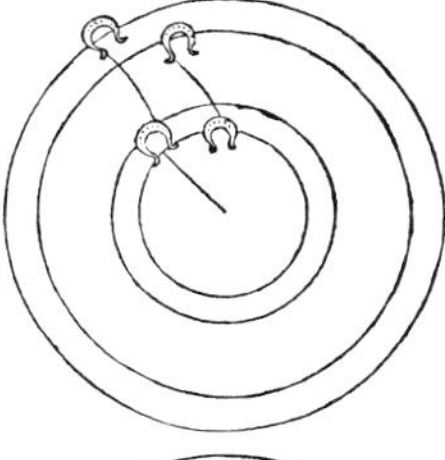

within the croupe notwithſtanding.

This figure is both for Curvets to the right and left with the horſe's head to the pillar, and his croupe out. You ought always to draw the inward rein of the bridle to

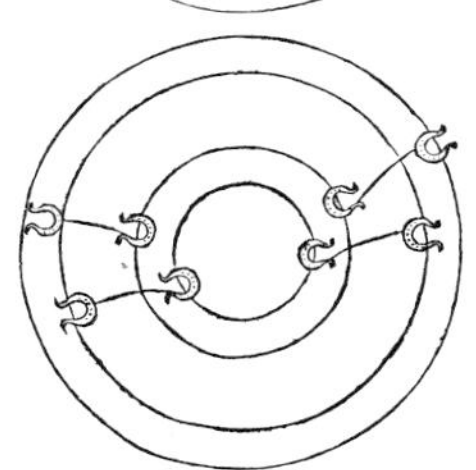

which ſide ſoever the horſe goes, by putting the bridle-hand on the outſide the volte, or the outſide of his neck, helping him gently with the leg without the volte.

The old way of making a horſe go in Curvets, two or three in the ſame place, then making him advance upon a walk, then curvetting, increaſing the

BOOK III.

the curvets, and diminiſhing the walk, till he has made an entire volte, is a mere trifle: for if you have worked him well at the pillar my new way, and have afterwards faſtened the inward rein of the caveſon to the pommel of the ſaddle, the horſe's croupe to the pillar; I ſay, you need do no more, for this alone will make him go perfectly in airs upon the voltes, with the greateſt eaſe and facility, without any thing elſe.

CHAP. XIV.

Of the Aids for Curvets, and the Horſeman's Seat.

TO the right, the bridle ought to be held on the contrary ſide, the hand turned a little upwards, that you may hold him up each movement in right time; every horſe ſhould be let take his own. Your body ſhould be a little forward, that his croupe may have liberty to work, your legs even, a little bent in the ham, that you may help him with your thigh, which is the moſt gentle aid you can uſe: being thus ſeated, the horſe's own air will help him more than any help you can give him. It is very certain, that the ſlower the time is a horſe takes, the higher he will go; and if he does not go as quick as he can, he will preſerve his ſtrength and breath the better, and go truer and with more eaſe to himſelf. But ſome may perhaps object, that by leaning the body a little forward, it is impoſſible to put a horſe upon his haunches; ſince he is put upon his haunches by putting the body backwards, according to the writings of the moſt excellent maſters in the art; and in order to convince you of the truth of that doctrine by example, they ſay, that when you ſtop a horſe upon a walk, you put him upon his haunches by leaning backward, and the ſame in the trot, gallop, &c. ſay they, is undeniable; from whence they conclude, that nothing puts a horſe more upon his haunches than leaning the body backwards, and conſequently that leaning forwards muſt be falſe. This is their manner of reaſoning, but it is eaſily anſwer'd. I confeſs, that in ſtopping it is neceſſary the body ſhould go back, both in the walk, trot, gallop, or in the carriere, for the ſame reaſons they give, that the horſe may be upon his haunches; this certainly puts him upon them, and nothing does it more, nor ſo well, when you ſtop him. But herein lies their abſurdity; they would uſe the ſame helps to make a horſe advance, as to ſtop him; whereas it ought to be conſidered, that when he is ſtopped there is an end of his motion, and that will always ſtop him, but never make him advance. They have not capacity to conceive, that the fore part is confined in all ſorts of airs, and the croupe ought to be free, not only that he may advance, but may likewiſe have liberty of beating with truth the right time of his air; and for this there is no better way to give the croupe room to play, than to bend the body gently forward, as I ſhewed before. Moreover, the inclination of the body forward forces the legs a little backward, which is their proper place for all kinds of aids; the contrary brings them forwards, puts them out of their place, and the rider upon his buttocks, when he ought to be upon his twiſt; now leaning forward puts him there. I would not be thought to mean that he ſhould bend his back, but on the contrary, his breaſt ought to be thruſt out, and his belly drawn in; and it ſhould be a gene-

ral

ral ply of the body from head to foot, but ſo little, that the lookers on ſhould hardly perceive it. This has not been a little ſtudy'd and conſider'd, and there is more in it than to gallop from St. Alban's to London, or to make a horſe trample with a ſnaffle and martingal the old Engliſh way. Thoſe too are miſtaken vaſtly, who think themſelves great maſters, becauſe they have learned to ride a month or two, and have not been thrown. To ride a horſe with the bridle only, the ſeat ſhould be as I directed before; to the right hand, the bridle ought to be on the contrary ſide, which is to the left, the nails turn'd upwards to the left ſhoulder, holding the hand high, turning the face a little into the volte, putting the left ſhoulder in, bending the legs a little in the ham, that the helps may be with the thighs, which is the gentleſt aid of all. To the left, the bridle muſt be on the contrary ſide, which is the right, the nails of the hand turned upwards to the right ſhoulder, the hand high, and firm or eaſy, as occaſion requires; the hand muſt be held ſo to command the inward rein, the rider muſt look into the volte, putting his right ſhoulder a little in, and be ſeated as I directed before, with his hams a little bent, that he may help the horſe with his thigh, which is the moſt gentle aid he can give.

CHAP. XV.

To change in Curvets upon the Voltes.

TO the right, the croupe to the pillar, and the pillar within the croupe, the bridle being on the ſide without the volte, which is the left, you muſt help the horſe with your hand each time, the nails of it turned upwards toward the left ſhoulder, and more or leſs according as there is occaſion, holding your legs even, your hams a little bent, that the aid may be with your thigh, which is the gentleſt can be given, looking a little into the volte, and bringing your left ſhoulder likewiſe in.

When a horſe is thus going in curvets to the right, you muſt help with the right leg, and change your hand at the ſame time to the right ſide beyond the neck of the horſe, making him advance a little; and ſo he will change perfectly without breaking his time. We are now curvetting to the left, the hand on the right ſide without the horſe's neck, that the right rein may be drawn. If you would change him again, you muſt help him with the leg within the volte, which is now the left, and change your hand at the ſame time to the left ſide without the neck of the horſe, making him advance a little; ſo he makes his changes regularly, without breaking time. One may change in this manner as often as one pleaſes. The figure here ſhews it.

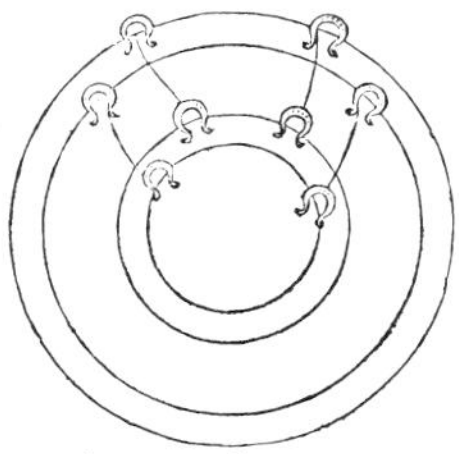

The changes near a wall are thus: when one goes in Curvets, the left ſide to the wall, the hand ought always to be towards the wall, that you may draw the rein, which is to be within the demi-volte. And when you would change, you muſt help the horſe with your leg from the wall, and at the ſame time put your hand a little towards it, which puts his croupe a little out, and brings his fore-part in, and ſo he changes regularly without breaking his time. The wall is at preſent on the right ſide, the bridle-hand towards it, and the horſe ſtill in curvets; when you change you muſt aid him with your leg from the wall, and with your hand, putting it at the ſame time a little to the wall, which puts his croupe ſomething out, and gives more liberty to his fore-part to turn, and ſo he won't break one time of his air. This way one may change him as often as one pleaſes.

CHAP. XVI.

Some more excellent Obſervations for Curvets.

THE action of the curvet is a little leap, in which, when a horſe raiſes his fore-legs, his hind ones fall, and all his four legs then are in the air at the ſame time; and when as his fore-legs fall, thoſe behind riſe, all his four legs will be likewiſe then in the air, and he touches the ground with his fore-feet firſt, and afterwards with the others.

The horſe is only upon two legs at a time, firſt upon thoſe before, and afterwards upon thoſe behind; and altho' two move upwards and two downwards, nevertheleſs they are all four in the air at the ſame time, thoſe behind immediately following thoſe before. He has his fore-legs nearer each other, becauſe they are more confined; and his croupe is larger, becauſe his hind legs are more at liberty; ſo that his fore-legs are within the lines of the others, and his hind-legs are in the lines of nature notwithſtanding, and therefore he deſcribes four circles with his four legs, as I ſaid before.

If you make him advance a little, you will perceive that his fore-part gets ground, and his croupe follows in the manner I have deſcribed; as he lowers his fore-part, he gains a little ground, and when he riſes, his hind-legs follow, to keep what his fore-legs have got; but then the action from the ground is done briſkly, and he ſtays a little in the air. The horſe that is the longeſt time up, that is, that goes the ſloweſt, ought to go the higheſt.

He reſembles a ſhip moved by the waves, or two buckets let down into a well, the one is coming up whilſt the other is going down; in the motion of the two buckets, they are both diſtant from the water at the ſame time, when one is coming up and the other is going down; it is exactly the ſame with a horſe's curvets, and no otherwiſe, altho' he goes low, which is properly a *Curvete rabattuë.*

CHAP. XVII.

Of the proper Helps in Curvets upon the Voltes.

TO the right hand, the rider being ſeated upon his twiſt with his breaſt out and his belly in, which he ought to draw a little back each time, and lean his body gently forwards, to give room to the horſe's croupe to play, his bridle-hand ſhould be on the outſide of the volte, turning the nails of it up to the left ſhoulder, putting that ſhoulder in, by which the horſe's croupe is thrown out a little when he raiſes him; and eaſe it afterwards, that his fore-part may have liberty to advance, and his croupe to follow when he raiſes him again. The inward rein of the bridle muſt be pulled, that the horſe may look into the volte, and that his ſhoulders may be worked.

The

The horſe going thus, his croupe to the pillar, and the pillar within, the croupe will be a little out, which few people can perceive. This is the very quinteſſence of curvets upon the voltes, in which the ſhoulders are worked, and the croupe very little; wherein many are miſtaken, who imagine that the croupe only is, and not the ſhoulders.

In curvets upon the voltes to the left, the bridle ought to be held on the outſide the horſe's neck, with the nails turned upwards towards the right ſhoulder, and the ſame ſhoulder ought to be in, putting the oppoſite leg a little nearer the horſe, and backwarder, though but very little, than that within. Working thus at the ſame time with leg and rein contrary, the ſhoulders and croupe will be both worked, which is right, ſince the croupe is to the pillar, and a little out, but ſo little that many don't ſee it, for the reaſons I gave you before for the right hand, where the pillar is within the croupe.

CHAP. XVIII.

To work a horſe in Curvets backwards upon the Voltes.

THE pillar being on the right ſide, to the right you muſt advance your breaſt and pull in your belly, your bridle-hand on the contrary ſide, putting it very much out and back at each time, and helping him at the ſame time with the oppoſite leg. This is to make him go in a circle; but all the aids muſt be given in the right time. The rein and contrary leg here works the horſe's croupe, and his ſhoulders are at liberty.

For Curvets upon the Voltes to the Left Hand.

The pillar ought to be on the left ſide for the left hand, the nails of the bridle-hand upwards, to the right ſhoulder, putting your left a little in, and helping with the contrary leg. All theſe aids ought to be given in time; for there is difficulty in ſubjecting the croupe ſo as to go backwards in a circle. By leg and rein contrary, the horſe's croupe is worked, and his ſhoulders are at liberty.

CHAP. XIX.

To work in Curvets along a Wall, the Wall on the Left Side.

THE wall being on the left ſide, and the bridle hand on the contrary ſide of the horſe's neck from the wall, you muſt turn the nails of your hand towards the left ſhoulder, that you may keep the inward rein tight, which is fartheſt from the wall, putting your left ſhoulder a little in, and your right leg ſomething nearer the horſe's ſide, ſhould there be occaſion for it, and not otherwiſe; for ſo the horſe ought to take the demi-volte to the right hand. But the aids ought not to be ſo ſtrong as upon the voltes, an inclination is enough, ſince he goes directly forwards and to the right; you ought to put your breaſt out and draw your belly in, which makes your body advance, to give liberty to the horſe's croupe to do ſo. He begins upon his fore-part, and his croupe follows. His fore-legs gain ground, and his hind-legs keep it; his fore-legs make room for thoſe behind, as they follow immediately. He makes four ſtrait lines forwards in curvets. His fore-legs are confined, and

and his hind-legs at liberty; his fore-legs are within the lines of thoſe behind, as this figure ſhews.

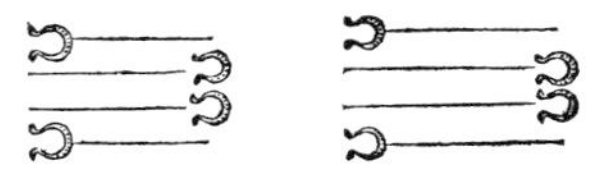

CHAP. XX.

To make a Horſe go backwards in Curvets by a Wall in a ſtrait Line, the wall on the Left Side.

THE left ſide of the horſe being to the wall, I have already told you, that in going ſtrait it was only an inclination towards it, tho' he goes forward, to prepare him for the demi-volte to the right hand; ſo that the ſame helps ought to be given, as for the right hand upon the voltes, but gently and eaſy, becauſe he goes in a ſtrait line. But here the left ſide being ſtill to the wall, you are to make him go in curvets backwards, not forgetting that the left ſide of the horſe to the wall, when he advances, is for your right hand; and continuing the ſame poſture, the left ſide towards the wall, in going backwards in curvets, is for the left hand. When he advances to the right, you help him with the rein from the wall, and the leg on the ſame ſide, confining his ſhoulders, and giving liberty to his croupe, keeping his croupe likewiſe towards the wall, putting your breaſt out, and keeping your belly in, which gives the croupe room to play.

But now when you make him to go backwards in curvets, it is to the left hand, and therefore the helps are to be theſe; you muſt draw the rein next the wall, which you do by putting the bridle on the right ſide of his neck, the nails of your hand turned upwards to your right ſhoulder, your left ſhoulder a little in, and your oppoſite leg a little backward, that you may conſtrain the croupe and give liberty to the ſhoulders, aiding him in time with your hand at each motion, your right leg cloſe to his body, and a little back. He ſhould be pulled back when he riſes, and the hand eaſed as he comes down, that his croupe may have room to go backward; for the horſe gains ground with his croupe, and his fore-part follows to keep it; if he did not make room for his fore-legs to follow, he could move but in the ſame place. You muſt put your body forward, and your breaſt out, with your belly a little in. As to the old method of leaning the body back, it is very wrong, ſince it is giving a horſe the ſame helps to go backwards, which are to make him advance. Certainly, if I draw ſomething towards me, I lean back, and if I puſh any thing from me I lean forward. Theſe aids are to make him keep the line of the wall, with his croupe towards it, and it is the true method of making a horſe go backward in curvets along a wall, preſſing his croupe and giving liberty to his ſhoulders. So you ſee, that what is for the right hand forwards is for the left hand backwards, and that all the aids are changed; for example, when you go forward, the rein and leg on the ſame ſide are to confine the ſhoulders, and give liberty to the croupe; and when you go backward, the rein and contrary leg are to confine the croupe and give liberty to the ſhoulders. Beſides, in going forwards your left ſhoulder, which is oppoſite to the rein you work, is brought in to preſs the ſhoulders; but in going backward backwards, the rein and ſhoulder on the ſame ſide are brought in to work the croupe. Thus you have the truth of Curvets backwards, your left ſide to the wall; and a horſe cannot keep the line of the wall any other way; for he cannot go through the wall, and therefore goes backward as if he went to the left. The caſe is different round the pillar, for there he advances to the right, and goes backwards to the right, as there is no wall to confine him: the aids backwards are the ſame, excepting that he goes in a circle.

CHAP. XXI.

To make a Horſe go ſtrait forwards in Curvets by a Wall, the Right Side to the Wall.

THE horſe here is to be helped with the inward rein, the rider having his bridle-hand towards the wall, on the right ſide the neck, with the nails of his hand turned upwards towards the right ſhoulder, aiding him with the leg on the ſame ſide, his breaſt out, and his leg in. So his ſhoulders are worked, and his croupe is at liberty, which is only an inclination to the left hand, in preparing him for his Demivolte.

CHAP. XXII.

To make a Horſe go backwards in a ſtrait Line by a Wall in Curvets, the Right Side ſtill to the Wall.

WHEN your left ſhoulder was to the wall, it was for the right hand in going forwards, and for the left in going backwards: therefore your right ſhoulder to the wall is for the left hand forward, and for the right backward. The aids are theſe: The horſe ſhould be helped with the rein next the wall, putting your bridle-hand on the left ſide his neck, the nails turned upwards towards the left ſhoulder, putting that ſhoulder a little back each time, and helping him with the contrary leg (for leg and rein contrary work the croupe) the breaſt and body ought to advance a little, helping him back with the hand every time he riſes. When you raiſe him, the curb will be a little looſe, and when he comes down it will be a little tighter; ſo that all horſes are light upon the hand when they are upon their haunches. If your left ſide is to the wall, for the Demivolte you ought to help him more ſtrongly on the right, both with the rein and your leg on the ſame ſide, which is the leg from the wall in Curvets: but if your right ſide is to the wall, for the Demivolte help him ſtronger on the left ſide, both with the rein and leg on the ſame ſide, which is that from the wall in Curvets.

End of the Second Diviſion of Leſſons for CURVETS.

The Third Diviſion of Leſſons, which is to dreſs a Horſe for CAPRIOLES, BALOTADES, GROUPADES, *and* DEMI-AIRS.

CHAP. XXIII.

For Caprioles.

A HORSE muſt be worked at the pillar my new way for Caprioles. Firſt, the rein of the caveſon ought to be faſtened ſhort, and then he muſt be helped with two ſwitches, one upon his fore-part, the other upon his croupe,

BOOK III. in right time, ſtanding on which ſide one pleaſes. This will make him go ſurpriſingly true, as well in the ſame place *ferme à ferme*, as upon the voltes, and with an aſtoniſhing eaſe and facility. One may make him go either ſideways or backwards; but a horſe is not graceful in leaping backwards. For the left, you need only faſten the left rein of the caveſon ſhort to the pillar, and work him as you did for the right before. When he is perfect, the button of the reins down, without any body upon his back, you may ride him to both hands with the rein faſtened to the pillar, but then it muſt be a little longer. When you firſt mount him, you muſt uſe him gently, and not work him too much at a time, for all new things ſurpriſe a horſe very much. In a ſhort time you will find the wonderful effects of the pillar, my new way, for Caprioles *ferme à ferme*, forwards, ſideways, and backwards upon the voltes, if you pleaſe; therefore I adviſe you to practiſe this new method of the pillar in all kinds of airs.

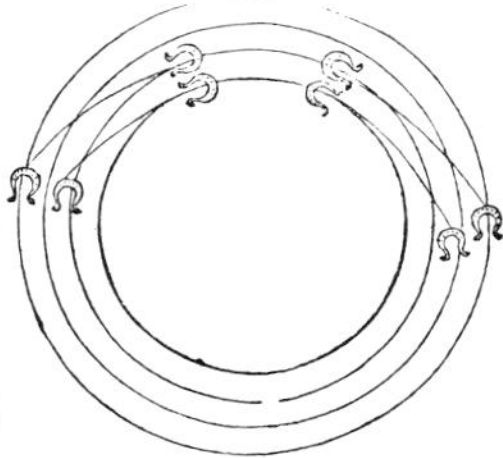

The above Figure is for Caprioles to the Right and Left Hand.

CHAP. XXIV.

To dreſs a Horſe for the Balotade.

A Balotade is a leap that is taught in the ſame manner as the Capriole, and differs only in this; a horſe in the Capriole ſtrikes out equally with both hind-legs at the ſame time, when he is at the height of his leap; in a Balotade he only ſtrikes half out, and makes only an offer; for in effect he does not ſtrike at all, the ſhoes of his hind-feet are only ſeen, and this is called a Balotade. The ſingle pillar will make him perfect in it, as I have ſhewn you in the Caprioles.

CHAP. XXV.

To dreſs a Horſe for the Groupade.

THE Groupade is a leap which is taught in the ſame manner as the Capriole, and differs from the Capriole and Balotade only in this, that he does not ſtrike out as in the Caprioles, nor does he offer to ſtrike, ſhewing the ſhoes of his hind-feet, as in the Balotade, but draws up his hind-legs as if he drew them to his belly.

With regard to the height of theſe three airs, it is the ſame, and differ only in the poſture of the hind-legs, as I ſhewed before: the method of teaching them is the ſame. Nature ſhews you this diverſity in the hind-legs of a horſe better than art, being more diſpoſed by her to one than another. My new way of the pillar will do for this, as I ſaid of the Caprioles.

CHAP. XXVI.

To dreſs a Horſe for a Step and a Leap.

THIS air is taught in the ſame manner as the other airs in leaping horſes. I muſt only ſay, that a horſe naturally takes this air of his own accord, for he is never taught it. Firſt, if he has not ſound feet, he won't always leap; ſecondly,

ſecondly, if he has not a good *appuy*, and a very good mouth, but is too light upon the hand, he is more proper for a Step and a Leap, than to leap continually, ſince the Step ſtrengthens his mouth, and gives him *appuy*. Beſides, if his reins are weak, he is fitter for it; the Step helps him to leap higher, as a man that runs before he leaps, leaps higher than one who takes a ſtanding leap; it is the ſame with a horſe in a Step and a Leap. A horſe in this air does three different actions, viz. *Terre-à-terre*, a *Curvet*, and a *Leap:* the Step reſembles *Terre-à-terre*, his riſing before, a Curvet, and then a Leap follows.

With reſpect to two *Steps* and a Leap, and three *Steps* and a Leap, it is the ſame thing, as it is only adding one or two *Steps* more; but this air is old and out of faſhion, and in reality very ridiculous.

The gallop *galliard* is worſe, for a horſe leaps when he ought to gallop. A gallop *galliard* is only proper for thoſe who have not the art to make a horſe leap true. A horſe with ſtrong reins and fed with good oats, when you prick him after a little reſt, if he gallops, will leap if you hold him up with your hand, and help him a little with your legs; but this is by accident, and becauſe he has reſt, though ignorant riders attribute it to their own dexterity, by idle impertinent talk, and to what dexterity God knows; it conſiſts more in words than in horſemanſhip, and deceives only the ignorant. This gallop *galliard* is fitter for a groom to brag on, than a horſeman; I leave it therefore to theſe tatlers and their ignorance. This is all as to the Step and the Leap: I ſhall only add, that my new method of the pillar will bring it to perfection, as I have ſhown in the Caprioles and other airs.

CHAP. XXVII.

The proper Helps for a leaping Horſe, either forwards or upon the Voltes, in Caprioles, Groupades, Balotades, &c. and how the Rider is to be ſeated.

THE rider being placed in the middle of the ſaddle, his breaſt out and his legs ſtrait, as if they were upon the ground, and well fixed upon his ſtirrups, he ought to raiſe his horſe, and as ſoon as he has done that, help him with the ſwitch in the following manner, holding the point of it behind; give him one ſtroke only upon the croupe in right time, helping with the outward rein of the bridle, which, when a horſe goes along a wall, is always the rein next to it, and is eaſily done by keeping the hand a little from the wall, placing it on the other ſide the horſe's neck, the nails turned upwards, to whichever hand he goes. If you are in an open field, and no wall near, you may make uſe of whichever outward rein you pleaſe. I call that *which outward rein you pleaſe*, that gives liberty to his croupe on either hand, conceiving the wall to be placed on either ſide: from hence it is no falſe way of reaſoning to ſay, that you may help him with which outward rein you pleaſe: according to this truth in horſemanſhip, I call it which rein you pleaſe, becauſe it puts out both haunches, either on one ſide or the other, when one works with one of the reins in this manner. Thus the croupe is a little out, that it may have liberty to play, as it ought to do in Caprioles; for how otherways can the croupe be at liberty? and if it is not, it is impoſſible to raiſe it.

BOOK III.

At the ſame time you raiſe the horſe, and help with your ſwitch as I mentioned before, you muſt ſit firm upon your ſaddle with your thighs and knees, but muſt be eaſy from the knees to the ſtirrups: for if your legs were ſtiff from the knee downwards, and in the hams, you would rather make the horſe fling himſelf forward than make a regular leap; therefore you muſt keep a firm ſeat with your thighs and knees, and be free and eaſy from the hams to the ſtirrups, your toes pointing a little downwards, which relaxes the muſcles of the leg and the hams, and the bent of the ham makes the legs eaſy, as they ought to be in all kinds of airs, and whenever a horſe leaps; and that you may ſupport him in the air with your hand, you muſt help him gently with the calf of your leg, but ſo as not to be perceived by the ſpectators. And in reality, if you ſit in the poſture I have deſcribed, the bare motion of the horſe will make your legs help him; the bending the ham gives the aid with the thigh. Should it be neceſſary to pinch him with the ſpurs, the bent of the ham puts them ſo much the nearer to him; and that motion ought to be very little, and performed with ſecreſy, as if you did not help him at all.

Juſt when the horſe takes his leap, you muſt thruſt your breaſt very much forwards, which flings your ſhoulders back with ſtrength, and yet no body can perceive but that you ſit upright, and move but very little. You muſt not do as ſome that I have ſeen, who put their heads back almoſt to his croupe every time the horſe leaps, as if their reins were broke, or as if they had difficulty to keep in the ſaddle. You ſhould be careful to take the exact time, as you do the bound of a ball at tennis, giving juſt then the aids I have told you. When the horſe is at the height of his leap, you muſt ſtop him there a little, as if he was held in the air, which is called *ſoûtenir*.

You may help him with the ſwitch each leap, if you pleaſe, not over the ſhoulder, but over the bending of the arm that holds it, a little under the ſhoulder, your arm at a ſmall diſtance from your body, and a little bent at the elbow, and ſo the end of your ſwitch will fall directly upon the middle of the croupe; this aid is graceful for a leaping horſe. If he goes freely, and you find his croupe light, you may extend your right arm upwards at a ſmall diſtance from your body, waving your ſwitch up and down, which is graceful enough. But the beſt way is, to have the ſwitch under your hand, the point downwards, and help with it upon the croupe in exact time when he leaps, that is, when he raiſes himſelf. This aid ought not to be only a ſingle ſtroke, but a continual touching upon the horſe's croupe, till he riſes again from the ground; and do thus every time he riſes. This is the moſt certain and trueſt help, but is the leaſt graceful of any. As you help with the rein without the volte in Caprioles to the right hand, and bring the ſhoulder on the ſame ſide in, ſo the croupe and both the haunches will conſequently go a little out, which makes room for his croupe to play. He likewiſe deſcribes four compleat circles with his four legs, but different to thoſe in Terre-à-terre or Curvets; for here the fore-leg next the volte deſcribes the leaſt circle, the other fore-leg the ſecond; but the fore-leg without the volte is a little before that within it, becauſe the aid is with the outward rein; his hind-leg within the volte deſcribes the third circle, and his other hind-leg the largeſt; but the hind-leg without the volte is a little before that within it, and

and becauſe the help is with the rein without the volte. His legs ought to be in this manner, if they go right, and if you have ſuppled him to each hand, as you may ſee by the figure here, which is both for the right and left.

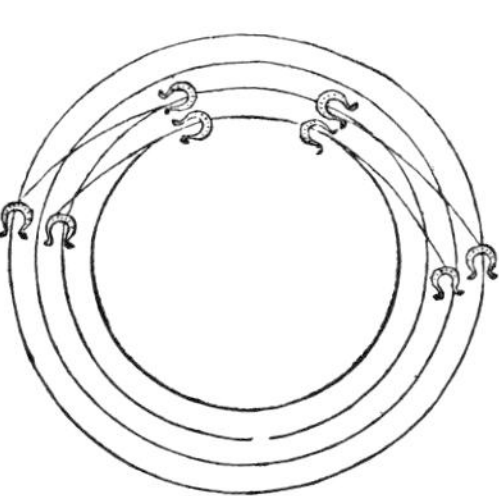

You muſt do the ſame for the left hand; it is only placing your bridle-hand within the volte on the inſide his neck, to work the outward rein; you muſt help ſomewhat more with the left leg, which is that within the volte, leaning a little more upon that ſtirrup and do in every thing elſe as you did for the right hand, thruſting out your breaſt and putting your ſhoulders back; but the right ſhoulder ſhould come in when you are going to the left.

I have now given you the very quinteſſence of the art of making horſes go in leaps either forward or upon the voltes, in Caprioles, Balotades and Groupades, which makes both the horſe and horſeman compleat. You ſhould remember to work him at the pillar. A Capriole is a gallop in the Air.

End of the Third Diviſion of Leſſons upon AIRS, *which is to Dreſs a Horſe in Caprioles, Balotades, Groupades, and Demi-Airs.*

The Fourth Diviſion of Leſſons, upon AIDS *or* HELPS.

CHAP. XXVIII.

Of the Helps with the Bridle-Hand.

THE bridle-hand, contrary to the old maxims, ought never to be juſt over the neck of the horſe, in any of his actions; as for example, if you gallop along a wall, with the wall on the left hand, your hand ought to be on the outſide the horſe's neck towards the wall, the nails upwards, to draw the right rein, that is, the rein fartheſt from the wall, to prepare him for the demi-volte. The wall on the right ſide, you muſt put your hand a little without the horſe's neck on the ſame ſide, the nails upwards, that you may draw the rein which is the fartheſt from the wall, to prepare him for the demi-volte, ſtill helping him with the ſame rein, till he has finiſhed it, and then change.

If you go upon one *piſte*, as it is termed, upon large circles to the right hand, you muſt place your bridle-hand on the contrary ſide, which is the left, that you may work the rein within the volte. If you gallop upon one *piſte* to the left, you muſt place the bridle-hand on the contrary ſide, which is the right and without the volte, to work the rein within it.

If you go Terre-à-terre to the right hand, you muſt place the bridle-hand on the contrary ſide, which is the out and left ſide, the nails upwards, keeping it high towards the left ſhoulder. If you go Terre-à-terre to the left hand, your bridle-hand muſt be without the horſe's neck or volte, the nails upwards to the right ſhoulder, holding it higher or lower, as there is occaſion.

BOOK III.

The Helps with the Bridle for Caprioles, Balotades, and Groupades.

For leaps, the hand ſhould be held otherwiſe; for going along a wall, with your left ſide towards it, you muſt place your bridle-hand a little on the contrary ſide of his neck, which is the ſide from the wall, the nails of your hand turned to the right ſhoulder, holding it high to ſupport him: by this you pull the outward rein of the bridle to work his ſhoulders, which forces his croupe out, that it may have the more room to play. The aids for the hand will be here directly contrary to my foregoing inſtructions; for in thoſe, you work with the inward rein to ſubject the croupe, and here you work with the outward rein of the bridle, to give liberty to the croupe.

When a horſe goes to the right upon the voltes, or along a wall his left ſide to it, you muſt place your bridle-hand within the volte, the nails of your hand upwards to the right ſhoulder, to make ſure of the ſhoulders, and give room to his croupe to play. For it is moſt certain that the outward rein of the bridle forces his ſhoulders in, and conſequently his croupe out.

When you go to the left hand upon the voltes, you muſt place your bridle-hand within the volte, the nails of your hand upwards, to the left ſhoulder. Thus I have given you the true way of working with the bridle, and the reaſons why you do ſo, and how you are to uſe the inward rein, which till now was never known.

CHAP. XXIX.

Of the Helps of the Body.

YOU muſt ſit upon your twiſt, having your breaſt out and your belly in, your knees and thighs cloſe to the ſaddle, and your legs ſtrait down. Being ſeated in this manner, it follows from a man's natural make, that when the ham is bent the thigh grows bigger, which is the help of the thigh, and is the moſt gentle can be given, and the moſt proper in all airs, (not but it is ſometimes neceſſary to help him with the legs, tho' very rarely.) Bending the ham puts the thigh cloſe to the ſaddle, and throws the calf of the leg from it. The ſecond help is with the calf of the leg, and then the ham muſt be ſtiff, and cloſe to the horſe, by which the thigh is put from him; this aid being ſtronger than that with the thigh, it is properer for Terre-à-terre. The third help is pinching with the ſpurs, and is the ſtrongeſt; it is done thus: the legs being cloſe to the horſe, muſt be a little bent in the ham (this aid is proper in all airs) and being bent, the toes will be down, which will bring the ſpurs up, and the calves of the legs being a little farther from the horſe's ſides by bending the ham, the ſpurs will be nearer, and then pinch him gently with them, and in time. This is an excellent aid, and very proper in all airs; it is very good too in Terre-à-terre, and ought to be kept for the laſt, as it is the ſtrongeſt. It is not ſpurring; for ſpurring is not an aid, but a correction. Here I have given the three principal aids of the body; that of the thigh, calf of the leg, and the gentle pinching with the ſpurs.

I don't mention them, as others have done before, without teaching you in what manner they are to be uſed; if they intended to teach you, they did it wrong, not for want of good will, or that they meant to deceive you, (for I am convinced that many worthy gentlemen have wrote upon this ſubject) but

but it was certainly for want of knowing better. I have given you now the helps of the hand, the thigh, the calf of the leg, and the heel, and hope you will be able to put your letters together, that is, theſe aids, which muſt be by never giving any help with the hand, without adding one of the others in a greater or leſſer degree, as there is occaſion; but the gentler the better, both as to hand, thigh, calf of the leg, and heel; for a horſe generally goes better with gentle than with ſtrong helps: a ſtrong aid confounds and ſurpriſes a weak horſe, makes a ſtrong one go too much upon the reins, giving him a *contre-temps*, and makes him lean upon his fore-part, and be heavy upon the hand. Beſides, ſtrong aids make a horſe full of fire almoſt mad, and a dull one reſty and lifeleſs; therefore the moſt gentle aids are beſt for all horſes.

The hand, thigh, leg, and heel ought always to go together; for example, ſuppoſe a man playing upon the lute, and he touches the ſtrings with his left hand, without touching the others with his right, he muſt make but a very indifferent harmony; but when both hands go together, and in right time, the muſick will be good. It is the ſame with reſpect to this excellent art; what you mark with your hand ſhould be touched at the ſame time either with your thigh, leg, or heel, or the muſick of your work will be bad. We are at preſent ſpeaking of muſick, and he that has not a muſical head can never be a good horſeman. A horſe well dreſſed moves as true, and keeps as regular time as any muſician can. Thus you have the aids of the hand, thigh, leg, and heel, ſeparately and together.

CHAP. XXX.

Of the Helps with the Switch.

THE ſwitch is both uſeful and graceful, nevertheleſs I would not have it much uſed to any horſe whatſoever, unleſs it be to thoſe deſigned for pleaſure or for airs; for a ſoldier's horſe ought to go with the hand and heel only, ſince the rider is to have a ſword in his hand.

But if you would uſe it in working a ſoldier's horſe in the open field, you muſt to the right hand help with it in the following manner: Put your ſwitch acroſs to the left towards the eye of the bridle, or hold it up with the end of the bridle in the right hand, to whichever hand the horſe goes. It is graceful too to hold the ſwitch up without the end of the bridle. If you find that your horſe does not riſe ſufficiently, you muſt give him a ſtroke or two upon the neck or ſhoulders on either ſide, as there is occaſion. Theſe aids are likewiſe good in Terre-à-terre. If he does not put his croupe in enough, you muſt give him two or three ſtrokes over the bridle-arm upon the left ſide of the croupe, or upon the flank, to keep it in. But this I don't much like, nor do I think it graceful, and ſeems as if the horſe did not obey the heel. However, when a horſe goes Terre-à-terre to the left, nothing looks better than to hold the ſwitch down by the right thigh, your arm a little bent, ſo that it ſeems hollow from the body. This is an excellent aid. Theſe are the helps with the ſwitch in Terre-à-terre, or in riding a ſoldier's horſe.

The Helps with the Switch in Curvets and Demi-Airs.

The ſwitch ought rather to be ſhort than long, and your arm not ſo cloſe to the body as to appear ſtiff and confined; for it looks like affectation, which is wrong in every thing: befides, it has an aukward air; and a good horfeman ought to fit in as eafy a pofture as poffible, doing nothing however inconfiftent with the rules of riding. The fwitch ought to be fhort, and when the horfe goes in Curvets to the right, you muft hold it acrofs the horfe's neck, the elbow high, but a little lower than the hand, fometimes upon a level with it, keeping an exact time with grace, fometimes touching his neck, and fometimes only making as if you would, as occafion requires. If he fhould not rife high enough, give him a ftrong ftroke or two upon the fhoulders. This aid will ferve for both hands, but beft for the right.

When he goes to the left, you may help him upon the right fhoulder, as before, keeping your horfe's time with grace, having your elbow bent, as when one takes a ball upon the bound at tennis.

If the horfe does not raife himfelf fufficiently, you muft give him a hard ftroke or two upon the right fhoulder, and then gently again as before. There is another help with the fwitch, which is called *de tous temps*, and that is, helping him with it continually; all thefe aids are both for the voltes and the ftrait line forwards. There is another that is very graceful, but it muft be with a fwitch fomething longer than ordinary, that bends a good deal: hold your right hand up, the arm bent at the elbow, and move it backwards and forwards without keeping time as long as the horfe works. This aid ferves upon the voltes forward, backward, and fideways in Curvets like the former.

When a horfe goes along a wall, with his right fide to it, if you ftrike the wall gently with your fwitch conftantly and without time, with your elbow a little bent, it enlivens and animates the horfe, and nothing can be more graceful. Thefe are the aids with the fwitch for Curvets.

The helps with the Switch in Groupades, Balotades, and Caprioles.

You muft help the horfe with the fwitch over the right arm, having it a little bent in the elbow, and the arm from the body, fo that the point of the fwitch may touch the middle of the croupe, taking care to do it in the right time of the leap, and as the horfe rifes. But the fureft aid is to turn it in your hand, holding the point behind, and help him with it in right time, and as he rifes.

If the horfe leaps freely, it is fufficient to wave the fwitch backwards and forwards, which is graceful enough.

The Rider that is on Foot may help the Horfe in this manner:

He may help him before to rife with the fwitch either upon his cheft or fhoulders, or upon the knees to make him bend his legs; though perhaps the bending of your knees will make him do it fufficiently. This is for the fore-part.

He may help with the Switch upon the Croupe thus:

If the horfe is touched upon the middle of his croupe, it will make him put himfelf together, and draw his legs in without lafhing out: if you touch him upon the end of his croupe, he will lafh out with both legs; and if you ftrike him on the outfide his hind-legs, a little above the hock, he will draw his legs under hs belly. Thefe three different aids with the fwitch have thefe different effects.

The

The help at the ſingle pillar with two ſwitches the new way, one to raiſe him before, and the other to help him at the ſame time under the belly, works wonderfully to put a horſe upon the haunches.

The helps upon the hind-legs, whether within or without, are very ridiculous, and occaſion more confuſion than they do good; and ſo do all the others, excepting thoſe I have laid down for you to uſe.

The ſwitch is excellent to raiſe a horſe, to animate him, and make him keep his time. The voice is ſometimes good, but ought to be ſeldom uſed; not to be like the riders of ſome countries, that are always calling to their horſes like carters.

I have here made a kind of abridgment or repetition of what you ought abſolutely to remember; therefore take it in good part, without criticiſing upon it, ſince I have done it more for your ſakes than my own, for I myſelf knew all this before; don't therefore find fault with what I write for your ſervice. As to the new method I have here given you, I dare venture to ſay, that he that does not approve of it is like never to underſtand it. For my part, I addreſs it to the reaſonable part of mankind; and ſo have done.

CHAP. XXXI.

A new Invention for putting a Horſe upon his Haunches, which is the beſt in the World, for without it they will hardly be made to go well.

NATURE, that we ought to follow, has made a horſe's legs thus: His fore-legs are made like ours, the knees are before and the hams behind: his hind-legs are as our arms, the elbow behind, and the bending part before, and from the paſtern to the hoof it is the ſame; that is to ſay, the heels of the fore-feet are behind like ours, and the toes before as our toes; and the heels of the hind-feet are behind, and the toes before as our hands. Tho' the heels of a horſe's fore-feet are towards his hams, and the toes towards his knees; and the heels of his hind-feet towards his elbow, and the toes towards the hams, which is directly contrary; nevertheleſs his paſterns and feet make the bending of all four feet to be alike, which is by the contraction of the nerves.

So that to put a horſe upon his haunches, one ſhould raiſe the heels of the hind-feet, by having the ſhoes turned up at both heels a good deal more than uſual, which will oblige him to bend his hocks, as the heel will be higher than the toe of the foot. A gentle deſcent of ground will put him upon his haunches, as you may ſee in the ſtable, when a horſe is turned upon the ſnaffle, that part next the manger is higher than the other; and if you make him go there in curvets, ſo turned upon the ſnaffle, the croupe being higher than the fore-part, it puts him upon his haunches. Therefore by raiſing the hind-part of his foot, by turning up his ſhoes, higher than the toe, it anſwers the ſame end as the deſcent of ground, to place him upon his haunches. As in going up-hill you make the horſe's hind-legs ſtiff, by keeping them ſtretch'd backwards, which throws him off of his haunches; ſo in going down-hill you make him bend his legs at the hocks, placing them under his belly, which puts him upon his haunches. Theſe turn'd-up ſhoes produce the ſame effect as when a horſe goes down-hill. When a horſe goes down a hill his croupe is higher than his ſhoulders, which puts him mightily upon his haunches; and therefore theſe ſhoes, which raiſe him higher behind than before, ought to put him upon his haunches for the ſame reaſon.

It may be thought, that a horſe may hurt himſelf by treads with theſe ſhoes, but I have always made uſe of them without the leaſt accident; though with common ſhoes ſometimes horſes get treads, and it even happens to the fore-legs, where they are never uſed. My new method of faſtening one of the reins of the caveſon ſhort to the pillar puts a horſe very much upon his haunches, eſpecially when he goes de *ferme-à-ferme*, or upon the voltes backwards.

Helping a horſe with a ſwitch upon the cheſt, or upon the bridle, ſtriking him upwards with it, or ſometimes upon the noſe, tho' ſeldom, will put him upon his haunches. I approve moſt of aiding him upon the cheſt or upon the noſe, ſince theſe aids make him advance his cheſt, which he can never do without being upon his haunches; for when the cheſt advances, the croupe muſt of neceſſity be drawn in. Aiding a horſe upon the cheſt, noſe, or bridle, forces his cheſt out, and puts him upon his haunches; helping him upon the knees makes him ſo timorous that he withdraws his breaſt, and therefore it puts him off of his haunches; but aiding him upon the cheſt with one ſwitch, and with another under the belly, places him ſtrongly upon them; for one ſwitch makes him advance his cheſt, and places him upon his haunches, whilſt the other tickling him under the belly makes him draw in his haunches and hind-legs, ſo that both working together have the better effect. When you raiſe him too high, he ſupports himſelf upon the toes of his feet, to prevent his falling backward; and his heels not touching the ground, it makes his hocks ſtiff, and conſequently throws him off of his haunches: therefore thoſe who raiſe a horſe very high to place him upon his haunches are much in the wrong. And though a horſe puts his hind-legs under his belly, if he ſupports himſelf upon his heels with the fore-part of his foot from the ground, his hocks are always ſtiff, and he is not upon his haunches: therefore theſe ſhoes, for the reaſons I have given, make the whole weight of the croupe to fall equally upon the heel and fore-part of the foot, and conſequently upon the whole foot, which gives him ſtrength, and makes him bend his hocks as much as poſſible with eaſe and facility.

As to the fore-part of a horſe, you muſt take care in fitting him with a bitt, that he does not arm himſelf againſt it: for this not only makes him hard upon the hand, becauſe it touches his cheſt, and you have no room to pull him; but if he carries his head low and round, he muſt of neceſſity raiſe his croupe, which will put him off his haunches. You muſt therefore give him a gentle bitt, that he may not carry low, but in a good place. The branches of the bridle ought to be neither too ſtrong nor too weak, that is to ſay, they muſt ſlope towards you, but not fall quite back, that you may have room to pull the reins with advantage, and this poſture puts him upon his haunches; or otherwiſe you muſt work with your hand going to the right, as I ſhewed you before, keeping it up pointing to the left ſhoulder. And to the left, you muſt keep your hand up and to the right ſhoulder. If you go ſtrait forward, hold it forward and high near your ſtomach. By drawing your hand low to your body, you pull the horſe's head down, and put him off his haunches; therefore you ought rather to advance it towards his head, and ſo the branches

will

will have leſs force, and won't be ſo tight, which will put him upon his haunches, which is the beſt aid.

I don't mean that you place your hand ſo much forwards, as to be almoſt upon the horſe's head; if it be only a little forward it is ſufficient; you muſt have his head up, as I ſaid before, that he may not harm himſelf againſt his bitt. If you hold the bridle up towards one of your ſhoulders (viz. towards the left when you go to the right, and towards the right when you go to the left) without leaning forwards, the branches of the bridle will have the more power, not only as a lever to keep him up, but likewiſe to put him upon his haunches. It is true, that he may be apt to go backwards.

It is a good way to put his head to the pillar, not only to walk him ſo, but likewiſe to raiſe him, provided you don't let him riſe too high. I have already ſhewed you how to make him riſe. Nothing makes a horſe go better Terre-à-terre, than to make him do it his head to the wall all round the covered Manege, and it will put him upon his haunches.

A ſlow gallop with the croupe in, puts him likewiſe upon his haunches, and ſo does Terre-à-terre.

You muſt gallop him in one *piſte*, as it is termed, upon his haunches, your hand out, helping a little with your leg on the ſame ſide, to make him bend his ſhoulders: if you put his croupe too much out, you put him off his haunches. The *walk* or *paſſage*, which is the action of the trot, is the beſt of all to put him upon his haunches.

It is good, and in the beginning very neceſſary to ſtop a horſe, and make him go backwards, to put him upon his haunches; but they are both very diſagreeable to horſes. You may meet with leſſons enough of this ſort in old FREDERICK GRISON, and many other ſuch authors, who have wrote upon this ſubject.

All the leſſons I have ſhewed you, as plainly and clearly as poſſibly I could, are new inventions; and I can aſſure you, that you will find them true and excellent, to put a horſe upon his haunches, without which, none can go as they ought.

And therefore our only aim in this long, laborious, and painful work, is to put a horſe well upon his haunches, in order to have him well dreſſed, and compleat the art of the Manege. Receive it therefore in as good part as I communicate it heartily.

End of the Fourth Diviſion of Leſſons for AIRS, *and of the Third Book of the New Method of Dreſſing Horſes.*

THE

NEW METHOD OF DRESSING HORSES.

BOOK IV.

Which treats of all the Vices belonging to Horſes, and the ſureſt Ways to cure them.

The Firſt Diviſion of Leſſons.

Whenever a Horſe in working does wrong, it muſt be either in the fore or hind Part, in the Shoulders or the Croupe; he muſt be diſobedient either to the Hand or Heel. We ſhall therefore firſt treat of the Diſobedience of the Shoulders, to prevent his being entier, *which is to refuſe to turn, and is the worſt Vice of all: Here follows the Method therefore of making the Shoulders ſupple.*

CHAP. I.

Leſſon the Firſt, to work a Horſe's Shoulders.

A HORSE ſhould be walked, trotted, and galloped upon large circles at firſt, uſing the inward rein of the caveſon, and the leg on the ſame ſide, which to the right hand is the right rein and right leg. I have often told you, that rein and leg on the ſame ſide work a horſe's ſhoulders, but not the croupe; that they confine the fore-part, and leave the croupe at liberty, becauſe the ſhoulders are ſubjected, and the croupe not. This ſhould be upon large circles, to make it more eaſy to him.

In

In the ſecond leſſon to work the ſhoulders, you muſt walk the horſe in his own length, drawing the inward rein, and helping with the inward leg, which always work both the ſhoulders, ſo that the croupe is neceſſarily at liberty. This is an excellent leſſon to ſupple the ſhoulders. Horſes generally reſiſt what you would have them do, not from a natural ſimplicity, but with malice and ſubtilty. Very often when they find their croupe is to be put out, they endeavour to put it in. You ought therefore to draw the inward rein very ſtrong, giving him the inward ſpur at the ſame time, and very ſuddenly, which is rein and leg on the ſame ſide ; but when he is to the right, it is the right rein and right leg: this makes the ſhoulders ſupple, and is a moſt excellent leſſon.

But if he ſtill continues to be ſtiff in the ſhoulders, and refuſes to turn to the right hand, put his head to the pillar to the left hand, and draw the outward rein, which is the right, helping with the leg on the ſame ſide. Tho' here the horſe goes to the left hand, nevertheleſs both his ſhoulders are worked to the right; for the leg and rein are uſed of the ſame ſide, which always works the ſhoulders. This is an excellent leſſon to ſupple the ſhoulders, tho' it is a falſe one; for the horſe goes to one hand, and looks to the other ; he goes to the left hand, and his ſhoulders are worked to the right, and his legs go falſe; ſo that this ought to be uſed only when the other leſſons won't do. This is a good remedy to cure a horſe that refuſes to turn, but ought to be uſed no longer than till you have got the better of that vice.

There is another leſſon to ſupple the ſhoulders, which is this: Faſten the right rein of the caveſon my way to the pommel of the ſaddle on the right hand, and tye it ſo ſhort, as to bring his head as much in as poſſible, when there is no danger of his coming over; then work him with the leg on the ſame ſide, which is the right, (leg and rein thus always work the ſhoulders) and the croupe for the ſame reaſon is loſt. You may work him in this manner, in all the leſſons I have taught you.

If you work with falſe reins, you muſt work with the rein and leg on the ſame ſide, to work his ſhoulders.

If you work with the bridle reins, you muſt work with the rein and leg on the ſame ſide, to work the ſhoulders.

There is another way of working the ſhoulders, with the rein of the bridle: you muſt ſeparate your reins and hold one in each hand, and draw the inward rein towards your left ſhoulder going to the right, and advance the outward rein near the horſe's head, and bend it as much as poſſible within his neck, turning the nails of your left hand upwards, and putting your inward leg a little to him. This being done in time, and with force, will bend his ſhoulders, or make him ready to break his neck. But I rather recommend the other aids to ſupple the ſhoulders, as they are more gentle, and work with more eaſe to the horſe without injuring his mouth. The rein and the leg on the ſame ſide, whether the croupe is in or out, always work the ſhoulders and not the croupe, altho' it yields a little to the heel.

For the left hand, you ought always to work with rein and leg on the ſame ſide, and put the bridle in your right hand, and the caveſon in the left, and remember that your outward ſhoulder always works the horſe's ſhoulders. The left hand requires no farther explanation. Thus I have given you all the aids for ſuppling a horſe's ſhoulders to both hands, which is the principal thing.

End of the Firſt Diviſion of Leſſons for ſuppling the Shoulders.

The Second Division of Leſſons, which is to correct a Horſe that does not obey the Heel.

CHAP. II.

To make a Horſe obey the Heel.

AS rein and leg of a ſide work the ſhoulders of a horſe, ſo rein and leg contrary work the croupe. If you would put a horſe's croupe in, and he obſtinately thruſts it out, give him a good ſtroke or two with the ſpur on the outſide to keep it in.

If he refuſes to keep it in notwithſtanding this, and is obſtinately diſobedient to the ſpur, put his croupe in, by drawing the contrary rein to the way he is going, helping him with your leg on the ſame ſide, which is the outward, and this will make him comply tho' he be very vicious and obſtinate. Theſe aids ought not to be continued, but are to be uſed only in caſe of neceſſity, ſince they are falſe; therefore when you have done what you wanted, you muſt return to the true aids.

The rein of the caveſon, and the leg on the ſame ſide, whether the croupe be out or in, always work the ſhoulders, and only half the croupe; the ſhoulders always to the contrary ſide to which he goes, and the half of his croupe to the ſide he does go of. But if the croupe is in, the hind-leg within the volte is entirely loſt, and there is no help for it, ſo that it is to be feared that he will be *entier*,(that is, reſty) by putting his croupe too much in, becauſe he has there too much liberty. Therefore you muſt turn the bridle-hand, and aſſiſt him with it, working with the rein of the caveſon, and the leg on the ſame ſide, which preſſes his ſhoulders and fore-part, puts his croupe out, and will neceſſarily put him upon his ſhoulders, whether his croupe be in or out. When he goes in this manner upon the Paſſage, his legs move as true as when he is worked as he ought to be; but when he goes Terre-à-terre, or upon the Gallop, if he goes to the right, the fore-leg without the volte leads, which is falſe, and the hind-leg within the volte follows it, which is a Trot upon the ſwiftneſs of a Gallop, and makes him ready to fall; therefore I would adviſe you not to work him in this manner, but upon a walk, and not then neither but in caſe of neceſſity, that is, when a horſe's ſhoulders are ſo ſtiff that he will not turn, or that he obſtinately reſiſts the ſpur, and will not obey it. Then, I ſay, there is no better way than this, with rein and leg on the ſame ſide, not only to make the ſhoulders ſupple, but to make him obey the heel without violence. But this ought to be uſed like a medicince; when you have cured the diſtemper, it is neceſſary to return to the true method, for fear of accuſtoming him to go falſe and look out of the turn. You muſt always work him, where he ſeems to find the greateſt difficulty.

When you work with the rein and leg on the ſame ſide, the croupe to the pillar, the horſe has too much liberty within the volte, and there is no way to hinder it but by turning the hand in: but horſes are ſo cunning and artful in their diſobedience to the rider, that, when you work them with the rein and leg on the ſame ſide with the croupe to the pillar, they find their hind-leg within the volte at liberty; therefore, that they may reſiſt the rider, they put their croupe ſo much in, that they don't turn their ſhoulders, and are *entier*.

It

It is the ſame when you work with rein and leg contrary; for then they find their liberty without the volte, and defend themſelves againſt the rider, taking that advantage, and thruſt the croupe vigorouſly out. The more you ſpur them, the more obſtinately they reſiſt, and will often ſooner die than yield. In this caſe you muſt work with the leg and rein on the ſame ſide, and that will eaſily cure them. Thus you ſee the cunning and ſubtilty of horſes, as well as their vicious defence againſt the rider. But this aid ought not to be long uſed.

Another Way of putting a Horſe's Croupe in, which is as good as the preceding one.

You muſt work with the rein within the volte, and the leg without in the following manner: If you go to the right, and find that your horſe's croupe does not come in enough, you muſt put the rein of the caveſon entirely croſs his neck towards the left hand, in order to put his croupe in; as much as you put his croupe in, ſo much almoſt do you force his fore-part to the left, which is right, ſince you put his croupe in. But ſo the inward rein of the caveſon works his outward haunch, which does not belong to it, as much as if you drew the outward rein; for only the inward haunch belongs to the inward rein. It works the outward haunch as much as if you drew the outward rein; ſo that the inward haunch is loſt to you as much as if you had drawn the outward rein, which is likewiſe falſe; for half his haunches go before his ſhoulders, and his legs go as wrong, the fore-leg within the volte leading, and the hind-leg without the volte following it, which is croſs-ways, and is the action of a Trot upon the ſwiftneſs of a Gallop, or Terre-à-terre. Beſides, you are placed wrong in the ſaddle, the right ſhoulder being forward to the right hand, when the left ſhould be ſo, and the whole ſeat falſe, thighs and legs, and all. But this way leg and rein contrary have as much effect in forcing the horſe's croupe in, as by working with the outward rein and the leg on the ſame ſide; it has even this advantage, that it makes the horſe look into the volte, which the other does not, for that makes him look very much out of it. In every thing elſe this is as falſe as the other, and therefore ought to be uſed only in caſes of neceſſity, as you do good medicines to cure a diſtemper, which are diſcontinued when the cure is compleated.

If one works a horſe upon a Walk in his own length, with his croupe very much in, he is mightily preſſed in that part, for tho' the ſhoulders go more ground than the croupe, the croupe is the moſt confined, and the ſhoulders moſt worked. There is no better leſſon than this, to ſubject a horſe's croupe. The rein and contrary leg, the horſe's head to the wall, either to the right or left; to the right hand you muſt draw the rein of the caveſon towards the left ſhoulder, or the falſe rein, if you uſe it, in the ſame manner; if you have only the bridle, you muſt place your bridle-hand on the left ſide the horſe's neck, that you may draw the inward rein, helping him with the contrary leg, which to the right hand is the left, putting your right ſhoulder in, for that helps greatly to work the horſe's croupe. This is an excellent leſſon.

Another Method of working a Horſe's Croupe.

To the right hand, put the horſe's head to the pillar, and the falſe rein, or rein of the caveſon within the volte, draw towards the left ſhoulder; or if you

ride

ride with the bridle only, you muſt place your bridle-hand on the left ſide the horſe's neck, turning the nails of it up towards your left ſhoulder, helping him with the contrary leg, that is, the left, and putting your right ſhoulder in, which will put his croupe in. This ought not to be long uſed, only for a certain time, to make him obey the heel, ſince it is falſe. The pillar ought to be on the inſide, when you work a horſe's croupe with his head towards the pillar, which works the croupe, but he goes falſe.

All the ſame aids ſerve for the left hand, only changing the rein, the leg, and the ſhoulder. The horſe's head is to be to the pillar for the left hand, the pillar on the inſide,which works the croupe, but it is (as I ſaid before) falſe. Therefore you ought only to uſe this leſſon till you have brought him to obey the heel.

Thus I have given you all the ways of reducing a horſe, whether the fault be in the ſhoulders, or the croupe, before or behind, whether he reſiſts the hand or the heel: nothing more can be upon a circle.

CHAP. III.

How a Horſe's Croupe or Shoulders are to be worked occaſionally.

IF you go to the right, and draw the inward rein of the caveſon, or the falſe rein towards your left ſhoulder, helping with the contrary leg, either more or leſs as there is occaſion, your inward leg being very ſupple; if the horſe's ſhoulders don't come ſufficiently in, by putting your left ſhoulder in you will make his ſhoulders very pliant: for the caveſon rein, or falſe rein within the volte, only keeps back the hind leg within the volte, which gives the ſhoulders room to turn, and conſequently makes them more ſupple.

If you ride with the bridle only, going to the right, put the bridle-hand on the contrary ſide, or left, turning the nails of it upwards as much as you can, and bring your left ſhoulder in, which will work the horſe's ſhoulders and make them ſupple, for the ſame reaſons I gave you before, ſince it produces the ſame effect.

But if the ſhoulders of your horſe turn too much to the right, and his croupe goes out, which it will then neceſſarily do, you muſt draw the inward rein of the caveſon, or falſe rein, or rein of the bridle, as much as you can above the neck, towards the outſide of the volte, putting your right ſhoulder in as much as you poſſibly can, looking a little out of the volte, which works the croupe of a horſe, and thruſts his ſhoulders out, and therefore his croupe will conſequently come in. This will make him obey the heel, tho' it is falſe with reſpect to his movement, but at length will make him go as he ought, when he is brought to obey both the hand and the heel.

From hence it is evident, that the rider's ſhoulder works the croupe, or ſhoulders, and nothing elſe: for inſtance, when I work a horſe upon a Walk, if I don't find his ſhoulders ſupple, I put my contrary ſhoulder in, to work thoſe of the horſe; and if I find he does not obey the leg, I put my ſhoulder in, (that is, within the volte) in order to work his croupe, helping him all the time with the contrary leg more or leſs, as there is occaſion.

I work him in this manner in all his leſſons, according as I find he does or does not obey. This is the quinteſſence of working a horſe in the hands of an able

able man. He ſhould be worked in the ſame manner to the left hand, only changing the hand and the leg.

CHAP. IV.

To work a Horſe, the Croupe either in or out.

YOU muſt work him with rein and leg contrary; but you ought not to lean more upon the outſide, than the inſide of the volte, becauſe you would make the horſe lean ſo much on that ſide, that he would avoid the aid or ſpur on the other ſide; for when a horſe leans much on the outſide, his legs within the volte will be up, like the legs of a form or bench, ſo that they muſt of neceſſity be ſhorter than his legs without, which is wrong, ſince they ought to be the longeſt to lead the way.

A horſe therefore ought to go ſtrait, and if you find he leans, give him a good ſtroke or two with the ſpur within the volte, and that will redreſs him. The rider has no better way to keep him thus, than to ſit ſtrait in his ſaddle; for the horſe continually follows the action of the rider. It is impoſſible to ſit ſo ſtrait upon a circle, as when the horſe goes forwards; nevertheleſs, if you will ſit upon the circles as I have taught you, you will ſeem to ſit ſtrait.

To put a horſe's head to the wall is an excellent leſſon, not only to put him upon his haunches, and to make him light in the hand, but alſo to bring a light horſe to bear the hand, and to put him too upon his haunches. Nothing is better than to paſſage thus ſideways, or curvet ſideways, to raiſe him in one place in Peſades; or to make him go Terre-à-terre with his head to the wall, three ſides or all, or the whole of the covered manege, is an excellent leſſon, and makes a horſe more obedient and readier, than any thing elſe can.

You may ſee now how preſumptuous thoſe are, who only want to ſee a maſter ride a horſe once, to underſtand the art inſtantly, and ſteal from him all his ſcience. Without diſpute theſe people are very fond of themſelves, ſince they imagine that by ſeeing a horſeman once ride they can find out the myſteries and ſecrets belonging to this dextrous art. It is equally probable, that one who had never been taught to play upon the lute, ſhould only by ſeeing ſome great maſter of that inſtrument play once, play inſtantly as well as he: He may put the lute out of order indeed: but I leave ſuch people to their own opinions.

End of the Second Diviſion of Leſſons.

The Third Diviſion of Leſſons.

CHAP. V.

The abſurd Faults of ſome Horſemen, who by ſeeing imitate, and imagine they ride as I do.

TO faſten the rein of the caveſon my way, and the rein within the volte very ſhort to the pommel of the ſaddle, not only puts the horſe's inward hind-leg back, and brings the half of his ſhoulders in, which is right; but alſo being tyed very ſhort, it acts upon both ſhoulders, which is wrong. Therefore to put his outward hind-leg or haunch in, they ſpur him without the volte, which is the moſt ſtupid ignorance imaginable; for they would

BOOK IV.

perform impoſſibilities, and things contrary to nature, for ſo they would have him obey two contrary aids at the ſame time, which is impoſſible. That is to ſay, they throw the outward haunch out with the rein, and at the ſame time they would force the ſame haunch in with the ſpur, which are two contrary actions, and utterly impoſſible at the ſame time.

But let us ſee what happens by it to the poor horſe; why, he having more ſenſe than the rider, finds that the rider would make him perform what he cannot, and therefore rebells, and reſiſts the ſpur, and throws his croupe out in ſpite of ſpur or ſwitch, ſo that he is thereby made both malicious and reſty, committing all manner of extravagancies to hurt his rider.

Their next abſurdity is, that they draw the rein within the volte (when the croupe does not come in enough) ſo tight to the pommel of the ſaddle, that it throws the outward hind-leg out, and they ſpur him with the outward leg to force it in, which are (as I ſaid above) two contrary actions at the ſame time; ſo that if the horſe does not put his croupe out, but is of a heavy diſpoſition, as are the Flanders horſes, he puts his outward haunch in, by the violence of the ſpur.

But he commits here a greater fault with his inward hind-leg; for the poor horſe has no other way of relieving himſelf, but by bringing it before his ſhoulder, which is utterly falſe, and ſo forced, that it is ridiculous to ſee a horſe's head drawn againſt his ſhoulder, and his hind-leg within the volte before his ſhoulders, by the violent conſtraint he is put to. Theſe are abſurdities in horſemanſhip. Can one imagine, that a horſe can go thus againſt nature, having his ſhoulders thus drawn in and confined? and nevertheleſs they expect that his croupe ſhould go before his ſhoulders!

The third error is, for example, when they go to the right, and draw the rein within the volte, fearing leſt the outward haunch ſhould not go ſufficiently in, they put the ſhoulders with the left rein as much as they can to the left: it is very certain that it brings the outward leg in, and they imagine, that becauſe they draw the rein towards the inſide, that they put the hind-leg within the volte back, ſeeing me work in that manner, as they think; but they are therein much miſtaken. For, altho' the rein be drawn towards the inſide, putting his ſhoulders to the ſide contrary to that he is going to, it works his hind-leg without the volte as much as the common outward rein; and is ſo far from working the hind-leg within the volte, that it allows it as much liberty in every reſpect, as if they worked with the rein to the contrary way to which the horſe goes. The inward rein does juſt the ſame, when the horſe's ſhoulders are put on the ſide contrary to that to which he goes; the effects are alike, and his legs move as falſe, ſince it is the action of a Trot upon the ſwiftneſs of a Gallop, which is abſolutely wrong, and ought to be avoided.

Theſe are errors and miſtakes, which are daily commited by imitation and preſumption.

Theſe remedies may be uſed, particularly the laſt, but the other hardly ever. When the croupe is out, you may faſten the inward rein as ſhort as you pleaſe, for then he is at liberty, and not at all forced. This laſt aid is only a ſort of correction, when he refuſes to obey the heel, and not properly an aid, and ought only to be uſed as ſuch. Therefore we ſhall now return to the truth of the Manege.

CHAP.

CHAP. VI.

The Way I took to reduce a Horse, that was extreamly Resty.

A Horse's restiness, when it is in a high degree, does not consist only in his refusing to advance, but also in his opposition to the rider, in every thing he possibly can, and with the utmost malice: for if one would make him go forward, he will go back; and if one would have him turn to one hand, he will turn to the other. Thus he avoids and opposes whatever he is required to perform, and all is the effect of his ill-will to the rider, which makes him refuse whatever he would have him do.

One must endeavour therefore to gain the horse; for the perfection of a well-managed horse consists in his following the will of his rider, so that the will of both shall seem to be the same. He must be forc'd a little, but not long, because force will make him worse. I have never yet seen that force and passion have prevailed the least upon a horse: for the horse having less understanding than his rider, his passion is so much the stronger, which makes him always get the better of the horseman, and shews that violent methods will not do. For when the horseman thinks himself victorious, he is deceiv'd, for we find that it is the horse. Because, when the horseman has spurred the beast so much, that he has made him all over blood and sweat, and put himself into a great heat and out of breath, still so long as he torments the horse, the horse will resist. He will run against a wall, lie down, bite, kick, and commit a thousand such like disorders. But as soon as the rider ceases to beat and spur him, the horse will leave off his tricks: and then the rider thinks himself conqueror, but is mistaken, since he himself gave up the cause by ceasing to beat and spur. The horse therefore finding he has the better, is altogether master of the field.

If the rider begins again to beat and spur, the horse will resist again: it is not the beast then that is vanquished, but the man, who is the greater brute of the two: the whip and the spur serve only to continue the quarrel even to death, as in a duel. The whole therefore is to make the horseman and his horse friends, and bring them to will the same thing.

If you can't gain your point therefore in one way, you must have recourse to another: I mean, that if in this extremity the horse will not agree with you, you must agree with him in the following manner. You would make your horse advance, and he to defend himself against you runs back: at that instant pull him back with all your strength. And if to oppose you he advances, immediately force him briskly forwards. If you would turn to the right, and he endeavours to turn to the left, pull him round to the left as suddenly as possible: if you would turn him to the left, and he insists on the right, turn him as smartly to the right as you are able. If you would have him go sideways to one hand, and he inclines more to the other, immediately second his inclination. If he would rise, make him rise two or three times. In a word, follow his inclinations in every thing, and change as often as he. When he perceives there can be no opposition, but that you always will the same thing as he, he will be amazed, he will breathe short, snuff up his nose, and won't know what to do next, as it happen'd with the horse that I cured this way.

This, I say, is the method of curing a horse that is desperately restive: in other cases, the common way is to reward your horse when he does well, and punish punifh him when he does ill. But you ought to be lavifh of your rewards, and fparing of your corrections, otherwife you will fpoil your horfe. You fhould pardon him a great many faults, as proceeding from ignorance: For how fhould a horfe know what he has never been taught? Inftruct him then by frequent repetitions. When you have taught him, if he malicioufly rebells, correct him, but let it be feldom, and the correction fhould not laft long. If the horfe obeys ever fo little, ftop him, and make friends with him by fome prefent recompence. If he rifes too high, do not fail to flacken your reins extremely, and as he comes down give him firmly both fpurs when he is almoft at the ground, and make him advance. This is what I had to fay concerning a horfe exceffively reftive, and the common corrections.

CHAP. VII.

Of the Correction and Cure of feveral Vices.

AS to a horfe that thro' reftivenefs will not advance, that flings himfelf down, or in rifing throws himfelf back with two or three fprings of his fore-legs when he is up, or that runs away, thefe are things that all the world is acquainted with. Spurs are faid only to make a horfe the more reftive; but that the fwitch will never cure him: For this reafon fpurs muft be made ufe of till he is broke, and pretty fmartly too. One fhould firft try the gentle ways, and if thofe have no effect, we have no other remedy, none that are more certain than the fpurs. But firft walk, trot, and gallop him without any other aid than a flack bridle, and a moderate cavefon. If this has no effect, add the calf of the leg, and let your fpurs be kept for the laft extremity only. When he would lie down make ufe of the fpur, and have fomebody behind you with the *chambriere*. When a horfe is reftive, it is not proper to ftop him, or to put him upon his haunches, for fear of making him more fo. But you muft put him upon the fhoulders as much as you can, to make him advance: for it is enough to cure one vice at a time; and when he is cured, you may eafily put him afterwards upon the haunches. No horfe ever has this vice, if a good rider has had him at firft. If he rifes too high before, it is good to ftrike him hard on the legs with the fwitch: but this ought to be done in right time, or it will do no manner of good.

If a horfe is given to throw himfelf back with his man (a very dangerous vice) it is a proof that he was very ill rode at firft, and that they taught him to rife before he could walk, trot, or gallop; which is a thing contrary to nature, and ridiculous. When a horfe rifes in this manner, he may in fome fenfe be called reftive; becaufe, when he ought to advance, he rifes in order to avoid it. There are fome jades fo vicious, that they rife on purpofe to throw themfelves, and kill their man. The only way to cure them is to hold the bridle flack, and the cavefon fo too, and to walk them a long while ftrait forwards, and afterwards in large circles, that they may be infenfible of their turning; for a horfe often plays his tricks only to avoid being turned. You muft never ftop him, but put him entirely upon his fhoulders, which is contrary to his vice. By being worked thus upon the walk, trot, and gallop, without giving him any ftop, he may be reclaimed. Every time that he would rife, give him entirely the reins of the bridle, and alfo thofe of the cavefon, till you find him half way down, and then give him the fpurs to make him advance;

advance; for if you ſpur him when he is at the higheſt, he will throw himſelf over. You may thus eaſily conquer him by degrees, and afterwards you may put him upon the haunches. At firſt you ought to ſtop him gently, and by degrees; for a ſudden ſtop, without warning, is not good for any horſe; but it ought always to be done with two or three *falcades*, which is a ſliding gently upon the haunches at two or three times; it gives a grace to a horſe, and prepares him the better for his demi-volte.

One muſt not give a rough bit to a paſſionate run-away horſe, for that makes him worſe, and his mouth the harder. Such a horſe ſhould never be ſpur'd, in conformity to the old proverb: *A free horſe needs no ſpur.* The ſpur indeed but augments his vice, neither ſhould the bridle or caveſon be held hard: for the more you pull, the more he will pull in oppoſition. Even if he feels the hand, or the caveſon tho' but little, he will run to reſiſt it.

For this vice therefore, tho' it is contrary to what we call reſtineſs, you are to uſe the ſame aids, ſince they both proceed from a too hard hand; which in one hinders the horſe from advancing, for fear of hurting his mouth, or his noſe with the caveſon; and makes the other pull the harder, the harder you pull, to avoid and reſiſt the force. You ought therefore to ride them both with a ſlack and gentle hand, and an eaſy caveſon in all their paces, walk, trot, and gallop, without making any ſtop. For if in the beginning you would ſtop a run-away horſe, preſſing his mouth or noſe, he will endeavour immediately to run, finding you have a mind to hold him. Do not ſtop him therefore for a long time, and when you do let it be very gently, and by degrees, upon a ſlow walk, and win him in this manner. By which you may ſee, that it is an excellent thing to have a gentle hand (it is one of the greateſt ſecrets we have in managing a horſe) even ſo as ſometimes to let it be quite ſlack. But what for the generality I call a light or gentle hand, is at the ſame time as light as a feather, and yet firm, except in extraordinary caſes. The pillar with a long rein is ſometimes good for a run-away horſe, or for one that is heavy on the hand: For the pillar will hold him when one or more men can't, and with leſs danger to the rider, becauſe he can run but in a circle. Sometimes a horſe may be reſty, and refuſe to advance, becauſe ſomething hurts him; and the ſame thing may make another endeavour to run away. Thus much concerning theſe vices.

CHAP. VIII.

For a Horſe that is too light in the Hand, or which has not a good Appuy.

THIS may ſometimes proceed from the beard, on which the curb reſts, being too tender, or there not being room enough for it, or its being only cover'd with a very thin ſkin, or becauſe the bars are too tender, or becauſe the horſe's neck is not well placed, or that he has a throat like a cock, or has been ill rid before, or is not well fitted with a bit, or has been hurt by hard and rough ones. But all this may be remedied the following way.

You muſt firſt give him a good eaſy bit, that is, a canon or ſcatch *à la Pignatelle*, and branches *à la Connétable*, and a caveſon after my faſhion, and faſten the curb to the branches of the bit; for you muſt ride him ſome time without the curb, in order by degrees to give him the *appuy* upon the bars. But the bridle at the beginning ought to be very ſlack, and you ſhould work only with the caveſon till you have ſettled his head, and put it in a good place: when that is done you may uſe the curb, but it ought to be long and ſlack; and when he is accuſtomed to it, fix it in its proper place. The leſſons you give him ought to be either ſtrait forwards, or upon circles ſo large, that the horſe may not perceive he turns. Theſe leſſons ought to be in an open place, without limits, as a park, or an open field; for ſo he will get a better *appuy*. You ought never at firſt to force him to any thing, but work him upon a long trot, and trot him as much as you can upon the ſhoulders; which alſo will give him *appuy*. Do not ſtop him for ſome time, for that puts him upon his haunches; and when you do, let it be rather by gradually retarding by little and little, than a ſtop. When you gallop, let it be a ſhort gallop, for that gives *appuy*, provided it is gentle and without violence, and on the ſhoulders. Some uſe a martingal, but I do not approve of it; becauſe when it is taken away, the horſe is no better than before. When you have broke him, you may work him upon the haunches as you pleaſe.

But there is nothing to be done till a horſe's head is ſettled. It ought therefore to be the principal care, and the firſt work to fix that, or to give him a good mouth, or, which is the ſame thing, to put him in the hand; and this whether it be to a colt, a young horſe, a horſe of a middle age, or an old one; in ſhort, any one that is rode in a Manege: For without being in the hand he is good for nothing; and being once there, he is good for every thing, and it is the foundation of our art; and thus I finiſh this diſcourſe.

Another Diſcourſe concerning a Horſe that has not a good Appuy, *or is too light in the Hand.*

You ought to feel him more than with a full hand; and when you walk him, you ſhould have your hand yet a little firmer; if he pulls, you ought alſo to pull hard, and not by jerks: for when you pull he will do the ſame, and ſo give himſelf *appuy*. After you have uſed him thus upon a walk, do it upon the trot, and afterwards upon the gallop, never ſtoping him but very gently, and this you need not queſtion will give him *appuy*. If he is impatient, and ſeems diſguſted at the hand and at the heel, but eſpecially at the heel, he will be more ſo by confined and narrow leſſons, and quite furious upon his Airs, Curvets, and Terre-à-terre. Defer his airs therefore for ſome time, as well as the narrow leſſons of ſubjection, or thoſe which force the croupe either in or out. Work him only upon one *piſte* in large circles, making much uſe of your hand, but not at all of your legs or heels, for fear of offending and angering him.

If you work him only upon one *piſte* in large circles, it will make him forget his furious and choleric humour, and thoſe apprehenſions that he had before. When you find he is more patient and fit for the manege, try his obedience to the heel and to the hand; but let it be upon a ſlow walk, and without confinement, and by little and little, not obliging him for a long time to make an entire volte, nor putting at firſt more than one haunch into the volte.

As ſoon as ever he obeys, put him upon one *piſte*, and afterwards try him again. But be ſure to finiſh him upon one *piſte*, and large; keeping him quiet and eaſy, without fury or fear; making him always advance, whatever he does.

You need not doubt, but this leſſon will produce entirely the effects you deſire, whether it be to give him *appuy*, or to make him patient. Be very cautious likewiſe

wiſe not to correct him, tho' he ſhould incline to be choleric, and commit ſome fault. You ought to pardon him many, becauſe in deſpair he will commit thoſe faults to oppoſe you, and by that means become extremely enraged, from a dread of puniſhment. Pardon then and paſs them over in order to deceive him, and ſhow him how good you are; which will break him of them, when he finds you are not ill-natured. To keep a horſe in perpetual ſubjection and ſlavery, makes him either deſperately or ſtupidly reſty. Divert him therefore ſometimes, and give him liberty, riding him large upon one *piſte* in walk, trot, and gallop, finiſhing quietly, and you will find the good that will reſult from it.

I know nothing better to give a horſe *appuy*, than the falſe reins my way; for they work the bars, and eaſe the curb. A bit alſo without liberty, and of one piece, will give him *appuy*. This is what I had to ſay in this diſcourſe, about giving *appuy* to a horſe, and taking from him his furious and choleric apprehenſion.

CHAP. IX.

For a Horſe that is heavy on the Hand.

THIS proceeds ſometimes from a thick fleſhy neck, fleſhy ſhoulders, a thick fleſhy head, with a great deal of hair in the curb place; or from a thick ſkin in that part, or hard bars, or even ſometimes from the horſe's arming himſelf againſt the bridle, ſometimes from his obſtinacy in oppoſing the rider, in order to run away; and ſometimes a horſe is ſo heavy as to lean all his weight upon the bridle.

Yo may break him thus. Give him on an eaſy bit, as before directed, that fits him, with a caveſon after my manner, not forcing him either with the bridle or the caveſon. Trot him as ſhort as poſſible, becauſe the ſhort trot puts him upon his haunches; ſtop him often of a ſudden; make him go backwards; raiſe him before, walk him with his head againſt a wall; work him in a corner where two walls meet; ſtop him againſt a wall; work him with his croupe in, all which puts him upon his haunches. You may alſo gallop him upon the haunches. Never make him advance, or but very little at moſt, in his quarter and demi-voltes: And as you work other horſes forwards upon a line between the quarters of the volte, making the line ſo much the longer in proportion as they are light in hand; in like manner, a horſe that is heavy in hand, the line muſt be made more or leſs ſhort. You ſhould pull him back beſides in all the lines before the quarter, juſt as you make the others advance. Theſe are excellent leſſons to break him, and make him light in hand: but nothing puts a horſe ſo much upon his haunches, and conſequently makes him ſo light in hand, as my new method of the pillar.

If he has any imperfection in his legs, eſpecially in his fore-legs, or in his feet, his paſterns, his knees, his ſhoulders, &c. it is out of the rider's power to make him light in hand, and is properly the work of a farrier. For while he has any pain in thoſe parts, he will bear on the hand as upon a fifth foot, or as a cripple ſupports himſelf upon a ſtick. It is to relieve his pain, that a lame or weak horſe leans upon the hand. Nor is this all; for there is another imperfection of nature that admits of no remedy, and in which many horſemen are greatly deceived. They ſay, that a horſe that has a fine head

well

well placed, a ſlender neck, and lean ſhoulders, is always light in hand; and, on the contrary, that a horſe with a large head, a thick neck, and fleſhy ſhoulders, is always heavy in hand. Now this is ſo far from being true, that I have ſeen more large-headed, thick-necked, fat-ſhoulder'd horſes, that have been light in hand, than I have of thoſe that are ſlender and fine-ſhaped; and I have ſeen horſes with a little head, a ſlender neck, and fine ſhoulders, that were heavy in hand: ſo that nothing can be known from this. But here lies the whole ſecret. If an ill-ſhaped heavy horſe has good reins, he will be light in hand; and the moſt fine-ſhaped delicate creature on earth, if he is weak in the reins, will be heavy in hand: ſo that the being light or heavy in hand depends only on the reins, and the goodneſs of the chine. If his reins are good, you may put a horſe upon the haunches, becauſe he is able to bear it; and a horſe upon the haunches is light in hand: but one whoſe reins are weak, cannot bear to be put upon the haunches, but will go upon the ſhoulders to relieve the pain he feels in his reins, which is what we mean by being heavy in hand. The more you contend with him, the more will he lean upon your hand, and your labour will be like waſhing a black Moor with ink.

CHAP. X.

For a Horſe that is heavy in Hand, who will obey neither the Hand nor the Heel, but is ſtiff in the Shoulders, and won't obey the Spurs.

THE main ſecret for a horſe that is heavy upon the hand, is for the rider to have a very light one; for when he finds nothing to bear upon with his mouth, he infallibly throws himſelf upon the haunches for his own ſecurity. Either before or behind he muſt ſupport himſelf, and finding nothing to lean on before, he bears his weight behind. Now being upon the haunches (as he neceſſarily muſt be in this caſe) it is impoſſible but he muſt be light in hand, becauſe no horſe can be rightly upon his haunches without being ſo. And he that ſaid that a horſe was not dreſſed, whoſe curb was not looſe, ſaid right; and it is equally true, that the curb never can play, when in its right place, except the horſe be upon the haunches. No horſe therefore is well dreſſed that is not light in hand; ſo that an eaſy and gentle bridle, but firm, is the chief ſecret to make a horſe light. Your caveſon ought alſo to be eaſy. The ſtopping him ſhort upon walk, trot, or gallop, will contribute much to the ſame purpoſe, becauſe it puts him upon the haunches. To make him riſe once or twice, and then go forwards, ſo that when you raiſe him his haunches come in, will for the ſame reaſon produce the ſame effect. But my method of the pillar, as it throws the horſe yet more upon the haunches, is ſtill more effectual to this purpoſe, and beſides always gives him the ply to the ſide he goes of. The horſe's head to the wall puts him upon the haunches; turning upon very little more ground than his own length, puts him very much upon them, and conſequently makes him light upon the hand, quarter, and demi-voltes: the croupe in does ſo too; ſo does the croupe quite in, his head to all the four walls, for it puts him extremely upon the haunches. If the ſhoulders are not ſupple, the caveſon, the rein, and the leg of the ſame ſide will render them ſo, and make the horſe obey the heel, as I have told you often. But this is phyſick only, and not diet; that is to ſay, when the croupe is within

within the pillar, or the head to the pillar the croupe out; and ſhould be uſed only in the laſt extremity of the vice; it eaſily produces its effect however, without any conſtraint. Theſe are the ways of making a horſe light in the hand and obedient to the heel, and of ſuppling his ſhoulders, when the common ones won't do.

CHAP. XI.

Containing certain Obſervations.

REmember that my method reduces a horſe without beating or ſpurring him, and only by the rules already laid down; becauſe it obliges him to go well, whether he will or no.

Make him always advance, in whatſoever he does; for he will often put his croupe out, and go backwards, as if he was reſty to the ſpur. Uſe gentle means before you come to extremity, in whatever leſſon you work him, and never take above half his ſtrength, nor ride him till he is weary, but a little at a time and often. Be always laviſh of your careſſes, and ſparing in your corrections. When you do correct him, let it be to ſome purpoſe, but only one ſtroke at a time, whether it be with the ſpur, the ſwitch, the voice, or the *chambriere*, and even that not often repeated.

You may careſs him as much and as often as you pleaſe; as by patting him gently with your hand; talking kindly to him; ſtroking him; flattering him; or ſometimes by uſing a certain particular tone of voice, that is common to cajole ſkittiſh and unruly horſes. You may alſo reward him now and then in ſummer-time with graſs, green corn, beautiful and odoriferous flowers, pleaſant herbs, and ſuch fruits as horſes love. In winter give him in a ſmall ſieve made on purpoſe, a few oats, wheat, clean barly, the fineſt bran or bread. You may alſo give him bread with your hand, or ſugar, or ſweetmeats, or a little honey to lick off a ſtick; apples, carrots, or turnips cut in pieces, are alſo proper rewards in winter, when he has done well, and may be eaten in a ſhort time. You may have a groom to rub him, while he takes breath between his voltes. But if your horſe has a good memory, and is full of ſpirits, this is better let alone: for after having been worked, he will imagine he is to begin again as ſoon as the groom has rubbed him. Uſe none of theſe things therefore with impatient horſes; nor think to cure their eagerneſs by reſtraint, which only makes them worſe. Horſes take great delight in ſmelling to perfumed gloves, and in hearing of muſick, which refreſhes them very much.

CHAP. XII.

When a Horſe is ſo ſtiff-necked that he will not look into the Volte, nor turn his Head, or his Neck; when he holds his Head or his Neck out of the Volte; and when my Caveſon, which I commonly uſe, is not ſufficient, you muſt then have recourſe to this Invention.

THE caveſon has a ring on each ſide, and another in the middle; for which reaſon, my way, I have two reins, which have a little ring at each end, and I put the end of the rein thro' the ring, and faſten it to the pommel. I draw down the reins cloſe to the ſaddle-bow under my thighs, and paſſing them thro' the rings of the caveſon, bring them back ſtrait to my hands.

It muſt be obſerv'd, that the three rings of the caveſon divide it into four parts, and that (working with the left rein, that is in the ring next to me)

I have only a quarter force in pulling, and the horſe has three quarters againſt me: ſo that an oſtinate ſtiff-necked horſe may eaſily be too ſtrong for me. I faſten the rein of the caveſon therefore as before, except that inſtead of putting it thro' the left ring, I put it thro' the right, tho' I work my horſe to the left: Thus have I three times the force of the horſe, which is too much for him. I would have you faſten inſtead of holding it, the rein that comes back to your hand to the pommel of the ſaddle, becauſe it has the greater force. This irreſiſtibly draws the outſide of his head, and makes him look into the volte with both eyes, whether he will or no, which is the only way in the world to make him ſupple. For what uſually makes a horſe ſo ſtiff is, that he looks out with the eye without the volte, which the left ring cannot bring in; but the right will, drawing of it to the left ſide, as I told you, and it entirely does the buſineſs, and makes him ſo ſupple that it is a pleaſure to ride him. What I have ſaid of the left hand, is equally the ſame for the right.

This, believe me, is the beſt way in the world to make a horſe ſupple, tho' he were as ſtiff-necked as a bull: for the whole art lies in making him look in with both eyes. I muſt not omit to tell you, that you will find it difficult to work both the reins of the caveſon, becauſe by their croſſing they hinder and ſtop one another, and don't eaſily ſlip thro' the rings. But to prevent this, you muſt have your rings very large, ſo that the reins may not be ſtopped by the caveſon, nor by one another. Tho' they ſtop a little in your hand, the groom will eaſily draw the rein you want, and faſten it to the pommel: or, you may make uſe only of one rein, and when you have worked your horſe enough on one ſide, put it on the other, and ſo you will never be hindered.

Uſe this as the beſt help I know, for all ſorts of horſes to make them ſupple, and look into the volte with both eyes, which is the higheſt perfection of the manege. It is better for Terre-à-terre than the Paſſage.

CHAP. XIII.

The three following Leſſons are very efficacious, and moſt excellent in Terre-à-terre and Curvets. I call theſe the Rule of Three, or the Golden Rule.

Firſt, to work Terre-à-terre with the Caveſon, as I have directed in the preceding Chapter.

I. THERE is no better way to make a horſe obedient, both to the hand and heel, and to put him upon the haunches, than to draw the inner rein of the caveſon very high towards the outward ſhoulder, bringing that ſhoulder in, and helping ſtrongly with the outer leg; to put him together, teach him to obey both hand and heel, and put him upon the haunches.

To work with the Bridle only, the Reins ſeparated and in both Hands.

II. When the reins are ſeparate and in both hands, draw the inner rein very high towards the contrary ſhoulder, to which hand ſo ever you go, and put that ſhoulder in, helping at the ſame time with the contrary leg. This puts him together, throws him upon the haunches, and makes him obey both hand and heel. There is no better leſſon than this.

To work a Horſe with the Bridle in the Left Hand only.

III. The reins of the bridle, which ought to be ſeparated by the little finger only, are in this poſition: To the right hand the inner rein is above the little finger,

finger, and to the left hand the inner rein is under the little finger. To the right hand therefore you muſt put the bridle on the left ſide of the horſe, in order to draw the inner rein: but you need not turn up the nails of your bridle-hand, only hold it firm and ſtrait, the knuckles of your fingers without the neck of the horſe; and continuing this poſture, put out the knuckles of your little finger in ſuch manner, that the thumb may ſink a little, in order to draw the inner and ſlacken the outer rein: for when the little finger joints turn out, they ſlacken the outer rein, which is under that finger, and tighten the inner rein, which is above it; and this is according to art. Beſides, the horſeman's ſhoulder may naturally come in, which is juſt and eaſy; and thus the inner rein is in the ſame line with your left or outer ſhoulder, which is the whole affair.

You ought in Terre-à-terre to put your hand every time a little forwards; for if you keep it in the ſame place, or draw it towards you, you tighten the curb, and keep the horſe down, or upon his ſhoulders; but by putting your hand a little forwards, you looſe the curb, and neceſſarily put him upon the haunches. The elbow of the bridle-arm ought always to be much lower than the hand, in order to keep the horſe upon his haunches. It ought to be ſo in like manner, when the reins of the caveſon, the falſe reins, or the reins of the bridle are ſeparated and in both hands, or when they are in the left hand only.

It is quite otherwiſe to the left hand: for to the left you muſt pull the inner rein. You muſt therefore turn up the nails of your bridle-hand as much as poſſible towards your right ſhoulder, becauſe that rein lies under the little finger that works it. By turning up your hand in this manner, your inward rein comes into the ſame line as your right ſhoulder, which does the whole buſineſs. Bring your right ſhoulder a little in, becauſe that draws the inner rein, which lies under your little finger, and ſlackens the outer rein which is over that finger; in like manner as to the right hand you draw the inner rein that lies over that finger, and looſe the outer rein that lies under it.

In Terre-à-terre you muſt bring in the right ſhoulder a little for the left hand, and help with the outer leg. Here ends that moſt excellent leſſon, called the *Rule of Three*.

CHAP. XIV.

A very ſubtile and exact Rule to make a Horſe go Terre-à-Terre truly, or in Curvets, by which, when he fails, the true Cauſe may be known.

FIRST faſten the caveſon as I directed (the laſt way pleaſes me beſt;) then for the right hand, draw with that hand the rein of the caveſon, turning up the nails towards the left ſhoulder till they almoſt touch it; and ſo there will be an oblique line croſs the horſe's neck, from the right ſide of it to your left ſhoulder, which will give him the bent like a bow, or a ſemicircle; and the right rein of the caveſon, which is in your right hand, being drawn thus high towards your ſhoulder, is the middle or center of that ſemicircle made by the horſe: for if you meaſure from your hand to the horſe's noſe, and again from your hand to his croupe, you will find the diſtance equal; wherefore your hand is in the center of the ſemicircle.

If you faſten the rein to the pommel, it will be all one with regard to the line, only that the line perhaps will be a little ſhorter; for you ſee that the

pommel

pommel is in the middle of the horſe, as the rein will be if you draw it towards your left ſhoulder, by which you only make the line longer. This rein being an oblique line from one ſide to the other, which here is from right to left, it is in the middle of the horſe: ſo that between your legs and thoſe of the horſe's, by an exact and mathematical menſuration, there is a plain, which plain you carry with you. Now while you keep this line, your horſe can never go amiſs; but the moment you change or break it, all goes wrong. Nor does this line put him in the ſemicircle only, but, like a balance, it alſo weighs up the hind-leg within the volte, putting it out to a certain degree; and helping with your outer leg, to put out his hind-leg within the volte, it ſerves to poiſe the ſaid hind-leg in an equal manner with the other.

Thus the horſe will go regularly as in a ſquare, becauſe he cannot err while you keep this line exact and equal. Juſt as the four legs of a horſe make four circles Terre-à-terre, of which circles the pillar is the center. Thus the body of the horſe, bent in a ſemicircle by drawing the inner rein towards the outer ſhoulder, and bringing the outer ſhoulder in, ſo that the hand and the ſhoulder meet in a point, the center of the ſemicircle, which ſemicircle of the horſe, and center of the hand and of the ſhoulder, move in the four circles of the horſe's feet, as the ſun moves in the ecliptic line acroſs the zodiack, or the planets in their proper ſpheres or circles. This is an excellent leſſon.

For the Left Hand.

Put the bridle in your right hand, and with your left draw the left rein of the caveſon, turning up your nails towards your right ſhoulder, and helping it with your outer, that is, your right leg. In the reſt follow the inſtructions given for the right hand, taking great care to keep the line.

As to the falſe reins, which are faſtened in my manner to the arches of the bit, you muſt help the horſe with them as with the rings of the caveſon, always keeping the line.

The bridle in the left hand only, works as well to the right as to the left, as I have ſhewn you in the laſt part of the rule of three, which is the quinteſſence of working with the bridle in the left hand only. There you will find, if you work well, that the inner rein (which is the oblique line) is thus kept exactly. If you preſerve this line with care, your horſe cannot go amiſs Terre-à-terre, for which this is an excellent leſſon.

It is for this reaſon that I wonder, when I ſee horſemen put their right ſhoulder in when they go to the right, and their left when they go to the left: I pronounce boldly of ſuch riders, that they have ſufficiently broke the line.

Thus when they go to the right, they turn their hand up in the old manner towards the inſide of the horſe's neck, which draws the outward rein; and when they go to the left, they turn up their hand to the inſide of the horſe's neck, which draws and works the outer rein; ſo that they always turn their hand to the ſide the horſe goes of, which is very ridiculous and abſurd, becauſe it deſignedly breaks the line. But I pardon them all theſe faults, and many others, ſaying with St. STEPHEN, when he prayed for his perſecutors, *Lord forgive them, for they know not what they do.*

CHAP.

CHAP. XV.

Another Posture for a Horseman in Curvets and Terre-à-terre.

THIS differs not from what I before told you in the chapter of a horseman's seat, except that you must put your stomach out, hold your breast very stiff, and close your thighs at every curvet, which helps the horse with your fork, and puts your thighs forward, so that you cannot sit upon them, and consequently puts you upon your fork, and leaves a large space between the end of the saddle and your thighs, as there ought to be. Besides, thus your hand helps him up, which obliges him to be upon the haunches.

The same seat should be kept Terre-à-terre, except that you must not help your horse with your hand every time, as in Curvets. You have only to hold him up, in order to oblige him to be on the haunches.

CHAP. XVI.

To work a Horse with the Head to the Pillar, to make him sensible to the Heel, and put him upon the Haunches.

THE caveson my way makes the horse look into the volte with both eyes, puts him upon the haunches, and works his shoulders.

To work the croupe: To put a horse's head to the wall, but the croupe before the shoulders, to raise and stop him upon the hand, puts him upon the haunches, and works his croupe.

This way which here follows works the croupe more effectually. Fasten the caveson to the pommel in my last manner: For example, for the left hand, fasten the rein of the caveson in such manner, as to make the horse look into the volte with both eyes. Then put his head to the pillar to the left hand, and let the pillar be on the inside of his head; because that works the croupe, since it goes before the shoulders. When you find that the croupe is not supple enough, turn up the little finger of the left hand, with which you hold the bridle, towards the right shoulder, which draws the inward rein: give him at the same time a smart stroke with the right spur, bringing in your left shoulder, which is that within the volte.

This puts the shoulders so to the right, that the croupe must of necessity go to the left: and the croupe goes so to the left, that you cannot make him go far in this manner, because the pillar hinders, till you pull him back, which should be in a circle. Now by making him go backwards, you make him obey the heel, because the croupe goes before the shoulders; and besides, it puts him upon the haunches, and the more so, if you raise him sometimes circularly in Pesades.

I have often told you before, that if you bring into the volte your inward shoulder, and put your hand much out, tho' it puts in the horse's croupe, yet it makes him go as wrong with his legs as if you pulled the outward rein. You ought to understand this well; it means, that if your hand is without the volte, and beyond your body, then the horse goes wrong, because you have lost your line: but while your hand is within your shoulder, tho' you put in the inner shoulder, yet the horse will go right, in as much as you keep the line. This aid ought not to be used except in case of necessity, when the horse disobeys the heel.

CHAP. XVII.

To work a Horſe's Croupe to the left, the Croupe being to the Pillar.

THE caveſon ought to be fixed as before, and the reins of the bridle in the left hand. Now you go to the left, the pillar ſhould be on the outſide of the croupe, that it may go before the ſhoulders. Draw the bridle towards your right ſhoulder, turning up the little finger, and put in your ſhoulder within the volte, that is, your left.

If the horſe is not obedient enough to the heel, help him firm with your hand, in order to put his ſhoulders out, and at the ſame time give him a ſmart ſtroke with the right ſpur. This will neceſſarily put in his croupe, ſince his ſhoulders are without the volte, and his croupe put in at the ſame time. But the croupe will be ſo diſtant from the circle in which he ought to move, that you cannot bring it there again but by pulling him a little back.

His croupe being now within the pillar, you ought to put in your ſhoulder within the volte, as you did when he went backwards, in order to keep the circle when the head was without the pillar: you ought to do the ſame now, when his croupe is within the pillar, in order to ſubject it the more. Nothing will be falſe while you keep the line (that is, the bridle-hand) within your ſhoulder: but if you put it beyond your body, you will loſe the line, and the horſe will go wrong.

To raiſe him ſometimes in Peſades, the croupe within the pillar, and before the ſhoulders, puts him much upon the haunches. The diſobedience to the heel is in the outer haunch, which this leſſon works: You ſhould therefore continue it till you find the outer haunch very ſupple, and then return to the true method. Nothing in the world works the croupe and haunches like this; and you will find your advantage in it if you do it well. Uſe the ſame helps to the right hand, to ſubject the croupe and make him obey the heel.

CHAP. XVIII.

A Diſcourſe concerning the ſingle Pillar the old way, which is very falſe for Terre-à-terre.

I WILL ſhew you now the great error of him that firſt invented the pillar for Terre-à-terre, with the long rope or *longe*, and let you ſee that every oblique line does not work Terre-à-terre, but only mine, which is made in a croſs over the horſe's neck.

Let us take then, for example, the long rein to the pillar: They faſten one of the ends of this long rein or rope to the caveſon, and the other end to the pillar; or it is held by a groom, which makes an oblique line from the horſe to the pillar, and this indeed works the ſhoulders furiouſly, but no way affects the croupe, as my oblique line acroſs the neck does. This long cord beſides works the outer ſhoulder, which narrows the fore-part, and leaves the hind at large; and this in Terre-à-terre is a ſoleciſm. For I have told you often, that the fore-part Terre-à-terre ought to be large, and the croupe narrow. But the long rein and the pillar produce the contrary, and no way affect the croupe, as you will ſee by what follows. If the croupe is more at large than the fore-part, the horſe cannot go well Terre-à-terre; no more can he he when the croupe is out. For this reaſon they ſpur to put the croupe right, whereas they are as wrong this way with it in, as out; for the croupe is as large now, as it was before; and being now within, the inward hind-leg goes before the ſhoulder on the ſame ſide, which is quite wrong, and as much ſo as when the croupe was out, and that the hind-leg without the volte went larger than the ſhoulder of the ſame ſide. So that the long rope round a pillar is a ſilly invention, and very falſe Terre-à-terre; becauſe it does not at all work the croupe, but keeps the ſhoulders narrow, which is juſt the reverſe of what ought to be. Thus, you ſee, that this extraordinary invention is good for nothing.

CHAP. XIX.

A Diſcourſe concerning the two Pillars.

THE method of the two pillars is worth nothing; for it puts the horſe ſo off his bars and his curb, and ſo much upon the caveſon, that he will not go without pillars, as I have ſeen in many horſes. Neither is it good for Curvets, and it is yet worſe for Leaps: for it puts the horſe ſo upon the haunches, that his croupe has no liberty to play; and how ſhould he leap with the croupe confined? My way with one pillar gives all liberty to the croupe, and puts the horſe in the hand. You may alſo teach him to leap againſt a wall. As ſoon as he has made a leap, you muſt raiſe him immediately upon the hand, cauſing him to make a very high peſade, which puts him upon the haunches: for in all leaps a horſe ought to be in the hand. A nimble horſe will very ſoon learn this.

End of the Laſt Diviſion of Leſſons, and of the Fourth Book of the New Method of Dreſſing Horſes.

THE EPITOME of HORSEMANSHIP,

Which I desire may be not only read and studied, but learned by Heart; and it will give all the Advantage and Satisfaction that can be desired in this noble Art.

CHAP. I.

How to ride a Horse with Art. First, of the many Uses to be made of the inward Rein of the Caveson fastened to the Pommel of the Saddle.

IT is good for trotting and galloping a horse upon large circles, and *d'une piste*, upon smaller, or with the croupe rather out, working with the inward leg and inward caveson rein, and also with the inward rein of the bridle, sometimes with the outward rein of the bridle. This puts him upon his shoulders (because it draws his head down, and consequently makes him feel the bitt) brings in his outward shoulder, and narrows him before, and by the same means leaves his croupe large; it also works and supples the shoulders extreamly, but the croupe is then lost, because the horse is straitened within the volte, and at large without. A horse thus gallops as he ought, leading with the fore-leg within the volte, and his hind-leg of the same side following it, which is the true gallop. All these advantages come from the inward rein of the caveson fastened to the pommel my way, with these helps of the leg and rein of the same side, which makes the shoulders supple, and works them. This is the best lesson that can be for a young or ignorant horse.

Another Advantage of the inward Rein of the Caveson fastened my Way to the Pommel of the Saddle.

If you fasten it to the right, put your horse's head to the pillar, and go to the left, helping him in that posture with leg and rein of the same side, putting the croupe to the left. Tho' you go to the left, yet the horse's shoulders are made supple for the right. And if you fasten to the pommel the left rein of the caveson (putting the head to the pillar, and working with rein and leg of the same side) tho' you go to the right, and with the croupe out to the right, yet the shoulders of the horse are worked and made supple for the left. This lesson works well the shoulders, and makes him extreamly supple: but the croupe is lost, because one works with the rein and leg of the same side. It is done upon a walk.

CHAP. II.

The Rein of the Caveson being still fixed to the Pommel, to work the Shoulders and the Croupe together upon the Passage and Walk, with the Croupe or the Head to the Pillar; but in another Manner than before, for here the inward Rein and outward Leg are to be used.

WHEN the head of a horse is put to the pillar for the right hand, care must be taken that the pillar be without the head; and then the horse will never be *entier*, for his shoulders will always go before his croupe. This is the action of the trot, which is cross ways, and the horse is narrow and large every second movement for that reason. When he crosses the fore-leg without

without the volte over the fore-leg within it, his fore-part is narrow, and his croupe large, the hind-leg advancing a little. And when he croſſes his hind-leg without the volte over the other hind-leg within it, his croupe is narrow, and his fore-part large; ſo that every ſecond time he is large and narrow; and as he always bears upon that part that is narrow, one movement he is upon the ſhoulders, and another upon the haunches. That which is neareſt the center makes the leaſt circle, and therefore is moſt confined: the croupe then being out, it makes the largeſt circle, and is the moſt worked, in order to obey the heel.

If you faſten the rein of the caveſon to the pommel to the left hand, the head to the pillar, care muſt be taken that the pillar be without the head, working with the leg and the contrary rein as before, and for the ſame reaſons. The head being to the pillar, and the fore-part leading, the fore-part is to the center, and the croupe goes from it. This is done upon a walk, and works the outward haunch, making it ſupple to the heel. The horſe with his head to the pillar makes only two circles, the narroweſt with his fore-feet, and the larger with his croupe.

CHAP. III.

To put the Croupe to the Pillar, and work upon a Walk with the Leg and the contrary Rein, which ſhould ſtill be faſtened to the Pommel of the Saddle.

THE croupe here being to the center, care muſt be taken that the pillar is within the croupe, that the horſe may not be *entier*, becauſe ſo the ſhoulders will always go before the croupe. Tho' the croupe is to the pillar, the fore-part leading tends towards the center, and the croupe flys it, working leg and rein contrary.

The Paſſage is croſswiſe, which is the reaſon that the horſe is large and narrow every ſecond movement. When he is large before, his croupe is narrow; and when his croupe is large, his fore-part is narrow. This works his ſhoulders and his hind-leg without the volte, which makes him obedient to the heel. His fore-part makes the largeſt circle, and is therefore worked the moſt; but his croupe is the moſt preſſed and ſubjected, becauſe it makes the narroweſt circle, which puts him upon the haunches. This is a moſt excellent leſſon, becauſe it prepares a horſe for Terre-à-terre. For when he has the fore-part narrow, the hind-leg within the volte advances, which is half Terre-à-terre; and when he has the croupe narrow, the fore-leg within the volte advances, which is alſo half Terre-à-terre. His legs therefore in one movement perform the action of Terre-à-terre before, and in the other do the ſame behind; that is to ſay, that every movement, either before or behind, they perform this action, becauſe it is the action of the trot, and acroſs. There is no better leſſon than this.

The inward rein of the caveſon, fixed faſt and tight to the pommel, brings in (upon the Paſſage, which is done upon a walk) the outward ſhoulder. Now walking being the action of the trot, when the horſe is narrow before, his head is within his fore-legs, but at the ſame time his hind-leg within the volte is before his head; and when he is narrow behind, his fore-leg within the volte is before his head, but at the ſame time his head is before his hind-leg within the volte. The head therefore is always before one leg, and one leg at the ſame time before the head; that is to ſay, the head and the leg are alternately foremoſt every ſecond movement; and that becauſe it is a trot, which is an action in form of a croſs.

The outward ſhoulder ought to be brought very much in, which is the beſt thing that can be upon a walk, the croupe in; and the horſe will be in the hand and heel; for being convex without, he muſt endure the heel, and obey it, becauſe he cannot avoid it, the inward rein keeping him there. No better leſſon can be than this. His fore-part is worked, and his croupe ſubjected. He makes but two circles with his four legs, when he paſſages the croupe to the pillar; the fore-part makes the largeſt, and the croupe the leaſt.

CHAP. IV.

To paſſage a Horſe in his own Length, the Rein ſtill faſtened to the Pommel of the Saddle.

TO paſſage a horſe in his own length upon a walk works his ſhoulders, becauſe his ſhoulders are in the largeſt circle; but preſſes his croupe, puts him upon the haunches, and fixes them, becauſe they are in the narroweſt circle. It works the outward haunch, and makes it obedient to the heel; and there is no better leſſon.

CHAP. V.

The Rein of the Caveſon ſhould be ſtill fixed to the Pommel, and the Head to the Wall, working with the Rein and the contrary Leg.

THE head of a horſe to the wall, may be either as if the head, or as if the croupe was to the pillar. It is as if the head were to the pillar when the croupe goes before the head, becauſe then the croupe is worked, and the ſhoulders are preſſed and ſubjected. When the ſhoulders go before the croupe, they are the moſt worked, and the croupe is preſſed and ſubjected, ſo that the horſe is upon his haunches. To which hand ſoever you go, always work the inward rein and the outward leg. The wall puts the horſe upon his haunches, for he is afraid of hurting his noſe.

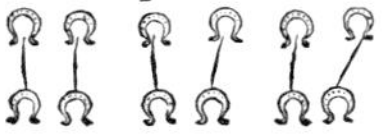

Here the ſhoulders are before the croupe, which works the ſhoulders, and ſubjects the croupe.

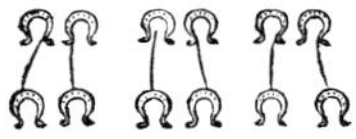

Here the croupe is before the ſhoulders, whereby theſe are ſtraitened, and that worked.

CHAP. VI.

To faſten the inward Rein of the Caveſon to the Pommel, and work with the Rein and the Leg of the ſame ſide.

THIS is moſt excellent upon a ſhort trot, to put a horſe upon his haunches (advancing upon one *piſte*:) for the hind-legs of a horſe being made like our arms, they make him bend in the ham, by putting out his inward hind-leg, and therefore he is upon the haunches. There is no better leſſon for that purpoſe.

All the preceding leſſons, and different manners of working a horſe with the inward rein of the caveſon faſtened to the pommel, are moſt excellent. There are ſix of them, all done upon a walk.

To

To draw the inward rein of the caveſon low towards your thigh in the horſe's length, is an excellent leſſon to work him upon a walk, in order to prepare him for the *pirouette*, becauſe it works the ſhoulders, and the croupe is more fixed. But then I have no feeling of the horſe, and it ſeems as if we did not move together.

CHAP. VII.

A true Obſervation as to the Walk, the Trot, the Gallop upon one Piſte *in a Circle; the Paſſage, either the Head or the Croupe to the Pillar; Terre-à-terre, the Croupe to the Pillar, Curvets, Demi-Airs, the Head to the Pillar; Groupades, Balotades, and Caprioles upon Circles; or the Horſe's Head faſtened ſhort to the Pillar my way by the Rein of the Caveſon, in Curvets de Ferme-à-ferme, forwards or backwards, working with the Rein and Leg of the ſame Side, or Rein and Leg contrary: whereby it will be ſeen, that what part ſoever leads the Way, the ſame tends to the Center, and the other part of the Horſe avoids it. This Rule never fails, whether the Fore-part or the Croupe leads the Way, as will appear from Example.*

THE inward rein of the caveſon being faſtened to the pommel, working with the leg and rein of the ſame ſide, whether upon a trot or gallop, one *piſte*, the fore-part leads the way, and comes in, and conſequently tends towards the center, and the croupe avoids it.

The head to the pillar, working with leg and rein of the ſame ſide, the croupe leads the way, and therefore tends towards the center, and the fore-part flies it.

Working with rein and leg contrary (the head to the pillar and the pillar without the head) the fore-part leads the way, and tends towards the center, and the croupe flies from it to which hand ſoever you go.

The croupe towards the pillar, and the pillar within the croupe, the fore-part leads the way, and therefore tends towards the center, and the croupe avoids it. This is upon a walk or paſſage.

Terre-à-terre the fore-part leads the way, and therefore tends towards the center, and the croupe avoids it. So in *pirouettes* or in demivoltes upon Paſſades, which are only half *pirouettes*, the fore-part leads the way, and therefore tends to the center, and the croupe ſhuns it.

In like manner in Curvets, Demi-Airs, Groupades, Balotades, and Caprioles upon circles or voltes, the fore-part leads the way, and for that reaſon tends towards the center, and the croupe avoids it. Thus at the pillar my way, the caveſon faſtened ſhort to the pillar, the fore-part leads the way upon the circles, and for that reaſon tends towards the center, and the croupe avoids it And it is the ſame when a horſe goes back upon curvets, his croupe then leads the way, and conſequently tends towards the center, and the fore-part ſhuns it.

It is an infallible rule, whether one works well or ill, that the part which leads the way, tends towards the center. For example, it is working ill when Terre-à-terre one makes the croupe lead the way; yet the croupe then tends towards the center, and the fore-part avoids it: ſo that the rule is always true, let a horſe be ever ſo badly rode.

General

General Rules.

That which leads the way, whether it be the fore-part or the croupe, always tends towards the center, and the other part of the horſe avoids it. And it is a rule equally general and true, that whatever makes the largeſt circle, whether it be the fore-part or the croupe, is the moſt worked, becauſe it goes the farther and is at liberty, whether it tends towards or avoids the center; and that whatever makes the ſmalleſt circle, is the moſt ſubjected and preſſed. For the head to the pillar, and the pillar without the head, the horſe leads the way with the fore-part; and for that reaſon the fore-part tends to the center, and the croupe avoids it; tho' the croupe is moſt worked, becauſe it makes the largeſt circle, which occaſions the fore-part to be moſt ſubject, and the horſe to be upon it, that is, upon his ſhoulders.

Thus the horſe's croupe being towards the pillar, and the pillar within the croupe, the croupe being in, the fore-part leads the way, and therefore tends towards the center, which the croupe avoids: yet the fore-part is the moſt worked, becauſe it is in the largeſt circle, and the croupe moſt ſubjected and preſſed, becauſe it is in the narroweſt circle; and conſequently the horſe is upon the haunches. It is juſt the ſame when you work in his own length.

An Obſervation.

It is better to faſten the caveſon my way, to the girth, becauſe it draws down the horſe's head, and conſequently brings the outward ſhoulder more in, which is the beſt way on all accounts for ſuppling a horſe; but is wrong for Terre-à-terre and Curvets.

All theſe leſſons are perfect and moſt excellent, and are the right methods of working a horſe with truth in the manege. For what can one have more? ſince a horſe can commit no fault, but it muſt be in the fore or hind-part, by diſobeying either the hand or heel. Now you have here excellent leſſons to make either the ſhoulders or the croupe ſupple, to make the horſe obey the hand or the heel, and to make him obey both together; and one can have no more.

CHAP. VIII.

Which contains a true Obſervation for dreſſing Horſes.

THE horſe being, after man, the moſt noble of all animals (for he is as much ſuperior to all other creatures as man is to him, and therefore holds a ſort of middle place between man and the reſt of the creation) he is wiſe and ſubtile; for which reaſon man ought carefully to preſerve his empire over him, knowing how nearly that wiſdom and ſubtilty approaches his own. This may eaſily be ſeen in the following example. When a horſe is much preſſed, he finds out how to avoid it ſooner than any man can ſhew him; and this the rider ſhould have particular regard to in working him.

If he is upon the ſhoulders when you ſtop him, he hurts his noſe with the caveſon, and his mouth with the bridle. Now to avoid all this, he puts himſelf upon the haunches, and draws in his head, which prevents the hurting his noſe or mouth, and makes him do what the rider deſires.

If

If between the two pillars he presses forwards, the caveson hurts his nose; if he runs back, it hurts his jaws; if he goes from side to side, he is hurt there too: the horse therefore having experienced all these inconveniences, keeps in the middle, and rises to save himself from being hurt, which is just what the rider wants.

In like manner, when the rein of the caveson is tied short my way to the pommel of the saddle, it bends and brings in his neck extreamly; which hurts him so much, that he finds himself eased in not pressing upon the caveson; consequently he bends his neck farther in, which is what the rider desires.

So the rein fastened so short to the pillar my way, that the horse cannot easily rise, because it still pulls him down, he is so subtile as to ease himself by going upon the haunches. This is indeed the only way he had to relieve himself, and just what the rider desires.

Thus when you put the head of a horse to a wall, he puts himself upon the haunches for fear of hurting his head against the wall, and to get farther from it. Now what the rider wants is, that he should be upon the haunches.

In whatever action the horse is upon the shoulders, if the rider hurts him with the caveson or the bridle, he puts himself upon the haunches to get relief, and so complies with the rider's wish: for no horse can be perfectly dressed till he is upon the haunches, and till the curb is loose and plays. But the curb may be slack, and yet the horse not upon the haunches: no horse however is upon the haunches unless his curb be slack; for which reason the horse should do it to find ease, and should not be forced to it by the rider.

CHAP. IX.

To make a Horse obey the Heels.

WHEN a horse is resty, and will not go forward, he must be spurred till he will: he finds himself eased from the spur by obeying, and therefore will continue to obey. If he is obstinate the first morning, he will submit another day: you should then pardon him many faults, and not be too severe, unless he commits those faults maliciously. If so, you must spur him again, and if he won't obey the heel, you must continue spurring till he does, for he will obey at last to find ease.

So that those are greatly deceived, and very ignorant, who think to make a horse obey the heel without following this method: and by the leave of those great philosophers, who have writ of this matter, and are altogether mistaken, this is not the way to make him more resty. It is neither the switch, the *chambriere*, the calf of the leg, nor gentle treatment, that will conquer a vicious jade: you might as well give him rose-water and sugar. But, to end all dispute, I have this way conquered all the horses I ever had. The medicine therefore is excellent, and proved so by experience.

CHAP. X.

To work the Croupe of a Horse before his Head, or his Shoulders, upon a Circle, is extreamly wrong; unless upon the most urgent necessity. As for me, I would never have it practised.

WHEN a horse's head is to the pillar, and the pillar on the inside of his head, the croupe goes before the shoulders. It is the same when the croupe is to the pillar, if the pillar is on the outside the croupe. Now this is wrong to all intents and purposes. For when his head is to the pillar, and both his legs are within it, he cannot make a quarter-volte without being *entier*. The ſame may be ſaid when his croupe is to the pillar, and the pillar without his croupe; beſides that he turns from the ſide on which he ought to go, and trots circularly backwards, quite contrary to what he does when he advances; and, what is worſe, he is bent in a circle to the right hand, his ſhoulders go to the left againſt that circle, his croupe to the right, and in reality he keeps neither center nor circle, but loſes them both. It is juſt the ſame to the left hand.

Tho' it may be thought that this works the croupe, it is a great miſtake; the croupe ſhuns the rider indeed, not that it obeys the heel, but becauſe the rider puts it from him, by putting the head on the contrary ſide. To ſay the whole of the matter, this works neither ſhoulders nor croupe, but both are loſt, and keep neither circle nor center, and the horſe goes backwards upon a falſe trot.

It is contradictory then to all reaſon, for the croupe of a horſe to go before his ſhoulders, in any caſe whatſoever, unleſs in Curvets upon voltes backwards, and in Curvets upon a ſtrait line backwards; becauſe the action of the curvet differs much from the action of a walk, which is that of the trot, and performed croſs-wiſe.

But it may be aſked, why a horſe is not *entier* when he goes with the croupe before the ſhoulders in Terre-à-terre? which he may do. I anſwer, it is becauſe he has but one haunch before the ſhoulders, and ſo he may go, tho' it be wrong. But if he had both his hind-legs within the pillar, he could not go at all without being *entier*.

However it be, avoid putting the croupe, or half the croupe, before the ſhoulders, it being one of the wrongeſt things in the world, and the moſt dangerous that can be for a horſe. He ſhould be brought indeed to bear and obey the heel; but ſo he obeys neither the hand nor the heel, nor are his ſhoulders at all worked.

CHAP. XI.

The Perfection of Terre-à-terre.

YOU muſt firſt put your horſe ſide-ways, his head in the volte, and his croupe to the center, leaning on your outer ſtirrup, your leg quite cloſe to the horſe, and the toes of your inner foot a little turned out, ſo that your body may be a little oblique; turning your head up (not in) ſo that the inward eye looks on the ſhoulder of the ſame ſide, which puts that inward ſhoulder a little forwards, and keeps the outward ſhoulder back.

The reins of the bridle ought to be ſomewhat long, and drawn without the pommel towards the outward ſhoulder, in order that with the inward rein you may draw up the head of the horſe, to make him look into the volte. This preſſes the horſe without, gives liberty to his inward legs, (becauſe they lead the way) and puts him upon the haunches, ſo that he always advances; for the horſe always follows the action of the horſeman that rides him.

Thus he will obey both the hand and the heel, be upon the haunches, and go eaſily and freely, agreeably, and not contrary to nature. This is the perfection of Terre-à-terre, which is to ſtop the ſhoulders with the hand, and preſs the croupe.

The

The ſame aids muſt be uſed for the left, changing the body, the legs, and the hand. They will alſo do in Demi-voltes, Terre-à-terre, and upon a ſlow Gallop upon the voltes, the croupe in, and in Curvets.

OBSERVATION.

To paſſage a Horſe upon a Walk, the Croupe without or within, working with Leg and Rein contrary, namely, the inward Rein and the outward Leg.

YOU muſt always pull up the horſe's head, to preſs him without the volte, and give him liberty within, which makes him always advance: his inward legs lead the way to prepare him for Terre-à-terre, which puts him upon the haunches, ſo that he is light in the hand.

When a horſe is preſſed within the volte, he muſt of courſe (when he is rode with the bridle only) look out and carry his head out, for his own eaſe; and when he is preſſed without the volte, he muſt neceſſarily look in and carry his head in, for the ſame reaſon. This is as it ſhould be, and the contrary to it wrong.

All that I have taught before is very good; but there is only one truth, which is this, and in its full extent ſo perfect for the Paſſage, Terre-à-terre, or Curvets, that one need have recourſe to nothing elſe.

I repeat very often what ſhould be done in Terre-à-Terre, that my inſtructions may be punctually obſerved.

If a horſe brings his ſhoulders too much in, in Terre-à-terre, he puts his croupe too much out; and the way to remedy this is to ſtop his ſhoulders, and preſs his croupe.

If he does not bring his ſhoulders enough in, he puts his croupe in too much; the way to help this is to bring in his inner ſhoulder, and aid him with both legs, but a little more within than without: for the ſhoulders ſhould always go before the croupe, which is the truth.

To change Terre-à-terre.

You muſt bring the ſhoulders of the horſe a little into the volte, to ſtop the croupe, and afterwards change, ſhifting the hand and the leg, and working always with the inner rein.

The ſame aids that are uſed Terre-à-terre, ſhould be uſed in demi-voltes Terre-à-terre; they are one thing, and differ only in being a half inſtead of a whole volte.

To change upon the Gallop à la Soldade.

Whether it be within or without the volte, whether it be a demi-volte or a quarter-volte, ſtill it muſt be a part of Terre-à-terre. You muſt always therefore aid the horſe with the inner rein and the outer leg: but whilſt you gallop, you muſt work with the inward rein and inward leg.

CHAP. XII.

The Conveniences and Inconveniences of the Caveſon-Rein tied ſhort my Way to the Pommel of the Saddle.

THE caveſon-rein tied ſhort, my way, to the pommel of the ſaddle, is to give the horſe *appuy*, fix him in the hand, and ſettle his head, drawing it down.

It is alſo excellent for a horſe that is too heavy in hand; for the caveſon-rein tied tight to the pommel of the ſaddle, always within the volte, hinders him from

bearing

CHAP. XII.

bearing too much on the bridle, which makes him very light, and fixes him in the hand.

The caveſon-rein tied ſhort to the pommel, is alſo excellent to ſupple the ſhoulders, which is the beſt thing that can be done.

Thus the caveſon gives *appuy* to a horſe that has none, takes it from him that has too much, and makes the ſhoulders extreamly ſupple, which is a great matter.

It alſo makes a horſe gallop with his legs right, ſo that he goes more eaſily afterwards Terre-à-terre: for it lengthens the legs within the volte, and ſhortens thoſe without, which is as they ſhould be.

The caveſon-rein therefore is good to work the ſhoulders of a horſe in every reſpect; and the croupe is loſt in working with the rein and the leg on the ſame ſide: it is alſo good in working with the rein and leg contrary, in almoſt all leſſons. This is the advantage you receive from the inner rein of the caveſon tied ſhort to the pommel of the ſaddle.

The Inconvenience in Terre-à-terre from the inner Caveſon-Rein tied to the Pommel of the Saddle.

The inner rein of the caveſon tied to the pommel of the ſaddle brings in the outward ſhoulder of the horſe very much, whereas Terre-à-terre the inner ſhoulder ought to be brought in. By drawing in the outward ſhoulder you narrow the horſe's fore-part, which neceſſarily makes the croupe large; but in Terre-à-terre the ſhoulders ſhould be large, and the croupe narrow.

If after you have brought in the outward ſhoulder, you put in the croupe, it goes before the ſhoulders; whereas Terre-à-terre the ſhoulders ought to go before the croupe.

Bringing in the outward ſhoulder, and putting in the croupe too, you make the horſe go backwards; whereas Terre-à-terre he ought to advance the ſhoulders firſt.

When you thus narrow the fore-part, and the croupe is in, the fore-part is within the lines of the hind-legs; whereas Terre-à-terre the hind-legs ought to be within the lines of thoſe before.

When you thus narrow the fore-part, and the croupe is in, the croupe leads the way, and the fore-part follows it; whereas Terre-à-terre the fore-part ought to lead the way, and the croupe to follow it.

When you thus narrow the fore-part, and the croupe is in, the horſe is preſſed within the volte, and at full liberty without it; whereas Terre-à-terre he ought to be preſſed without, and at liberty within, that he may the better embrace the volte. When the croupe goes before the ſhoulders, the horſe is as if he was reſty, and ſhuns the ſpur, becauſe he goes backwards. When the ſhoulders lead the croupe, and the horſe advances, he goes with freedom and alacrity, as if he deſpiſed the ground; but when the croupe leads the ſhoulders, every thing is wrong. Beſides, he acquires an ill cuſtom; for when one rides him with the bridle only, his croupe foremoſt, he looks without the volte, becauſe he cannot look within it: but when the ſhoulders go foremoſt, he looks within the volte as he ought to do, becauſe he cannot look without.

But, what is the worſt of all, when the croupe goes before the ſhoulders, the legs go croſs, which is the action of a trot upon the ſwiftneſs of a gallop; whereas Terre-à-terre the two legs within the volte ought to lead the way, which

which is a true gallop: for Terre-à-terre is nothing but a gallop in time. When you work a horſe with the bridle only, you muſt help with the inward rein; for if you uſe the outward, the horſe will go as wrong as with the rein of the caveſon faſtened to the pommel of the ſaddle, becauſe it narrows him as much before; and if you aid him with the outward leg, his croupe is as much before his ſhoulders.

Obſerve, that to faſten the caveſon-rein my way to the pommel of the ſaddle, within the volte, is the moſt excellent thing in the world for Terre-à-terre, if you preſs the horſe upon the legs without the volte: for the rein is wrong when the horſe is preſſed within the volte.

Note alſo, that the lower a horſe goes before, if he is preſſed without the volte, the more he will go upon his haunches.

CHAP. XIII.

For the Piroüete.

THE action of a horſe's legs in the Piroüette is very ſtrange; for by working violently with the outward rein of the bridle, you ſtreighten the fore-part, and put the croupe more in the way of being help'd with the outward leg. Now this is the action of the legs in the Piroüette to the right: when he lifts his two fore-legs, he lifts at the ſame time the hind-leg without the volte; ſo that he has three legs in the air at once, and ſupports himſelf only upon the hind-leg within the volte.

When he ſets his three legs down, his outward ſhoulder coming very quick in, he moves at the ſame time (almoſt in one and the ſame place) the hind-leg within the volte to keep the circle. At the ſame time, I ſay, that his three legs come to the ground, his hind-leg within the volte moves, to follow the circle, but moves as it were on the ſame place; ſo that this inward hind-leg touches the center: for tho' it moves, it moves almoſt always on one ſpot, and only turns round. When the horſe's head grows giddy, and he cannot continue this motion any longer for fear of falling, he puts forward his hind-leg within the volte to ſtop himſelf. Theſe are exactly the aids and movements of a horſe's legs in the Pirouette; otherwiſe he could not go ſo faſt as he ought.

CHAP. XIV.

For Paſſades.

DEMI-VOLTES upon Paſſades are only Demi-Piroüettes, and require the ſame aids; except that in Paſſades, upon a ſlow or full gallop, the horſe ought to make two or three falcades, or ſlides upon the haunches, before he turns.

The way to teach him, is to gallop him gently ſtrait forwards and ſtop him: after a little ſtop, you muſt turn him upon a walk, then gallop him again, ſtop him, and turn him as before. This will make him go perfectly well upon Paſſades.

CHAP. XV.

For Curvets.

THIS is the ſame thing, and conſequently has the ſame aids as Terre-à-terre; only you muſt ſupport the horſe a little more on the hand, ſo that he may advance very little, and he will be ſo much the more upon the haunches. You muſt help with the inward rein and outward leg, and the inward leg ought not to be quite ſo cloſe to him as the outward; it muſt not be ſtiff, and the toes of it ſhould turn a little out, but the toes of both feet ſhould be down, that the hams may be more pliant. The aids ſhould be delicate, and not ſo violent as in Terre-à-terre.

It is true, that the horſe's fore-legs are near together, and within the lines of his hind-legs, which are more aſunder; but at the ſame time it is alſo true, that the hind-legs are within the lines of the ſhoulders, which makes the horſe to be upon the haunches.

For Curvets along a Wall.

The left ſide of a horſe being againſt a wall, in Curvets forwards, you muſt help with the rein that is fartheſt from the wall, and put the left ſhoulder a little in, without giving him any aid with your legs. In Curvets backwards, you muſt help him with the rein that is next to the wall.

The right ſide to the wall, in Curvets forwards, you muſt aid the horſe with the rein from the wall; in Curvets backwards, with the rein neareſt the wall.

By obſerving all theſe rules the croſs will be eaſily made, it being done with theſe four aids, forwards, backwards, to the near ſide, and to the off ſide.

In the Saraband you muſt work with the outward ſhoulder and rein, but not at all with the legs.

CHAP. XVI.

Of the different Helps of the inward Rein of the Caveſon (or falſe Rein) in the Rider's Hand.

THERE are three different helps with the inward rein of the caveſon in the hand of the rider: the firſt draws the outward ſhoulder; the ſecond draws in the inward ſhoulder; and the third is to ſtop the ſhoulders.

In all theſe three different aids you muſt bring in your own outward ſhoulder.

OBSERVATIONS.

The leg and the rein of the ſame ſide work the ſhoulders, and the croupe is loſt. The leg and rein contrary, with the head to the pillar, and the pillar without the head, works the croupe, and preſſes the ſhoulders.

The croupe towards the pillar, and the pillar within the croupe works the ſhoulders, preſſes the croupe, and puts the horſe upon his haunches. It is juſt the ſame in his own length, and it puts him likewiſe upon his haunches; ſo does the head to the wall, and alſo the working with the rein and the leg on the ſame ſide upon a ſhort trot; the ſtopping a horſe, the making him go backwards, the raiſing him before, provided it is not too high, the ſlow gallop upon circles, and Terre-à-terre.

But a ſingle pillar my way, in Curvets, puts him extremely upon the haunches. Now to put a horſe upon the haunches is the quinteſſence of our art; for when he is there, he may do whatever your deſire of him, if he is obedient and has ſtrength enough.

When a horſe goes by rote, you are to take notice that he does ſo by the eye only. For it is not the hand or the heel that he minds, but the pillar, the wall, or the notice he takes of the particular place where you give him his leſſons.

leſſons. For this reaſon he who does not ride always in the ſame place, and who has neither pillar nor wall, finds his horſe the moſt obedient to the hand and the heel.

CHAP. XVII.

Of the uſe of the two Reins of the Bridle.

YOU muſt work with the outward rein of the bridle in the Piroüette, becauſe the fore-part of the horſe is confined, and the croupe at liberty. You muſt alſo work with the outward rein of the bridle in Demi-Airs, upon Paſſades along a wall; becauſe the fore-part is confined, and the croupe at liberty, this being but a Demi-Piroüette. In like manner you muſt work with the outward rein of the bridle in Curvets backwards, in a ſtrait line; becauſe the fore-part is ſtill confined and the croupe at liberty, ſo that the croupe leads the way in Curvets backwards. And by the ſame rule you muſt work with the outward rein of the bridle in all Leaps, Groupades, Balotades, and Caprioles forwards, or upon circles; becauſe the fore-part is confined and the croupe at liberty, otherwiſe the horſe could not leap. So much for the outward rein of the bridle.

As to the inward rein of the bridle, you muſt work with that in Terre-à-terre; becauſe the croupe is then confined and the ſhoulders are at liberty. For the very ſame reaſon you muſt work in like manner with the inward rein in Demivoltes, Terre-à-terre, and in Curvets upon voltes, the croupe being then confined, and the ſhoulders at liberty.

Curvets forwards likewiſe require the inward rein of the bridle to be worked; becauſe the croupe is ſtreightened, and the fore-part at large, to advance, as it leads the way. Upon the Trot, upon the Gallop, in Paſſaging, work ſtill with the inward rein; with which we have now done.

The caveſon my way ſubjects the head of the horſe more or leſs, according to the place to which it is fixed. When the rein is faſtened to the pommel, the head is leſs ſubjected; when it is faſtened to the girths, more, in proportion as the line is ſo much lower.

Concerning BITTS.

THE leſſons I give you concerning bitts ſhall be very ſhort, though there are many books already extant, and many riders now living, who think themſelves compleat maſters of this ſubject, and very wiſe in their great variety of bitts: Theſe people however, both authors and riders, appear to know little of the matter, in the judgment of men of experience; in as much as they imagine that a piece of iron in the mouth of a horſe can make him knowing. As well might they fondly believe, that a book in the hand of a boy would teach him to read the firſt time before he has been ſhewn his letters; or that ſpurs upon the heels of an ignorant fellow would be alone ſufficient to make him a good horſeman.

There is ſome art however in fitting a horſe with a proper bridle; according as the ply of his neck is long or ſhort, in giving him a large or ſmall mouth-piece, a large or narrow liberty, the eye ſhort or long, ſtrait or bent: the branches are either ſhorter or longer, ſtronger or weaker; mouth and liberty wider or narrower: the eye longer or ſhorter, ſtraiter or more bending;

ing; the hooks according to the juſt meaſure of the bitt; the curb equal, and conſiſting of three good round SS's, with one ring where it is fixed to the eye upon the far ſide, and two rings or mallions, whereby it is curbed or fixed upon the near ſide; the cheeks of the bitt handſomly furniſh'd with boſſes, not too big, and either rich or plain, according to your fancy; not two rows of little chains tied to the bitt within his mouth, but only one at the moſt.

But above all, this rule is chiefly to be obſerved, to put as little iron in your horſe's mouth as poſſibly you can. If his tongue be very big, the liberty muſt be the wider; if little, the liberty the leſs; but you muſt take heed that the *appuy*, or reſting-place of the bitt, be never made too near the liberty, for it would gall him: but the reſting-place muſt be where it ought, which is about a finger's breadth from the liberty upon each ſide of it; and the bitt muſt reſt upon the bars a finger's breadth above the tuſhes. Thoſe branches are weakeſt, whoſe extremities, when the reins are ſlackt, come neareſt to the horſe's neck; and thoſe ſtrongeſt, which go moſt forwards from his neck; and good reaſon for it, becauſe you have the greater pull.

If a horſe hold his head too much up and out, then they make uſe of ſhorter branches and ſtronger, to pull his head down and in, wherein they are pretty right. And ſo if a horſe hold his head too low, and bringeth it in ſo round that he arms himſelf againſt the bitt, which is to reſt the branches upon his breaſt, ſo that you have no farther pull or command of him at all; and becauſe this vice is contrary to holding up his head and out, for which they uſed ſhort branches and ſtronger to bring it in, they therefore think they ſhould make uſe of long and weak branches to pull it up; for they reaſon thus, that if a ſtrong branch pulled him down, then a weak branch will pull up his head: wherein they are mightily deceived, for when a horſe arms himſelf againſt the bitt, as it is certain that long branches will come ſooner to his breaſt than ſhort ones; ſo it is as certain, that weak branches will come ſooner to his breaſt than thoſe which are ſtrong. But, it ſeems, this they do not very exactly conſider, otherwiſe they would ſoon be ſenſible of their error.

For to a horſe that arms himſelf againſt the bitt, you muſt have not only a ſhort branch that will not ſo ſoon touch his breaſt, but alſo a ſtrong branch to keep it yet farther from his breaſt. The hooks of the curb ought likewiſe to be made a little longer, and ſo juſtly turned, as not to offend or hurt the ſides of his cheeks; and if the curb doth not lie in its right place, two little iron rings faſtened cloſe to the top of the hooks, to keep them ſteady and fixed, is the beſt remedy. I uſed it many years before I ſaw it in Mr. PLUVINEL's book; all other devices in bitts or curbs being inſignificant and to little purpoſe.

Now the bitts following are generally the beſt for all horſes whatſoever, *viz.* 1. A plain or ſimple *Canon*, with branches *a la Conneſtable:* 2. A plain *Scatch* with branches *à la Conneſtable:* 3. A *Canon à la Pignatel*, which is a bitt with a gentle falling and moving up and down, and the *liberty* ſo low as not to hurt the roof of the horſe's mouth, which is the beſt bitt certainly for all horſes which have any thing of a big tongue, which I am ſure they do not like to have preſſed; and therefore I recommend that *liberty* above all things in bitts, with the branches *à la Conneſtable:* 4. A *Scatch* with the liberty *à la Pignatel*, which I like better than a *Canon*, becauſe it don't fill a horſe's mouth ſo much.

much. 5. To difcharge a horfe's lips, I would have *Olives* with the liberty *à la Pignatel*; thofe *Olives* extending not fo far upon every fide of the mouth, as to the extremities of them, and having little rings at the ends of them, to give liberty to his lips, and difcharge them. 6. I would have alfo *Melons* to difcharge the lips, which are very good, and do it in the fame manner as the *Olives* above mentioned. But indeed I would have, in all, but two forts of bitts, which are, firft, the *Canon à la Pignatel*, and, fecondly, the *Olives à la Pignatel*, to difcharge his lips if need be, but the branches always *à la Conneftable*.

Thus you have the truth of bitts brought into a narrow compafs: There is little virtue in them to bring a horfe to underftanding, on which a man muft work, and that is his reafon, by the favour of the Logicians diftinction of reafonable and unreafonable creatures; for were they as good horfemen as fcholars, they would have made another diftinction. Well then, you fee it is not a piece of iron can make a horfe knowing, for if it were, the bitt-makers would be the beft horfemen: no, it is the art of appropriated leffons, fitting every horfe according to his nature, difpofition, and ftrength; punifhing and with good leffons rectifying his vices; rewarding him, and preferving him in his horfe-virtues, which will make him a juft and ready horfe; and not the trufting to an ignorant piece of iron called a *bitt*: for I will undertake to make a perfect horfe with a cavefon without a bitt, better than any man fhall with his bitt without a cavefon; fo highly is the cavefon, when rightly ufed, to be efteemed. I dreffed a *Barb* at *Antwerp* with a cavefon without a bitt, and he went perfectly well; and that is the true art, and not the ignorance and folly of a ftrange-figured bitt.

The famous *Pignatel* at *Naples*, never ufed but fimple bitts, which made the ignorant wonder how he could drefs horfes fo perfectly with fo few kinds of bitts; but he freely told them, *It was their ignorance made them wonder at his art:* and likewife that great mafter of his art, Monfieur DE PLUVINEL, faid the fame.

The cavefon ought to be full, and not too rough. It fhould be lined with leather, fingle or double, to make it more eafy. It rarely happens by my method that a horfe wrys his head, fucks up his bitt, or puts his tongue over it. The liberty *à la Pignatel* hinders the tongue from going over; and while you work with the cavefon in this good method, flacking often the bridle, you avoid the others.

If he puts out his tongue, and will not leave off that cuftom, cut it with a fharp round iron, made in the form of the end of his tongue. Let the iron be hot, and laying the tongue on a thin piece of board, you may cut it and ftop the blood at the fame time. But in fact, if you work according to the method of this book, fuch extremities will not be neceffary, becaufe the horfe will fall into none of thefe vices.

For my part, I always advife lenity and patience with good leffons; never to offend your horfe, if you can avoid it; never to ride him, or to exact from him above half fo much as he can bear. By this means you will not only preferve him, but make him take pleafure in all that he does: he will even love you, and the exercife you give him; whereas otherwife he will hate you, find the manage irkfome, and loth to come to it. It is your bufinefs to make both your perſon and the manage as agreeable to him as poſſible, by working him a little at a time, being bountiful in your careſſes and recompences, and very ſparing in your corrections, and without paſſion when you inflict them. So much concerning bitts and the caveſon.

I take it to be a great vice, when a horſe does not go as well to one hand as to the other; and I have ſeen very few that do ſo: but if you punctually follow my method, your horſes will go to perfection, and as well to one hand as the other, ſo that you will never ſee any difference.

One thing more I have to ſay; it is, that there is no horſe in the world that can obey the heel, if he has not a good *appuy*, a good mouth, and his head ſteady.

Obſerve alſo, that nothing is more ungraceful than to ſee a horſe ſhake his tail in every action. This vice is generally helped by faſtening a rein to his tail and then to the girths to keep it ſteady: but if the rein breaks, he ſhakes his tail as much as ever. Now the moſt infallible way to cure this, is to cut the great nerve that is under his tail, about the middle of it, which operation never does the horſe the leaſt prejudice.

I DO not here implore your pardon, but your juſtice, and that juſtice rather to yourſelves than to me. Thoſe things which to you, perhaps, ſeem not very conciſe, but too prolix, might if ſhorter have ſtill left you in darkneſs: whereas you have now a full ſunſhine to look on you with the ſplendor of the knowledge of Horſemanſhip; ſo that you have no occaſion to grope in obſcurity, ſince you have ſo clear a light to conduct you in the right way. This art does not conſiſt only in ſtudy and mental contemplation, but in bodily practice likewiſe. You ought to be well informed that the art of Horſemanſhip cannot be collected together in a proverb, or a ſhort aphoriſm, or reduced to a ſyllogiſm, or brought into as little compaſs as the poeſy of a ring; nor can there be one univerſal leſſon, as many deſire in this art, any more than a univerſal medicine for all diſtempers, or an ointment for all wounds. It is true indeed, that ſome dream of a univerſal medicine, which they call the Philoſopher's Stone; but this, I fear, is dreaming only.

For my part, I am very ſure there is nothing univerſal in Horſemanſhip, nor in any thing elſe that I know. If this work pleaſes you, I ſhall be thoroughly well ſatisfied; if not, I ſhall be content in my own mind; becauſe I know certainly that it is very good, and better than any thing that you have had before of the kind.

CONCLUSION,

CONCLUSION,

TO THE

READER.

Noble Horſemen,

I Have loved, practiſed, and ſtudied this art of Horſemanſhip from my youth upwards, and employed in it a great deal of time with pleaſure: for there is no exerciſe ſo good, nor is any attended with more honour and dignity, than that of Riding; provided a perſon rides with addreſs, which he cannot do unleſs he is well verſed in the art. Without it, nothing ſeems ſo ridiculous, ſo aukward, ſo irregular, as a man on horſeback. His members appear to be diſlocated, becauſe they are out of their natural ſituation; and his poſture uneaſy, becauſe it is conſtrained; whereas a good rider ſits in his natural place, and his poſture is eaſy, becauſe free and unconſtrained. It is in Horſemanſhip as in other things: regularity is beautiful, while diſtortion and compulſion muſt be without grace. There is an elegance moreover in Horſemanſhip, which looks as if it was natural, tho' it proceeds from art. Thus, tho' a perfect horſeman rides with art, it ſeems rather natural than acquired by practice; and he makes his horſe appear as if nature had produced ſuch a creature for no other end, but to be conducted, governed, and rid by man. What is more, a good horſeman rides as one may ſay with harmony; for his horſe being of the ſame mind with himſelf, moves in ſuch exact manner, ſteps ſo equally, and keeps ſuch juſt time; turns, piroüettes, riſes ſo equally, ſo eaſily, ſo lightly, that it is very agreeable to ſee, as well as a very profitable ſcience to learn. For whoever is not a perfect horſeman, can never ride either with grace or ſafety; and no man can be perfect in this art, unleſs he learns it at the Manege; becauſe that gives him a true and ſure ſeat, a firm hand, a heel that moves in juſt time, a free poſture, and a powerful command, that conſtrains his horſe. Without all this one cannot be a good horſeman, nor ride a horſe boldly, either for pleaſure, or in war; neither pleaſingly to others, nor with ſatisfaction to one's ſelf. I deſire therefore, my noble reader, that you would well underſtand my leſſons; which, I dare aſſure you, contain the truth and perfection of the Manege. I do not hereby cenſure others; but your induſtry and practice will ſhow you the difference between their method and mine. Endeavour to collect all the advantages from my inſtructions, and as much pleaſure. as I wiſh you.

FINIS.

ADDITIONS.

After this Work of mine was all printed, ſome very neceſſary Leſſons came to my Mind, which I give you here in Form of Appendix, or Additions, and particularly recommend them to your Study. They treat of the Actions of a Horſe's Legs; for without a perfect Knowledge of theſe, it is impoſſible for any Man to dreſs a Horſe well, unleſs by mere Chance.

I have before ſaid that the gallop is a leap forwards, in this manner: When the horſe brings down his fore-legs, before they touch the ground, he moves his hind-legs; ſo that the fore-leg which leads the way, on which ſide ſoever it be, is always followed by the hind-leg of the ſame ſide; this is the true gallop forwards in a ſtrait line. But it muſt be remarked, that tho' the horſe goes directly ſtrait forwards, the legs that lead the way are more preſſed than the two others; and that thoſe which are leaſt preſſed are moſt at liberty, and conſequently come firſt to the ground. For example, a horſe leads the way with the right-leg before, which is followed by the hind-leg of the ſame ſide; and the left-leg before being at liberty, he ſets it firſt to the ground: He then puſhes forwards, and leads the way with his right-leg behind; and the left-leg being at liberty, he ſets it firſt to the ground; ſo that he advances his right-leg behind, which leads the way. Thus the horſe keeps four perfect times (equal to one, two, three, four) with his four legs; that is to ſay the near leg before makes the firſt movement, and comes firſt to the ground; the other foreleg on the off-ſide, which is confined, and leads the way, makes the ſecond movement; the left hind-leg, which is not confined, moves in the third place; and the right hind-leg, which is confined, in the fourth place; ſo that his legs fall exactly in order, one, two, three, four; thoſe which lead the way being moſt confined, and the others moſt at liberty. This is the true gallop ſtrait forwards.

The Gallop of a Horſe in a Circle.

IF a horſe gallops to the right, the inner rein of the caveſon faſtened to the pommel and the croupe in, he is preſſed within the volte, ſo that his legs within lead the way, and thoſe without are at liberty, and come firſt to the ground, as I before ſaid, and the horſe leans a little upon the inſide. Thus he moves, and keeps the time of one, two, three, four. Obſerve here well, that the whole conſiſts in the outward haunch; for the horſe being preſſed within the voltes, is confined on that ſide, and at liberty without, narrow before and large behind, as the gallop ought to be. But he is more upon his ſhoulders than upon his haunches, becauſe the outward haunch is put out by the liberty it has, which is occaſioned by the preſſure within the volte. This is the true gallop, but not the true Terre-à-terre; for the horſe is always upon the movement of one, two, three, four, with his fore and hind-legs, which very much ſupples his ſhoulders: But

But if any man thinks in this manner to make him go Terre-à-terre, he is deceived; for it is only a ſwift gallop, preſſed upon the ſhoulders, becauſe the horſe is narrow before and large behind, the outward haunch being out; this, I ſay, is the true gallop, but not the true Terre-à-terre, as I ſhall ſhow preſently. It is right in Piroüettes, becauſe Piroüettes are nothing but a gallop in the horſe's own length, in which he is preſſed within the volte, and his outward haunch conſequently muſt be a little out. This gallop is alſo good in Demi-voltes upon Paſſades, ſince theſe Demi-voltes are only Demi-piroüettes. It is juſt the ſame to the left hand.

For Terre-à-terre upon Voltes.

THE inward rein of the caveſon being faſtened to the pommel of the ſaddle, for the right hand, you muſt as much as poſſible put in the outward haunch, in order to make the horſe bear on the outſide of the volte, to preſs his outward legs and put his inward at liberty; ſo that the inward legs are before the outward, and come to the ground in that manner. The action of Terre-à-terre therefore is directly contrary to that of the gallop: for the gallop is one, two, three, four, the haunch a little without, which will not do for Terre-à-terre; whereas when the outward haunch of the horſe is put in, and preſſed without the volte, he goes Terre-à-terre, but he cannot gallop; for the movement of Terre-à-terre conſiſts only of two times, as one, two, *pa*, *ta*, which is the ſame movement as in Curvets, but quicker, the fore-legs meeting at the ſame time in the firſt movement, and the hind-legs meeting in the ſecond movement; only the legs within the volte are a little before the others, notwithſtanding which the two fore-legs come to the ground at once in the firſt time, as the two hind-legs do in the ſecond time; juſt as in Curvets, where the croupe falls when the ſhoulders riſe, and the ſhoulders fall when the croupe riſes. The Curvet is a leap upwards, and Terre-à-terre is a leap forwards, preſſed and near the ground. This is the true Terre-a-terre; and thus you ſee that the outward haunch does the whole: when that is preſſed Terre-à-terre, the horſe is preſſed on the outſide; and when the outward haunch is put out a little, the horſe is preſſed within the volte, which is for the Gallop. This method of Terre-à-terre is excellent upon Demi-voltes by the wall; for theſe Demi-voltes are nothing but Terre-à-terre, as the Demi-voltes upon the Paſſades are nothing but Demi-piroüettes, which is only a Gallop in the horſe's length.

The following are the aids to make a horſe go Terre-à-terre. To which hand ſoever you go, you muſt help with the inward rein the hand without the volte, in order to draw the inward rein as much as you can towards the horſe's neck, helping him with the outward leg, by bearing hard upon the ſtirrup, turning out a little the toes of the inward leg, and making it ſhorter, by at leaſt a handful, than the outward; the outward ſhoulder ſhould be lower than the inward, and the face turned a little into the volte. This will make him go perfectly well Terre-à-terre, becauſe his croupe is narrow and his fore part large, ſo that he muſt be upon the haunches; beſides, being narrow behind and large before, he the better embraces the volte, and the hind-leg within the volte can never go before the ſhoulders.

It is ſo neceſſary to underſtand theſe things, that I would wiſh to have them ſtudied; for without them, nothing can be done but by mere hazard.

I muſt here inform you of one thing; which is, that even when a horſe goes on a Hand-gallop, his hind-legs advance beyond the place that the fore-legs had quitted: but when he runs full ſpeed, his hind-legs advance beyond the ſaid place a great deal more. But, tho' this be true of the gallop, in Terre-à-terre the hind-legs never go beyond the place the fore-legs left.

The following Remark with regard to the Bridle-Hand is of Importance.

THE horſe's neck is between the two reins of the bridle, which both meet in the rider's hand. When a horſe is upon his voltes, if one works or pulls the rein within the volte, this rein preſſes the outſide of the horſe, I mean his outward legs, eſpecially the outward hind one, and that puts in the outward haunch, and ſo throws the horſe upon his haunches. It muſt be noted, that when the outward haunch is thus put in, the hind-leg within the volte goes towards it, and the fore-leg within is in a manner pulled from the other fore-leg, which narrows the croupe, and enlarges the fore-part to embrace the volte ſo much the better, the hind-legs being within the lines of the fore. This is excellent for Terre-à-terre, Curvets, and Demi-airs: but a horſe cannot gallop in this manner.

If one works or pulls the outward rein of the bridle, it preſſes the horſe within the volte, his outward haunch being at liberty; he is more preſſed before than behind, and therefore is upon the ſhoulders, the fore-part being narrow, and the croupe large. Obſerve, that when a horſe is preſſed within the volte, the hind-leg within the volte is confined, and the hind-leg without the volte goes from it, and the fore-leg without the volte at the ſame time is brought near the other fore-leg, which narrows the fore-part and enlarges the croupe. This is wrong Terre-à-terre (becauſe he cannot go Terre-à-terre in this poſture) but very excellent in the Gallop.

Without knowing this, no man can dreſs a horſe perfectly. When a horſe has not a good *appuy*, or is not ſupple in the ſhoulders, you muſt preſs him within the volte, and that will cure him of both thoſe vices; if a horſe has too much *appuy*, and does not put himſelf upon the haunches, you muſt preſs him without the volte, which will cure him of both theſe. There is yet a third thing that will make him obey the heel, becauſe he cannot avoid it; which is, to faſten the caveſon in my manner to the pommel of the ſaddle. By this way you may dreſs all ſorts of horſes in the utmoſt perfection, if you know how to practiſe it; a thing that is very eaſy in the hands of a maſter.

The following Leſſons ſhould be obſerved, as the moſt excellent in the World.

IT is proper to gallop a horſe *d'une piſte* a turn or two very narrow, and, when he does not expect it, make him advance upon a ſtrait line: then make another narrow volte, and advance him in a right line: then

then make a third volte *d'une piſte*, and advance him ſuddenly; and after that a fourth; continuing this method as long as it ſhall be found neceſſary. Afterwards make a large circle, which may include them all. You ſhould ride him in this manner firſt on the trot, and when you find him ſo light that he begins to gallop of himſelf, proceed to gallop him according to the ſame method. There is nothing that ſo much helps the ſhoulders of a horſe, or ſettles him better in the hand, or makes him more freely obey the heel, and which is, in effect, better for all manner of purpoſes: But you muſt take care to have the inner rein of the caveſon faſtened to the pommel in my manner.

The beſt of all Leſſons to make a Horſe attend to, and obey, both Hand and Heel.

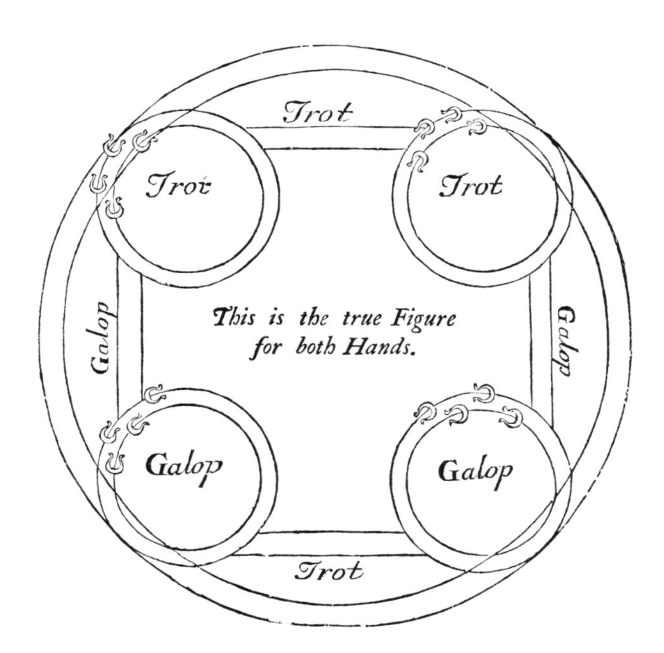

This leſſon is as good as the other, and differs from it only in that the horſe muſt go upon the Hand-gallop, or Terre-à-terre, the croupe in in each circle, and afterwards upon a ſtrait line. The caveſon muſt be faſtened, as before, to the pommel.

This leſſon is excellent to put a horſe in the hand, and upon his haunches; to make him obey either hand or heel, to make him free and without heſitation, which heſitation is often a kind of reſtiveneſs, to remedy which nothing better than this can be found.

It

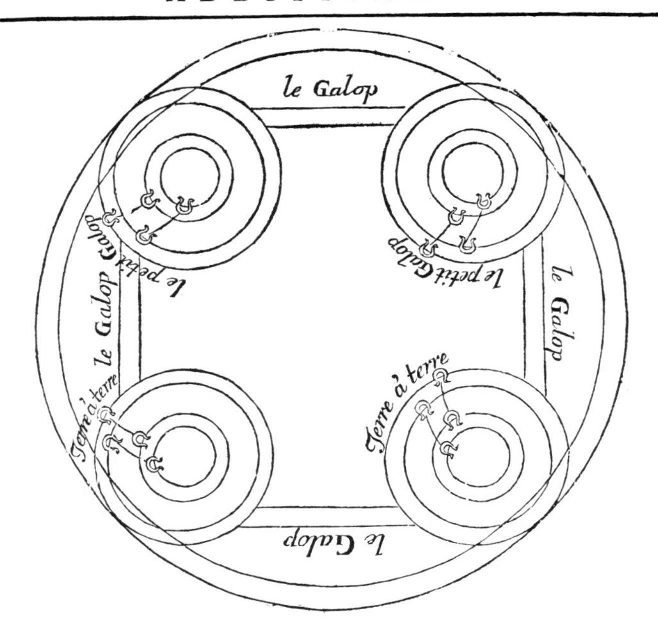

It is proper to remark, that all the rules of our art tend only to make a horſe ſubject to the ſenſe of feeling (which is the only ſenſe we ought to work upon) and that conſiſts in nothing but the feeling the hand and the heels, or having a ſenſible mouth and ſides. You muſt not let him work by the ſenſe of ſeeing, which is the uſe the pillar will give him; nor by the ſenſe of hearing, which the uſe of particular noiſes will do; but by that of feeling only, which is our only aim, and relates only to thoſe two places, the mouth and the ſides. It is by the ſight only that a horſe is taught a number of tricks and ſubtleties, which the ignorant admire; it can do nothing however in teaching a horſe to go well in the Manege. There is ſo much to be done by the ſenſe of feeling, and which requires ſo much art, wit, judgment, and long experience of the ſeveral diſpoſitions of horſes, that all men are not formed by nature to make good horſemen. One may much more eaſily teach a dog to dance, or even a horſe, by practiſing on his ſight. But I chuſe to let the ignorant ſpeak and think what they will, ſince their folly does not affect me, and ſince this noble art receives no real prejudice from their contemptible ignorance, or their impertinent railleries.

Remarks.

IT is impoſſible to dreſs a horſe before he obeys his rider, and by that obedience acknowledges him to be his maſter; that is, he muſt firſt fear him, and from this fear love muſt proceed, and ſo he muſt obey. For it is fear creates obedience in all creatures, in man as well as in beaſt, great

Great pains then muſt be taken to make a horſe fear his rider, that ſo he may obey out of ſelf-love, to avoid puniſhment. A horſe's love is not ſo ſafe to be truſted to, becauſe it depends on his own will; whereas his fear depends on the will of the rider, and that is being a dreſſed horſe. But when the rider depends on the will of the horſe, it is the horſe that manages the rider. Love then is of no uſe; fear does all: For which reaſon the rider muſt make himſelf feared, as the fundamental part of dreſſing a horſe. Fear commands obedience, and the practice of obedience makes a horſe well dreſſed. Believe me, for I tell it you as a friend, it is truth.

Of the Spur.

NOTHING has ſo much effect as the ſpur, in making a horſe fear his rider. Sharp ſpurs are better for correction than for aids. You muſt give the ſpur therefore for all vices, of what kind ſoever (all other corrections are ridiculous;) but then you muſt do it at the very inſtant the fault is committed, and properly: For if you do it out of ſeaſon, or for trifles, you will entirely ſpoil the horſe; otherwiſe, as I ſaid, the ſpurs are the only remedy for all vices, when you uſe them ſo that he knows for what, and is warned thereby to avoid the ſame fault.

The Aid of the Spur, called Pinching.

PINCHING with the ſpur is a moſt excellent aid. Aids are to be underſtood to go before the fault, in order to prevent it. This pinching is good in all airs, and better than for Terre-à-terre (becauſe it raiſes a horſe more than it makes him advance) tho' it may be made uſe of in both.

Another Aid with the Spur.

THERE is another aid of the ſpur, which we call an aid, becauſe it is not ſo violent as a correction (and that makes it an aid only) nor ſo ſevere as pinching, but preſerves the medium between both. It is thus done: When the horſe is upon the Hand-gallop, the croupe in, or upon Terre-à-terre, if he does not enough obey the leg that touches, or is very near him, you muſt move the leg as if you would give him the ſpur, but touch him with it very gently, only juſt to make him perceive it. This is the moſt delicate thing that is done with the ſpur; it makes him obey and advance, which is excellent Terre-à-terre, or on the Hand-gallop, with the croupe in; but the pinching is better in airs, for the reaſon before alledged.

If a horſe underſtands the correction and the two aids of the ſpurs, and is very ſenſible to them, you may be ſure that he will go without wanting them after ſome time; for he will be ſo ſenſible, that he will go freely, and obey voluntarily for the calf of the leg only. As for the aid of the thighs, it is but a ridiculous imagination. For, to ſpeak properly, there are no other aids but thoſe of the ſpurs and the calf of the leg, to which horſes can be any ways ſenſible. This is all I have to ſay of the ſpurs.

Of faſtening the inner Rein of the Caveſon to the Pommel of the Saddle.

THIS is the moſt excellent thing in the world for the dreſſing of all ſorts of horſes, of whatever age or diſpoſition they may be. When the croupe of a horſe is put in, and he is ſubject to bring in his ſhoulders, he is in the condition of a well-dreſſed horſe: For you have nothing to do but ſtop his fore-part with the inner rein of the bridle, and he will go well in all airs, and *à la Soldade*. To make the ſhoulders of a horſe ſupple is the whole affair, and this cannot be over-done; for I aſſure you that horſes are a ſtiff-necked generation. A horſe well ſuppled will beſides never be *entier*, a vice about which a great number of authors have blotted ſo much paper.

For a Reſty Horſe.

THE beſt remedy is to pull him back. If this fails, a good ſpur will certainly perſuade him: for that is the only argument.

For a Horſe that runs away.

I Have ſaid before, that you ought to treat a horſe with all the mildneſs imaginable; but that was to prevent his running away. If he does run away, and you are in an open field, the beſt method is to ſpur him ſmartly and continually on both ſides, till he voluntarily ſlackens his pace, and then to ſtop him. Serve him in this manner every time he begins again to run, and it will certainly cure him. If you are in a narrow place, the pillar with a rein will do the buſineſs, becauſe he can only run round.

Of the Imperfections of a Horſe's Mouth.

ALL our great writers, both ancient and modern, and the greateſt maſters who have treated of Horſemanſhip, think themſelves obliged to ſpeak of the vices and imperfections of a horſe's mouth. For example, when he draws up his tongue; when he puts his tongue over the bit; when he doubles his tongue round the bit; when he lets his tongue hang out of his mouth, either before or on one ſide. Our great doctors in Horſemanſhip, I ſay, have laboured much againſt all and every one of theſe vices, preſcribing many curious inventions, bits and engines for the mouth, and points for the curb; ſo that the remedy is worſe than the diſeaſe, and ſpoils a horſe. The truth, in few words, is, that I ſhould wiſh a horſe to have none of theſe faults; but if he has them, they are of no diſadvantage to him; for with all theſe defects his *appuy* will be as good as without them; his head as firm and ſure; his bars and the place of his curb as ſenſible as if he had none of them all: For the bridle reſts and works upon the bars, and the curb is in its uſual place, and where it ought to be, notwithſtanding the tongue. Be there a tongue or no tongue, or let that tongue hang where it will, it no ways affects the goodneſs of the *appuy*. We are now convinced then how vain and needleſs thoſe curioſities are, with which our great maſters have amuſed themſelves and their readers, and, what is worſe, have tormented the poor horſes to no purpoſe.

For Terre-à-terre.

YOU muſt aid a horſe with the inward rein and the outward leg, in order to preſs him without the volte, and make him bear upon his outward legs; that is, to put his outward haunch as much in as you can, tho' lookers-on perceive nothing of the matter. The horſe does not make

make a circle, and therefore there can be no center; but he makes a perfect quadrangle and a quarter-volte at each corner to come to the other line of this quadrangle; which is Terre-à-Terre in perfection. He must be light in hand, because he is much upon the haunches; and he is much upon the haunches because his outward haunch is put very much in; and thus all the croupe is put in upon a strait line, according to this figure.

A horse cannot go upon a perfect circle, unless he puts his outward haunch a little out; for which reason this quadrangle is the true figure of Terre-à-terre.

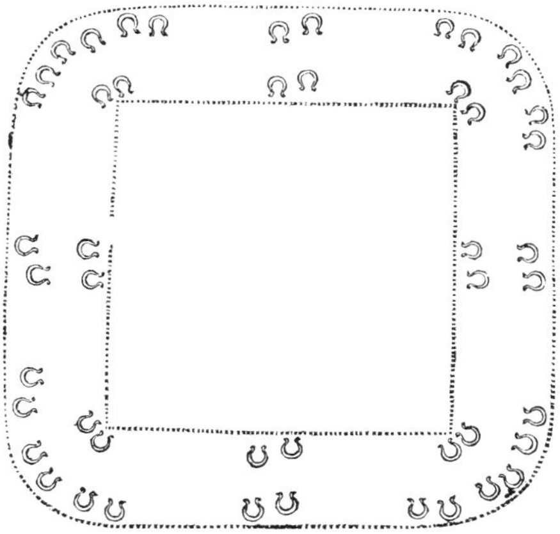

This may be easily seen when the head of the horse is to the wall, and he changes his line at an angle of it, or where the two walls meet.

Curvets upon Voltes.

THIS is another action; for here the horse must go sideways, the croupe a little out. The aids should be with the inward rein and the outward leg. When you first begin him upon this lesson, you must aid him with the inward leg, in order to keep his croupe out; for horses usually put the croupe too much in. If a horse makes five or six curvets forwards upon a strait line, and performs them well, you may without danger put him to curvets upon his voltes, which is no more than to turn a strait line into a circle; a thing that may be done without conjuration. If the horse presses a little upon the hand, so that you feel him, he will go perfectly well. I have yet one more thing to remind you of, which is, that in case he advances you cannot raise him too high, because he is then truly in the hand and the heels: But if you raise him high, and he does not advance, it is a Pesade and not a Curvet; for I deny that Ferme-à-ferme is the foundation of all Airs, or that it is good for any thing. This is the true method of making horses go in Curvets, and better than all the pillars in the world.

In Passades.

YOU must work with the outward rein, which is that next the wall, in order to keep his head from the wall, and his croupe to it. Upon the demi-voltes you must aid him with the same rein, and the leg of the same side, to keep his croupe near the wall. If one was to do otherwise, the horse would lose the line of the wall, his croupe being from it; which would not only be false, ſalſe, but very ungraceful beſides. For the outward rein in Paſſades narrows the fore-part, and enlarges the croupe; preſſes the one, and gives liberty to the other. Terre-à-terre the inner rein enlarges the fore-part and narrows the croupe, gives liberty to the former and ſubjects the latter. Thoſe are much deceived then who think the ſame aids that are for Terre-à-terre, will do alſo for Paſſades. I have before given you many reaſons, to ſhew why we work a horſe ſo much to put him upon the ſhoulders; but there is one more to add. It is, that the croupe or haunches of a horſe carry nothing but his tail, which is very light; but his haunches have a much greater load, namely, his head and his neck: It is for this reaſon we put him upon the haunches, to counterpoiſe, and to eaſe his ſhoulders, and make him light in hand. Be not diſcouraged when a horſe oppoſes you, for it is a ſign of ſtrength, vigour, and ſpirits: Now a horſe that has all theſe muſt be well dreſſed, if he is under a good hand, and learned heels; whereas a horſe that never reſiſts, ſhews his weakneſs, and his want of courage and ſpirits, and it is a very difficult thing for art to ſupply what nature is defective in. To ſpeak the truth, I have never known any horſe that did not very much withſtand the rider before he was compleatly dreſſed, and that too for a long time. Till he goes freely, he can't be brought to the perfection of the Manage, tho' he may ſometimes do right againſt his will. There is in reality no horſe that does not reſiſt at firſt, and that will not endeavour, almoſt thro' the whole courſe of his dreſſing, to follow his own inclinations, rather than thoſe of the rider. What is more, ſubjection is not agreeable to a horſe, nor to any other creature that I know; not even to men, who obey only becauſe they cannot help it. It is only the habit of obeying that brings a horſe to be dreſſed: But he will try all poſſible ways to avoid ſubjection, and it is not till he has no more ſtratagems to have recourſe to, that he gives up the diſpute: ſo that, in fact, you are not much obliged to him for his complaiſance. If the wiſeſt man in the world were put into the ſhape of a horſe, and retained his ſuperior underſtanding, he could not invent more cunning ways (I queſtion if ſo many) to oppoſe his rider, than a horſe does: Whence I conclude, that a horſe muſt know his rider to be his maſter, that is, muſt be afraid of him, and then he will obey him, which is what we call a dreſſed horſe.

The End of the Additions.

HONI SOIT QVI MAL Y PENSE
LA BATAILLE GAIGNEE

Apres l'homme le Cheval le plus noble animal,
Est rendu par ce Seigneur si juste et si égal,
Par cette Methode, que tout le monde admire,
Qu'on voit aisement, qu'il est sujet de Son Empire.
Son assiette si-belle, ses aydes si secrettes;
Tout à la negligence, encore si bien-faittes,
Nous sont un argument, assés valide et puissant,
Qu'il est à ses talons et Bride obeissant,
Et que tous les Chevaux sont assujettis à sa loy;
Puis qu'ils luy obeissent comme à leur propre ROY.
S'il montoit un Diable tres-robus te,
Ce Diable iroit en tous Airs fort Iuste.
M. D. V.
Abr. a Diepenbeke delineavit.
Petr. van Lisebetten sculpsit.
2

NEWCASTLE, c'est la force de ton genie,
Qui te fait triompher de la Cavalerie;
Qui au choc furieux pour l'amour de la gloire,
Dedans les combats emporte la victoire.
Dedans tes cercles tu ne fais que conjurer,
Quand tu monte tes chevaux, que Philosopher;
Puis que tu domte le fougueux, et le sage,
Et que tous ensemble ils te font hommage.
A.D.V.
Abr. a Diepenbeke delineavit
Petr Clouwet sculpsit

Il monte avec la main, les éperons, et gaule
Le Cheval de pegase qui volle en Capriole:
Il monte si haut qu'il touche de sa teste les Cieux
Et par ses merveilles ravit en extases les Dieux.
Les Chevaux corruptibles qui la bas sur terre sont
En Courbettes, demi-airs, terre à terre vont
Avec humilité soumission et bassesse.
L'adorer comme Dieu et auteur de leur adresse.
M. D. N.
4.
Ab. a Diepenbeke delineauit et Pet. Clouwet sculpsit

ROY DELA GRANDE
BRETAGNE
Que Pallas soit vôtre guide, Cupidon vôtre Page,
Mars le Capitaine qui conduise vôtre courage;
Que votre propre monture soit le Pegase aile,
Et Mercure, comme laquay, toûjours a vôtre côte
Que la Fortune soit en votre seul pouvoir soûmise,
Elle, qui sur nos tes tes ést jusques icy assise.
Abr. van Diepenbeeck inv. C. Caukercken fecit.

La Maison de WELBECK appartenant
à Monseigneur le Marquis
de NEWCASTLE, le quel est
dans la Province de
NOTTINGHAM.
Paragon un Barbe.
6.
Abr. a Diepenbeke delineavit
Petr van Lisebetten sculpsit

WELBECK.
Le Superbe Chevual De Spanie.
Diepenbeeck del:
7

WELBECK.
Le Manege couert vouté de bois large de 40 pieds, longe de 120 pieds.
La boutique du Mareckall.
Mackomilia un Turke.
Abr: a Diepenbeke delineauit
Lucas Vorsterman iunior sculpsit

WELBECK.
L'Ecurie voutée de pierre, les piliers de pierre, la mangeoire de pierre, a l'Italienne, et une fontaine qui coule le long de la mangeoire, et se rend dans une voute au dessous ou coule un petit ruisseau. Contre la teste de Chaque Cheval il y a une petite cheminée pour l'haleine du Cheval, laquelle s'ouure ou se ferme, selon la chaleur, ou froideur; Elle est pauée de pierre de taille.
Le Grenier de l'Ecurie.
Il y a d'autres Ecuries pour quatre-vint Chevaux.
Nobilissimo Coursier Nappolitain.
9.

Rubecan un Roussin.
Abr. a Diepenbeke delineavit.
Lucas Vorsterman iunior sculp.
10.

Les Haras.
Abr. à Diepenbeke delineavit
Petr. Clouwet sculpsit

Les poulins.

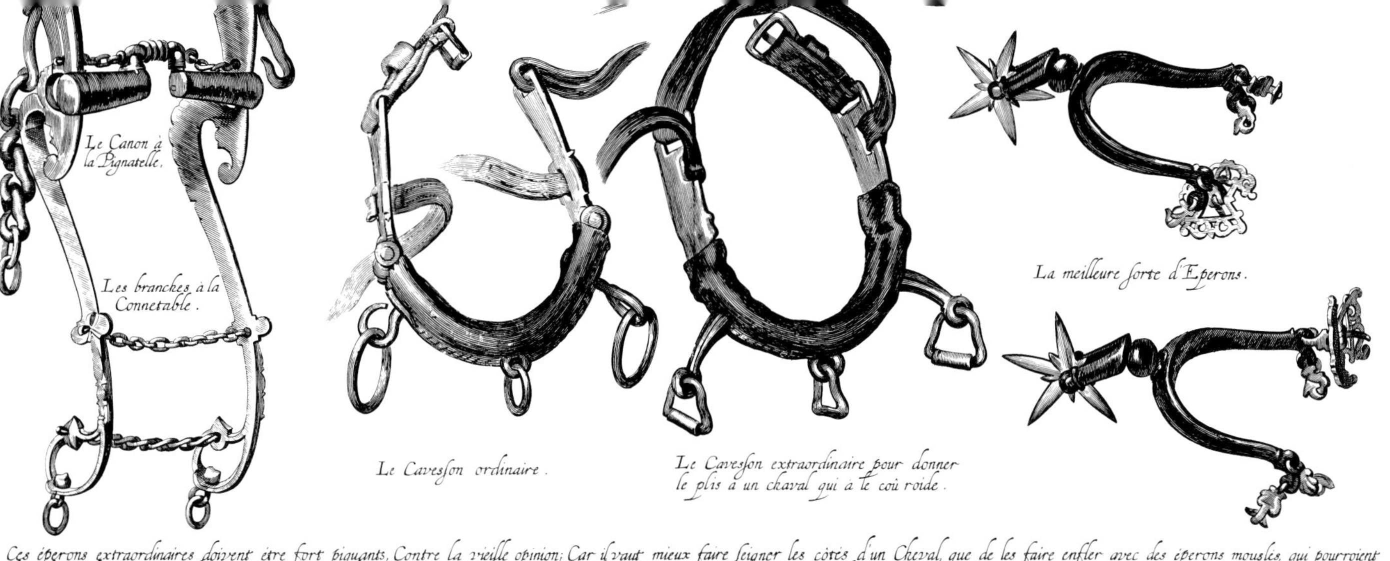

Le Cavesson ordinaire .

Le Cavesson extraordinaire pour donner le plis à un chaval qui a le coù roide .

La meilleure sorte d'Eperons .

Ces éperons extraordinaires doivent être fort piquants, Contre la vieille opinion; Car il vaut mieux faire seigner les côtés d'un Cheval, que de les faire enfler avec des éperons mousles, qui pourroient luy donner le farein. Qui plus est; rien n'a tant de pouvoir sur un Cheval retif, que de luy faire sentir un peu ses côtés; Il faut donc des éperons aigusmais ces éperons ne sont que pour des occasions extraordinaires. Vos éperons ordinairs doivent pourtant être piquants, affin que les côtés de votre Cheval en cuisent; Car le Cheval, de quelque pais que ce soit, qui ne peut souffrir les éperons, ne vaut à rien. La chambriere est trop lourde, et le nerf est encore pire; mais il sentira une bonne koussine, et le sang en viendra .

Les Eperons extraordinaires.

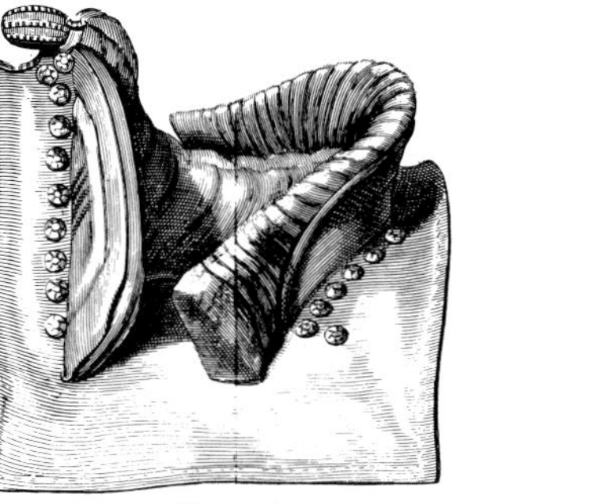
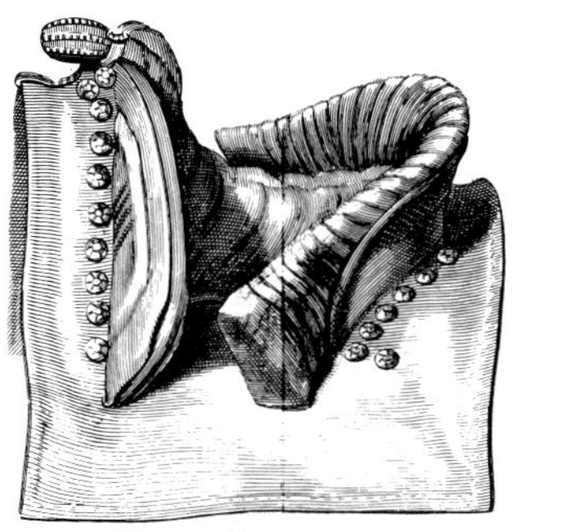

Voicy la plus excellente selle qui puisse être .

La meilleure sorte d'Etriés.

Abr. à Diepenbeke delineavit.   Lucas Vorsterman junior sculpsit

es tant à cheval, pour
môntrer la vraije assiette
du Cavallier.
plan naturel, pour faire
voir la plus parfaitte
posture du Cavallier.
M. Housley
14

et la Iambe dedans la volte, toutes deux
de mesme côté, pour trauailler et assouplir
les épaules sur le cercle large au trot,
et du galop et la test du Cheual contre le pillier.
Le Capitaine Mazin monte.
et
Monseig.r le Marquis donne leçon
Le galop a Gauche.
Le vray galop a Droicte.
Au pas a Gauche.
Monseig.r le Marquis.
Au pas a Droicte.
Trot a Gauche.
Trot a Droicte.
15.

Parade du trot pour
La Main Gauche.
Parade du trot pour
La Main Droicte.
Le Capitane Mazin a Cheual
Parade du Galop pour la Main Gauche.
Parade du Galop pour la Main Droicte.
Abr. a Diepenbeke delin.
Theod. van Kessel fecit aqua forti
16

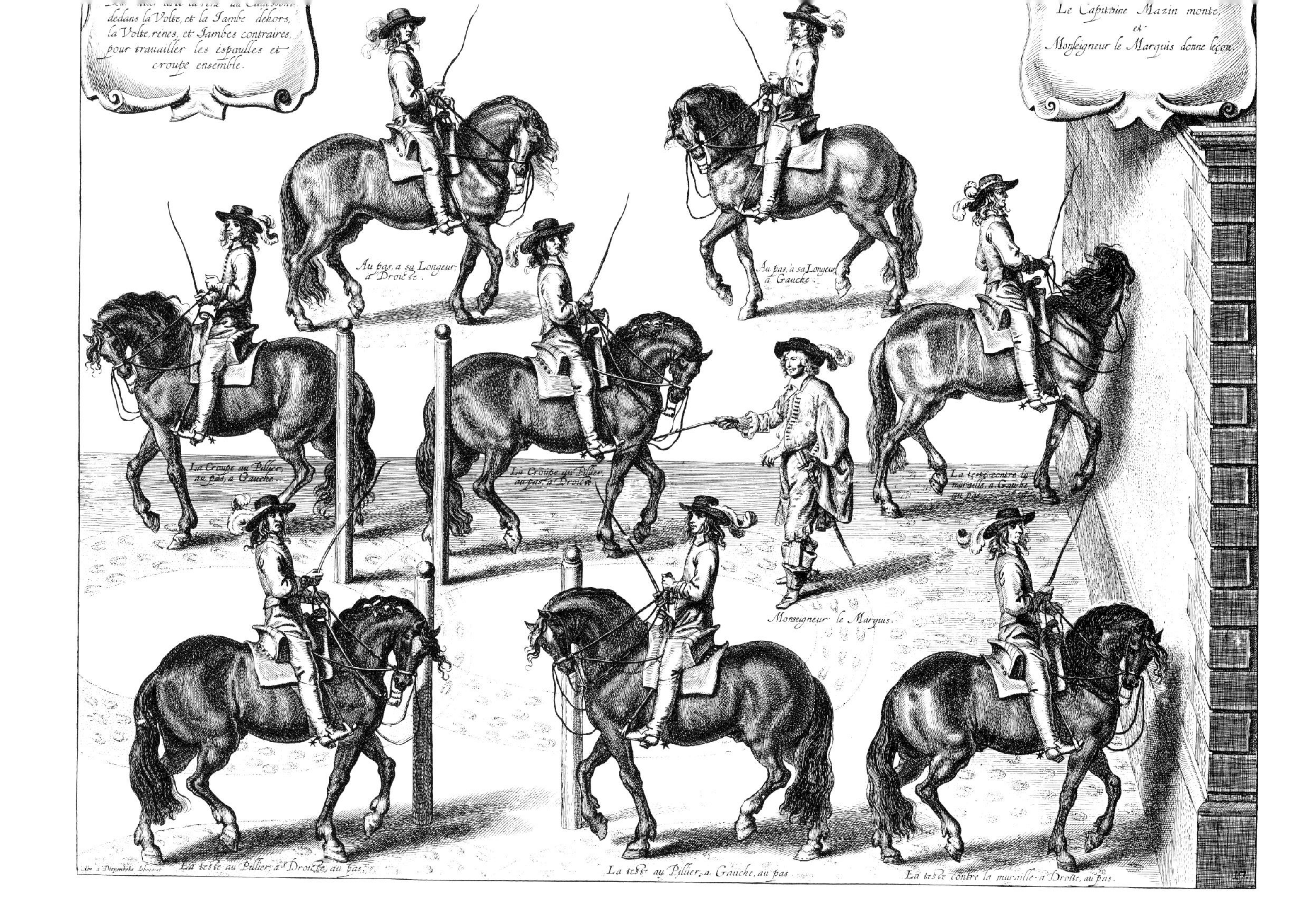
dedans la Volte, et la Iambe dehors,
la Volte, rênes, et Iambes contraires,
pour trauailler les espaulles et
croupe ensemble.
Le Capitaine Mazin monte,
et
Monseigneur le Marquis donne leçon.
Au pas, a sa Longeur, a Droitte.
Au pas, a sa Longeur a Gauche.
La Croupe au Pillier, au pas, a Gauche.
La Croupe au Pillier, au pas, a Droitte.
La teste contre la muraille, a Gauche au pas.
Monseigneur le Marquis.
La teste au Pillier, a Droitte, au pas.
La teste au Pillier, a Gauche, au pas.
La teste contre la muraille, a Droite, au pas.
17

cauesson dedans la volte et dans
la main, et la jambe hors la volte,
sur le terre à terre, a droite et
à gauche.
Monseigneur le Marquis donne leçon.
Terre à terre, à Main droite.
Terre à terre, à Main gauche.
Monseigneur le Marquis.
Terre à terre, la teste contre la muraille,
à Main gauche
Terre a terre la teste contre la muraille
a Main droite.
Abr. a Diepenbeke delineavit.
Petr. Clouwet sculpsit.
18

de la selle pour donner le ply au
Cheual et pour trauailler les barres
et la gourmette sur le trot et galop
des cercles larges
Le Capitaine Mazin monté
et
Monseigneur le Marquis donne
Le trot à Droite, sur
le cercle Large
Le galop à Droite sur
le cercle Large
La crouppe au pilier
de pas, à Droite.
Monseigneur le Marquis.
M.r Procter
La teste au pilier,
à Droite.
Le terre à terre, à Droite de sa Longueur
Le terre à terre, à Gauche.
Lucas Vorsterman iunior fecit apud
19.

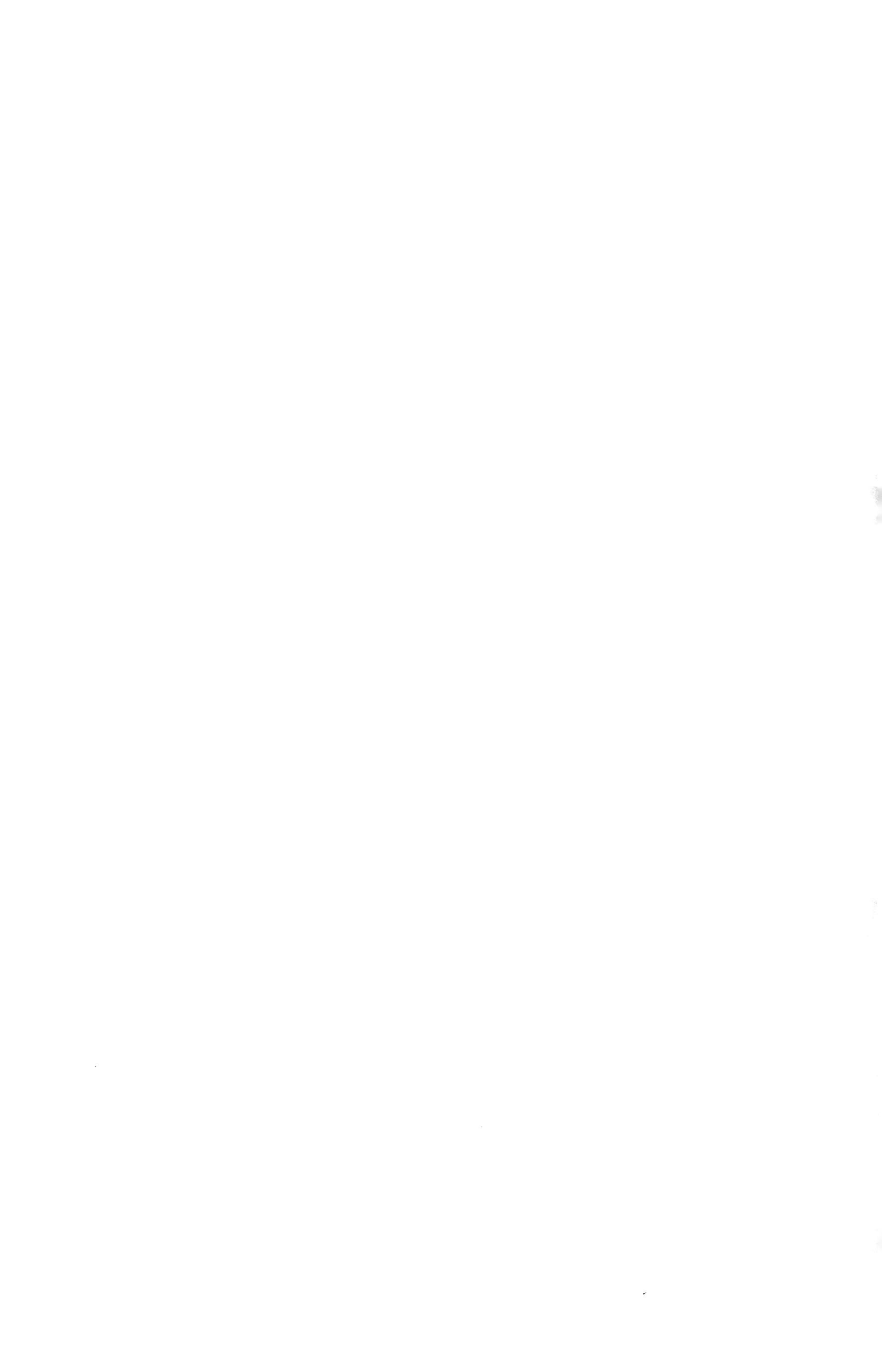

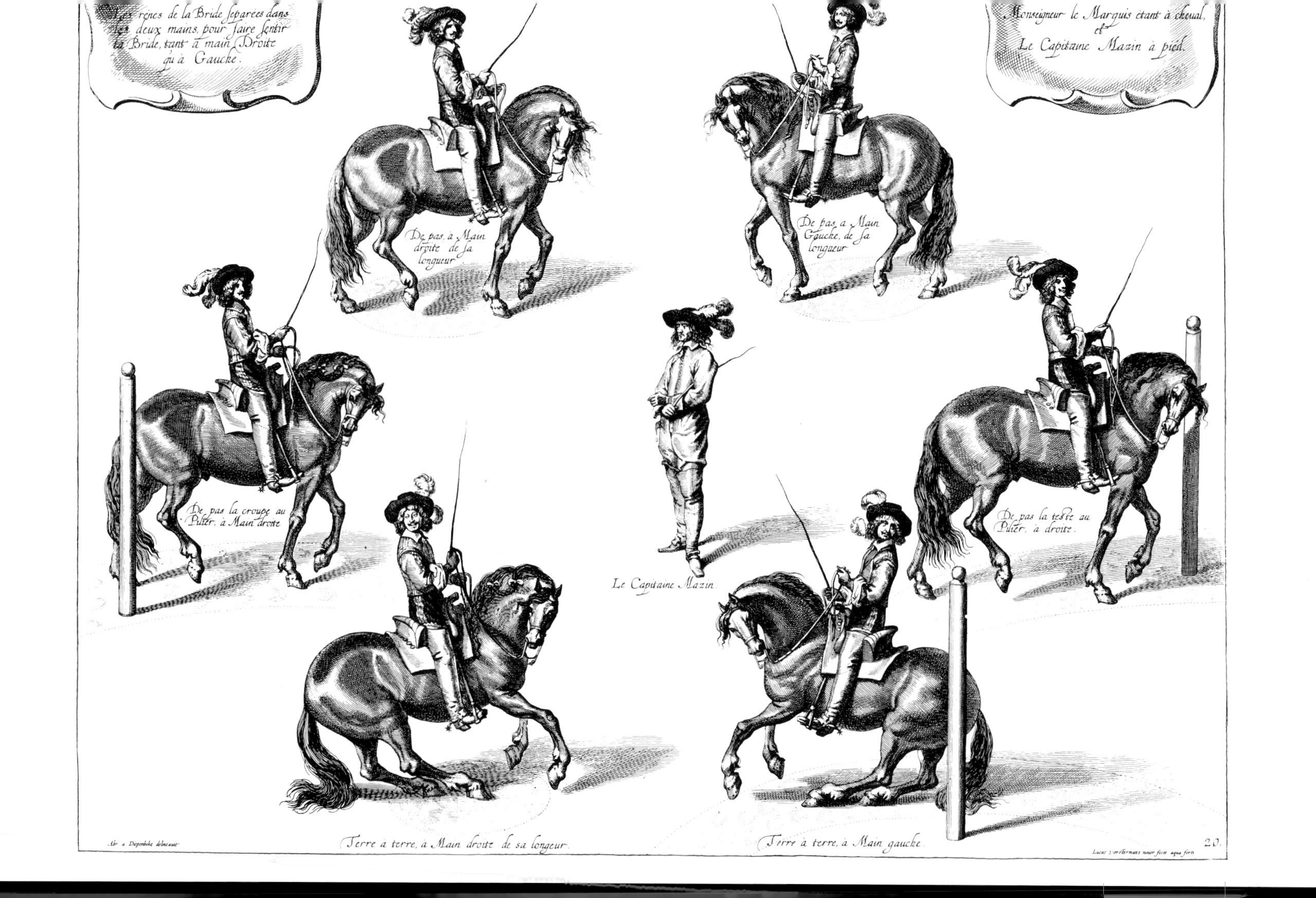
Les rênes de la Bride separées dans les deux mains, pour faire sentir la Bride, tant à main Droite qu à Gauche.
Monseigneur le Marquis étant à cheual, et Le Capitaine Mazin à pied.
De pas, à Main droite de sa longueur
De pas a Main Gauche, de sa longueur
De pas la croupe au Piliér, à Main droite
Le Capitaine Mazin.
De pas la teste au Piliér, à droite.
Terre à terre, à Main droite de sa longeur.
Terre à terre, à Main gauche.
Abr a Diepenbeke delineauit
Lucas Vorsterman iunior fecit aqua forti
20.

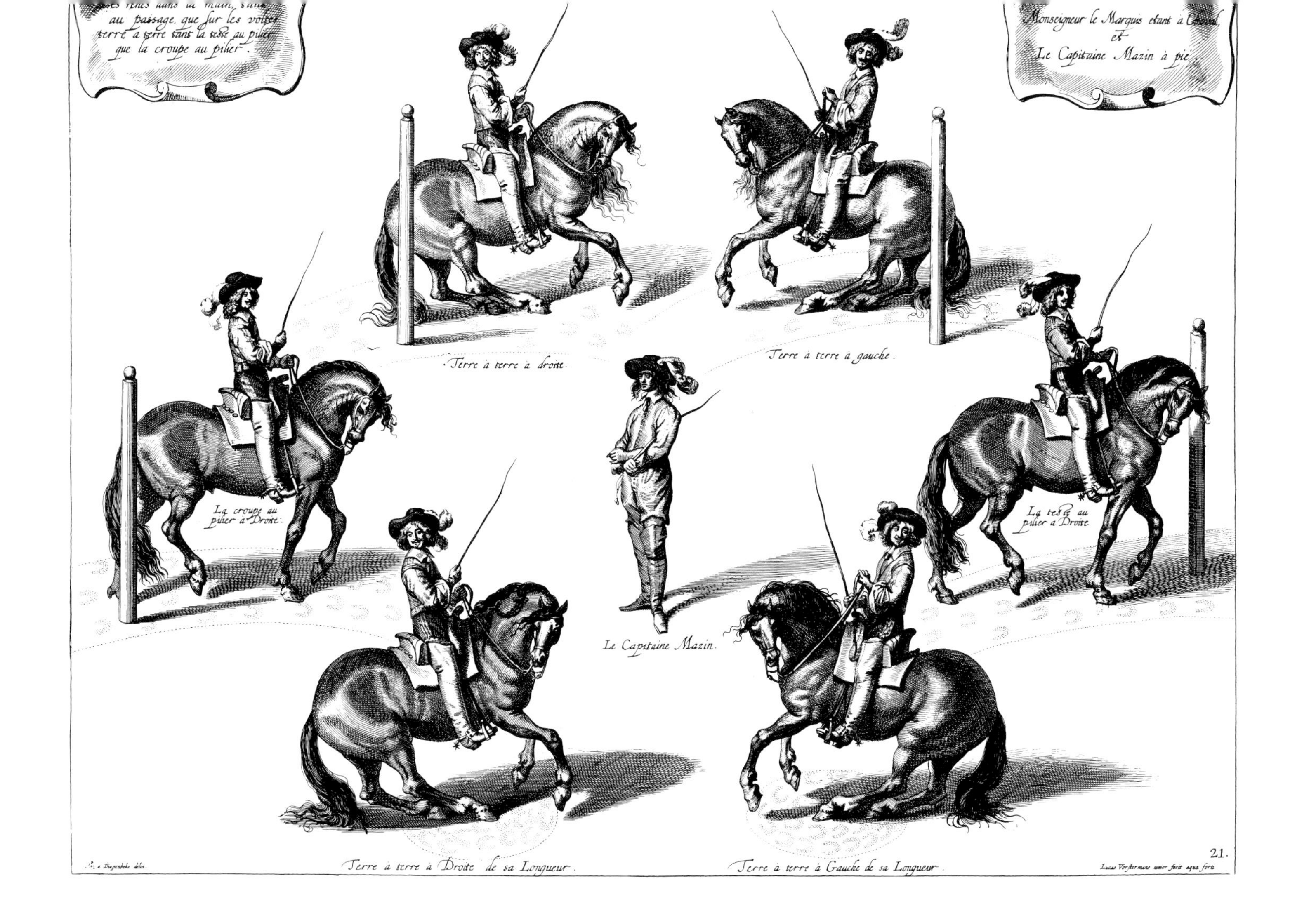
au passage, que sur les voltes terre à terre tant la teste au pilier que la croupe au pilier.
Monseigneur le Marquis etant à Cheval, et Le Capitaine Mazin à pie.
Terre à terre à droite.
Terre à terre à gauche.
La croupe au pilier à Droite.
La teste au pilier à Droite.
Le Capitaine Mazin.
Terre à terre à Droite de sa Longueur.
Terre à terre à Gauche de sa Longueur.
21.
Lucas Vorsterman iunior fecit aqua forti.

Passades au Petit Galop, la demy-volte a Main Gauche.
Passades a toute Bride, la demy-volte a Main Gauche.
Monseigneur le Marquis etant a Cheval. Passades au Petit Galop, la demy-volte a Main Droite
Passades a toute Bride, la demy-volte a Main Droite
Abr. a Diepenbeke delineavit
Theod. van Kessel fecit aqua forti
22.

airs a Courbettes, de ferme a ferme, sur les voltes a Droite, et en arriere, et de côté a Droite.
Monseigneur le Marquis travaille, estant a pied, et le Capitaine Mazin luy ayde.
Mg.r le Marquis
Le Capitaine.
Courbettes de ferme a ferme, a Droite.
Mg.r le Marquis.
Le Capitaine.
Courbettes sur les voltes, a Droite.
Le Capitaine.
Mg.r le Marquis
Palfrenier
Courbettes en arriere, sur les voltes, a Droite.
Palfrenier
Mg.r le Marquis
Le Capitaine.
Courbettes de côté, a Droite.
Abr. a Diepenbeke delineavit.
Theod van Kessel fecit aqua forti.

La nouvelle invention pour les airs à Courbettes de ferme à ferme sur les voltes à Gauche, et en arriere et de côté à Gauche.
Monseigneur le Marquis trauaille, estant à pied, et le Capitaine Mazin luy ayde.
Le Capitaine
Mg.r le Marq.
Courbettes sur les voltes a Gauche.
Le Capitaine.
Mg.r le Marq.
Courbettes de ferme a ferme, a Gauche.
Le Capitaine.
Mg.r le Marq.
Palfrenier
Courbettes de côté a Gauche.
Palfrenier
Mg.r le Marq.
Courbettes en arriere, sur les voltes a Gauche.
Le Capitaine.
24.
Abr. a Diepenbeke delineavit.
Lucas Vorsterman iunior fecit aqua forti.

La nouvelle invention pour les airs de Courbettes, de ferme à ferme, sur les Voltes à Droite, et en arriere, et de coté à Droite, le Capitaine étant à Cheval.
Le Capitaine étant à Cheval, Monseigneur le Marquis donne leçon.
Mg.r le Marquis.
Courbettes de ferme à ferme à Droite.
Mg.r le Marquis.
Courbettes sur les Voltes à Droite.
Mg.r le Marquis.
Palfrenier.
Courbettes en arriere sur les Voltes, à Droite.
Palfrenier.
Mg.r le Marquis.
Courbettes du Côté à Droite.
Abr. a Diepenbeke delineavit.
Lucas Vorsterman iunior fecit aqua forti

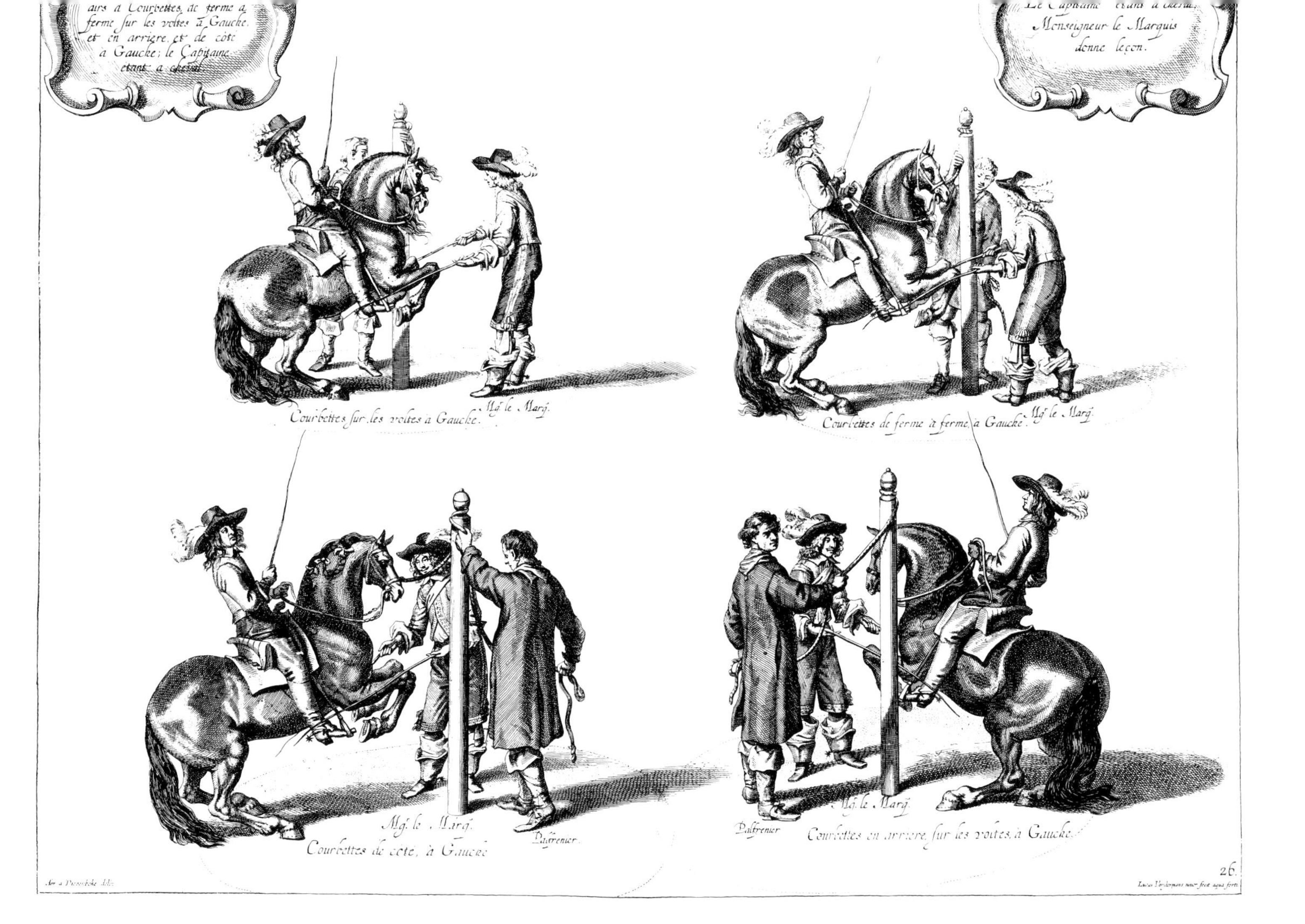
airs à Courbettes, de ferme à
ferme sur les voltes à Gauche,
et en arriere, et de côte
à Gauche; le Capitaine
etant a cheval.
Le Capitaine etant à cheval,
Monseigneur le Marquis
donne leçon.
Mg.r le Marq.
Courbettes sur les voltes à Gauche.
Mg.r le Marq.
Courbettes de ferme à ferme, à Gauche.
Mg.r le Marq.
Courbettes de côté, à Gauche
Palfrenier.
Mg.r le Marq.
Palfrenier
Courbettes en arriere, sur les voltes, à Gauche.
26.

Airs releves, demj Air Groupades, balotades, et caprioles de ferme à ferme, sur les voltes, à Droite.
Le Capitaine étant à Cheval, Monseigneur le Marquis donne leçon.
Demj Air de ferme à ferme, à Droite.
Groupades à Droite
Mg.r le Marq.
P.
Mg.r le Marq.
P.
Balotades à Droite.
Caprioles à Droite.
Mg.r le Marq.
P.
Mg.r le Marq.
P.
Diepenbeke delineavit.
Lucas Vorsterman iunior fecit aqua forti
27.

La Novelle invention pour les airs releues, Demj-airs Groupades Balotades et Caprioles de ferme a ferme sur les volbes a Gauche.
Le Capitaine estant a Cheval Monseigneur le Marquis donne leçon.
Groupades a Gauche.
Demj-air de ferme a ferme a Gaucke.
Mg. le Marquis
P.
P.
Mg. le Marquis.
Caprioles a Gaucke.
Balotades a Gaucke.
Mg. le Marquis.
P.
Mg. le Marquis
P.
Abr a Diepenbeke delineavit
Theod. van Kessel fecit aqua forti
28.

La Maison de Monseigneur
Le Marquis apellée Bolsover
en la Province de Darby
Monseigneur le Marquis a Cheval
Le Capitaine a pie
Courbetts sur les Voltes a Droict
Courbetts sur les Voltes a Gauche
Le Capne
Le vray pasaige sur les Voltes a Gauche.
Le vray pasaige sur les Voltes a Gauche.
Abr. a Diepenbeke delineavit
Petr. van Lisebetten fecit aqua forti
29.

Monseigneur le Marquis
à
Cheval.
Ma Maeson de Bolsouer
Demy air par le Droite

Bolsover
Monseigneur le Marquis
à Cheval.
Groupades par le Droite
Abr. à Diepenbeke delineavit
Petr. van Lysebetten sculpsit
31.

Bolsouer
Monseigneur le Marquis
à Cheval
Balottades par le Droite.
Abr. a Diepenbeke delineavit.
P. Clouwet sculpsit
32.

Bolsouer
De Monsigneur le Marquis à Cheval
Caprioles par le Droite

Bolsouer
Monseigneur le Marquis a Cheval.
Capriolles sur les Voltes a Main Gauche.
34
Abr. a Diepenbeke delineavit.
Lucas Vorsterman iunior sculpsit.

La gallerie
Balsouer
Monseigneur le Marquis acheual
Groupades sur les Voltes a main gauche
Thod van Kessel fecit. 35

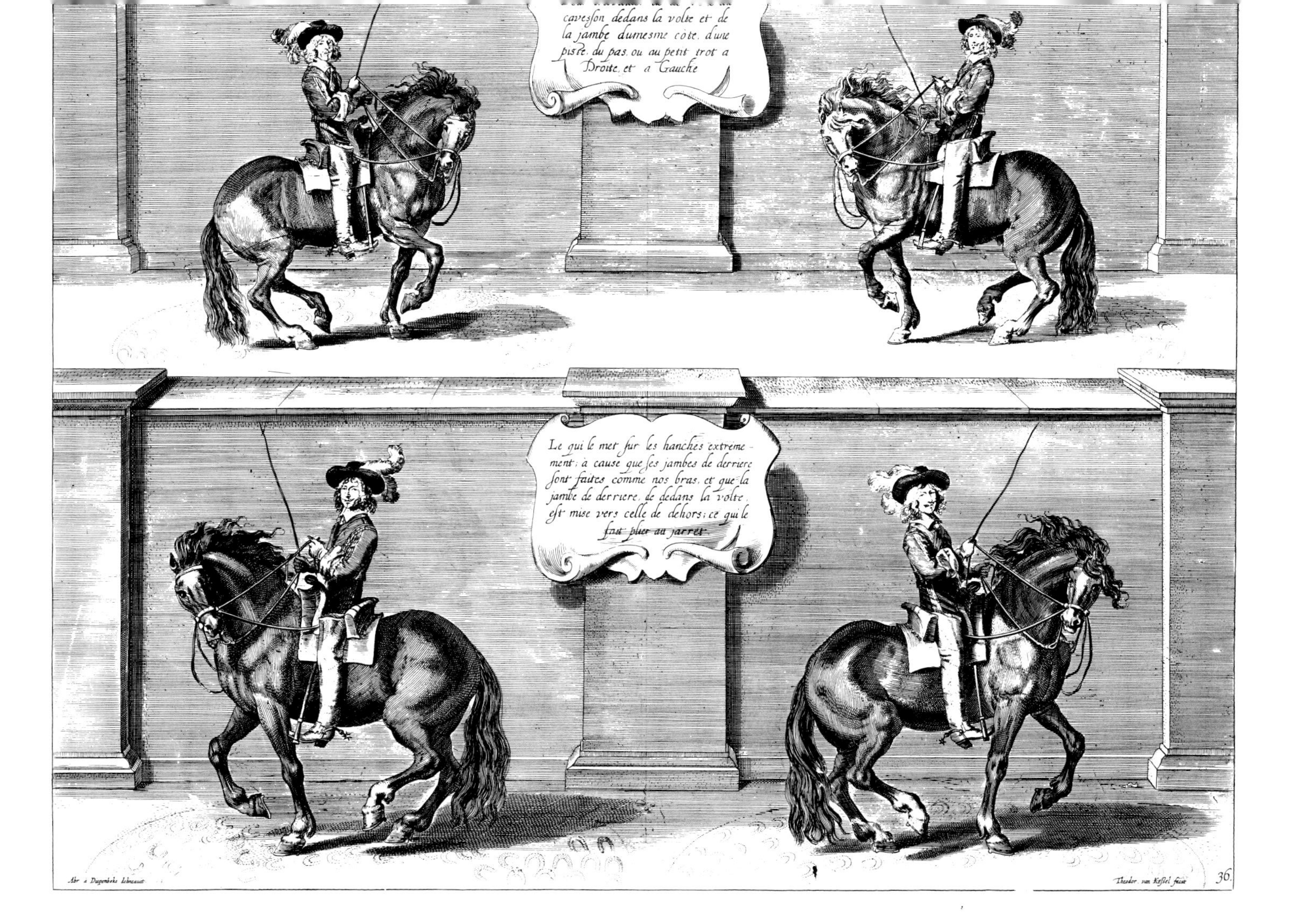
caveſson dedans la volte et de
la jambe dumesme côte, d'une
piste, du pas, ou au petit trot a
Droite, et a Gauche
Le qui le met ſur les hanches extreme-
ment; à cause que ſes jambes de derriere
ſont faites comme nos bras, et que la
jambe de derriere, de dedans la volte,
eſt mise vers celle de dehors; ce qui le
fait plier au jarret.
Abr. a Diepenbeke delineavit.
Theodor. van Keſſel fecit
36.

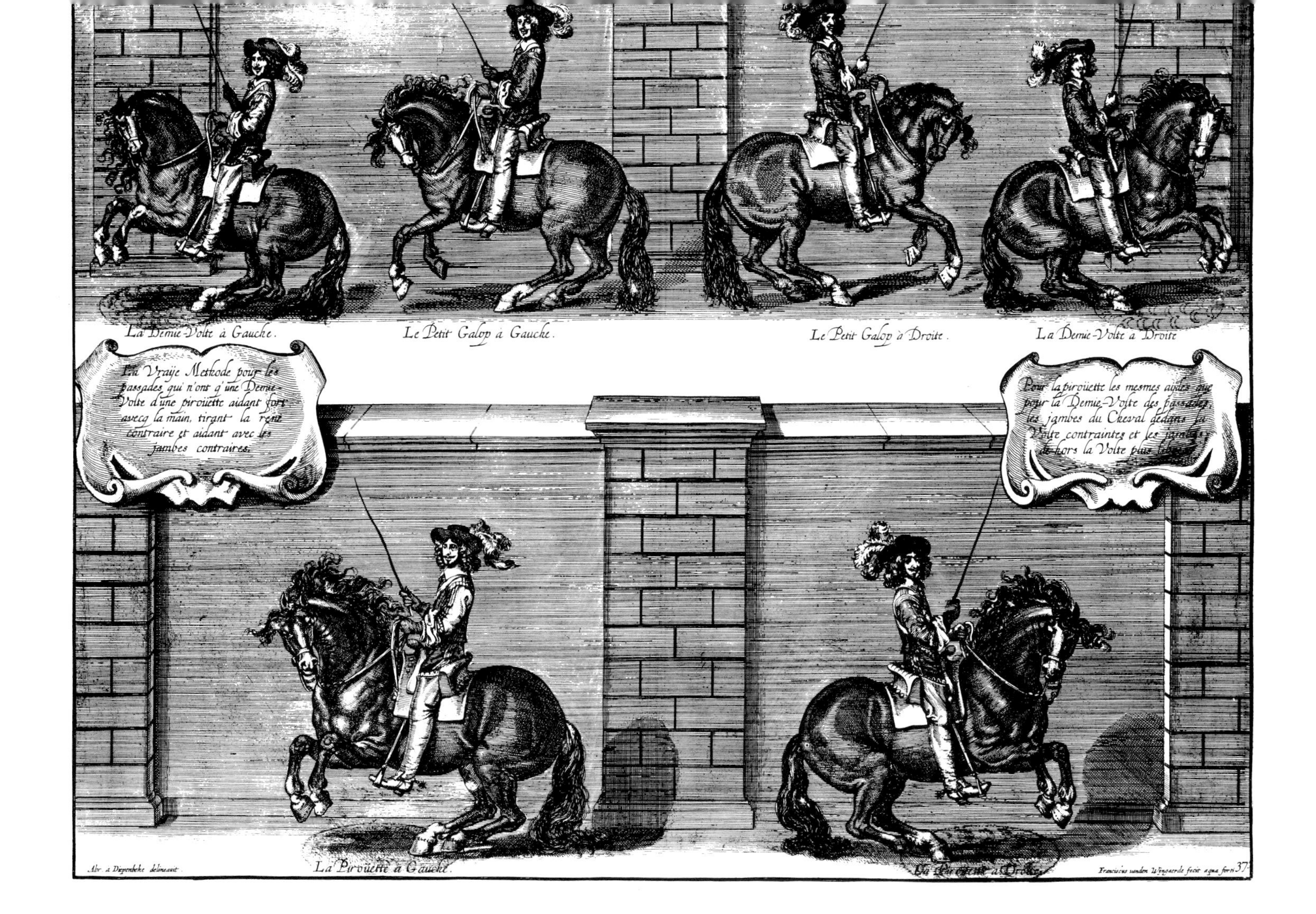
La Demie-Volte à Gauche.
Le Petit Galop à Gauche.
Le Petit Galop à Droite.
La Demie-Volte à Droite
La Vraije Methode pour les passades qui n'ont q'une Demie-Volte d'une piroüette aidant fort avecq la main, tirant la rene contraire et aidant avec les jambes contraires.
Pour la piroüette les mesmes aides que pour la Demie-Volte des passades, les jambes du Cheval dedans la Volte contraintes et les jambes de hors la Volte plus libres.
La Piroüette à Gauche.
La Piroüette à Droite.
Abr. à Diepenbeke delineavit.
Franciscus vanden Wyngaerde fecit aqua forti 37.

Parc de Welbeck appartenant a
seigneur le Marquis de
Nieucastle
est dans la Province de Nottingham.
Abr. à Diepenbeke delineavit
Theod. van Kessel fecit aqua forti
38

Abr. a Diepenbeke delineavit.

Theod. van Kessel fecit aqua forti.

LE CHATEAU D'OGLE,
qui fut à Monseigneur le Baron d'Ogle (le quel fut fait Baron par Edouard quatrieme Roi d'Angleterre) Grand-pere de Monseigneur le Marquis. Le quel Chateau est dans la province de Northumberland, et appartient apresent à Monseigneur le Marquis.

Abr. à Diepenbeke delineavit. Lucas Vorstermans iunior sculpsit. 40.

Le Chateau de Bothel
(dans la province de Northumberland)
qui fut à Mons.r le Baron d'Ogle,
et est apresent à Monseigneur
le Marquis.

MADAME LA VISCOMTES DE MANSFIELDE ET MADAME CAVENDYSSHE.
LE COMTE DE BRIDGWATER ET MADAME LA COMTESSE.
MONSEIGNEVR LE MARQVIS, ET MADAME LA MARQVISE.
LE COMTE DE BVLLINGBROOKE, ET MADAME LA COMTESSE.
MONSIEVR CHEYNE ET MADAME IEANE SA FEMME.
42.
Le Seigneur Charles vicomte de Mansfield l'Ené
Les deux Seigneurs qui sont à Cheval, et les trois Dames qui les regardent sont tous enfans de Monseigneur le Marquis; et les deux autres Dames sont femmes de ces deux Seigneurs, et les trois hommes sont maris de ces trois Dames filles de Monseigneur de Marquis.
Et le Seigneur Henrÿ Cavendÿsshe le Cadet

A

DICTIONARY

EXPLAINING THE

TECHNICAL TERMS

THAT BELONG TO THE

STUD, STABLE, MANAGE, AND FARRIERY;

Or Whatever elſe relates to HORSES.

A.

ABATE; a horſe is ſaid to abate, or take down, his curvets, when working upon curvets, he puts his two hind legs to the ground both at once, and obſerves the ſame exactneſs in all the times.

ABSCESS, proceeds from a blow, hurt, or ſome violence.

ACHE, a pain in any part of the Body; a diſeaſe that cauſes numbneſs in the joints, and proceeds from cold, taken upon hard and violent exerciſe or labour.

ACOPUM, a fomentation to allay the ſenſe of wearineſs; alſo a medicine for horſes, uſed for the ſame purpoſe.

ACTION of the mouth, is the agitation of the tongue, and the mandible of a horſe, that by champing upon the bridle, keep his mouth freſh. You may ſee by the white ropy foam, that a horſe has the action of the mouth, which is a ſign of vigour, mettle, and health.

ACULER, a French word, uſed in the academies, importing that a horſe working upon volts in the Manage, does not go far enough forwards at every time or motion, ſo that his ſhoulders embrace, or take in, too little ground, and his croupe comes too near the center of the volt.

AID; to aid, aſſiſt, or ſuccour, a horſe, is to ſuſtain and help him to work true, and mark his times or motions with a juſt exactneſs.

AIR is a cadence and liberty of motion, accommodated to the natural diſpoſition of the horſe, which makes him work in the manage, and riſe with obedience, meaſure, and juſtneſs of time. Some riding-maſters take the word Air in a ſtrict ſenſe, as ſignifying the manage that is higher, ſlower, and more artful or deſigned than the *terra a terra*; but others gives it a larger ſignification, including under that ſenſe *terra a terra*.

AMBLING; a motion in a horſe that is much deſired, very uſeful, but not eaſily to be obtained the right way, notwithſtanding the vain confidence of the various profeſſors of it, who, tho' they ſo confidently aſſert the ſucceſs, yet differ in their methods to affect it.

ANBURY, a kind of wen, or ſpungy wart, growing upon any part of a horſe's body, full of blood.

APPUI, or *ftay upon the hand*, is the reciprocal fenfe between the horfe's mouth and the bridle-hand, or the fenfe of the action of the bridle in the horfeman's hand.

ARCHED; a horfe is faid to have arched-legs when his knees are bended arch-wife.

To ARM; a horfe is faid to arm himfelf when he preffes down his head, as if he would check, and bends his neck fo as to reft the branches of his bridle upon his counter, in order to difobey the bit mouth, and guard his bars and his mouth, which are relieved by over-bending his neck.

ARMAN, a confection of wonderful efficacy to prevent a total lofs of appetite in horfes.

ARRESTS, are mangy humours upon the finews of the hinder legs of a horfe, between the ham and the paftern. They feldom appear upon the fhank finew.

ARZEL, a horfe is faid to be arzel, that has a white mark upon his far foot behind.

ATTAINT, is a blow, or wound, received by a horfe in his inner feet.

AUBIN is a broken going, or pace, of a horfe between an amble and a gallop.

AVERTI, a French word ufed in the manage, as applied to the pace or motion of a horfe; fignifying a motion that is injoined, regulated, and required in the leffons.

Pas ecoute, and Pas d'ecole, (*i. e.* liftening paces, or fchool paces) fignify the fame thing.

B.

BALOTADES are the leaps of a horfe between two pillars, or upon a ftraight line, made with juftnefs of time, with the aids of the hands, and the calves of the legs; and that in fuch manner, that when his fore-feet are in the air, he fhews nothing but the fhoes of his hinder feet without yerking out.

BANQUET, is that fmall part of the branch of the bridle that is under the eye, which being rounded like a fmall rod, gathers and joins the extremities of the bitt to the branch, and that in fuch a manner that the banquet is not feen, but covered by the cap, or that part of the bit that is next the branch.

BANDS of a faddle are two pieces of iron flat, and three fingers broad, nailed upon the bows of the faddle, one on each fide, contrived to hold the bows in the fituation that maketh the form of the faddle.

BARBLES are knots of fuperfluous flefh, that grow up the channels of a horfe's mouth; that is the interval that feparates the bars, and lies under the tongue.

BARDELLE, is a faddle made in the form of a great faddle, but only of cloth ftuffed with ftraw, and tied tight down with packthread, without either leather, wood or iron.

BARNACLES, horfe twitchers, or brakes; thefe are things which Farriers ufe to put upon horfes nofes, when they will not ftand quietly to be fhod, blooded, or dreffed of any fore.

BARS of a horfe's mouth, are the ridge, or higheft parts of that place of the gum that never bears any teeth, and is fituated between the grinders, and the tufhes, on each fide of the mouth: fo that the part of the gum which lies under, and at the fide of the bars, retains the name of gum.

BAY colour. A bay horfe is what we commonly call red inclining to chefnut.

This colour varies feveral ways; it is a dark bay, or a light bay, according as it is more or lefs deep: and we hawe likewife dapple bays. See MIROUETTE.

BAYARD, a bay horfe.

BEAT. To beat the duft or powder, is faid of a horfe that at each time, or motion, does not take in ground or way enough with his fore-legs.

BELLY; a thick-bellied, a well-bodied, a well thick-flanked horfe; that is, a horfe that has large, long, and well made ribs; or fuch as are neither too narrow nor too flat.

BELLY-FRETTING, is a grievous pain in the belly of a horfe, befides the cholic.

BISHOPING, a term amongft horfe-courfers, which they ufe for thofe fophiftications they ufe to make an old horfe appear young, and a bad one good, &c.

BITT, or horfe-bitt, in general, fignifies the whole machine of all the iron appurtenances of a bridle; as the bitt-mouth, the branches, the curb, the fevil-holes, the tranchefil, and crofs chains; but oftentimes it fignifies only the bitt-mouth in particular.

BITT-MOUTH, is a piece of iron forged feveral ways, in order to be put into a horfe's mouth, and to keep it in fubjection.

BLAZE. See STAR and WHITE-FACE.

BLEYNE, or Bleyme, [*in Horfes*] an inflammation occafioned by the blood's putrifying in the inner part of the coffin, towards the heel, between the fole and the coffin-bone. See HOOF-CAST.

BLINDNESS [*in Horfes*] may be thus difcerned: The walk, or ftep of a blind horfe, is always uncertain and unequal.

BLOOD-LETTING; the figns or indications of blood-letting in a horfe are thefe; his eyes will look red, and his veins fwell more than ordinary; he will alfo have an itching about his mane

mane and tail; and be continually rubbing them, and ſome times will ſhed ſome of his hair; otherwiſe he will peel about the roots of his ears, in the places where the head-ſtall of the bridle lies; his urine will be red and high coloured, and his dung black and hard; likewiſe if he has red inflammations, or little bubbles on his back, or does not digeſt his meat well; or if the white of his eyes be yellow, or the inſide of his upper or nether lip be ſo, theſe are ſigns he ſtands in need of bleeding.

BLOOD RUNNING ITCH, happens to an horſe by an inflammation of the blood, being overheated by hard riding.

BOAR; A horſe is ſaid to boar when he ſhoots out his noſe as high as his ears, and toſſes his noſe in the wind.

BOLSTERS of a ſaddle, are thoſe parts of a great ſaddle which are raiſed upon the bows, both before and behind, to hold the rider's thigh, and keep him in a right poſture, notwithſtanding the diſorders the horſe may occaſion.

BOUILLON is a lump or excreſcency of fleſh that grows either upon or juſt by the fruſh, inſomuch that the fruſh ſhoots out like a lump of fleſh, and makes the horſe halt; and this we call the fleſh blowing upon the fruſh.

BOULETTE; a horſe is called boulette, when the fetlock, or paſtern joint, bends forward and out of its natural ſituation; whether through violent riding, or by reaſon of being too ſhort jointed, in which caſe the leaſt fatigue will bring it.

BOUTE; a horſe is called boute, when his legs are in a ſtraight line from the knee to the coronet.

BOWS of a ſaddle, are two pieces of wood laid arch-wiſe, to receive the upper part of a horſe's back, to give the ſaddle it's due form, and keep it tight.

BRANCHES of a bridle, are two pieces of iron bended, which, in the interval between one and the other, bear the bitt-mouth, the croſs-chains, and the grub; ſo that on one end they anſwer to the head-ſtall, and on the other to the reins, in order to keep the horſe's head in ſubjection.

BRASSICOURT, or brachicourt; is a horſe whoſe forelegs are naturally bended arch-wiſe; being ſo called by way of diſtinction from an arched horſe, whoſe legs are bowed by hard labour.

BRAYE, an obſolete French word, made uſe of by ſome to ſignify the entry of the horſe's throat, or the extremity of the channel towards the maxillary bones.

BREAK; to break a horſe in trotting, is to make him light upon the hand by trotting, in order to make him fit for a gallop. To break a horſe for hunting, is to ſupple him, to make him take the habit of running.

BREATH, or wind. This word ſignifies ſometimes the eaſy reſpiration of a horſe, and ſometimes it implies the eaſe and reſt, or repoſe of a horſe.

BREED is a place where mares for breed, and ſtallions are kept in order to raiſe a ſtud.

BREEDING *of horſes.* See *Stud* in the *Index.*

BRIDLE is ſo termed when all it's appurtenances are fixed together in the ſeveral parts of it for the government of a horſe.

BRILLIANT; a briſk, high-mettled, ſtately horſe is ſo called, as having a raiſed neck, a fine motion, excellent haunches, upon which he riſes, tho' never ſo little put on.

BRING in a horſe, is to keep down the noſe of a horſe that bores and toſſes his noſe to the wind.

BROUILLER, is when a horſe, put to any manage, plunges, traverſes, and appears in diſorder.

BUTTERESS is an inſtrument of ſteel fitted to a wooden handle, with which they pare the foot, or cut the hoof of a horſe.

C.

CADENCE, is an eqal meaſure or proportion, obſerved by a horſe in all his motions.

CALADE, or Baſſe, is the deſcent, or ſloping declivity, of a riſing manage ground; being a ſmall eminence, upon which we ride down a horſe ſeveral times, putting him to a ſhort gallop, with his fore-hams in the air, to make him learn to ply and bend his haunches, and form his ſtop upon the aids of the calves of the legs, the ſtay of the bridle, and the caveſſon, ſeaſonably given: for without theſe aids he would throw himſelf too much upon his ſhoulders, and not bend his haunches.

CALKINS, a ſort of horſe-ſhoes for froſty weather.

CANNON-MOUTH of a bit, is a round but long piece of iron, conſiſting ſometimes of two pieces that couple and bend in the middle, and ſometimes only of one piece that does not bend, as in the cannon mouth a *trompe.*

CAPARASSON, or horſe-cloth, is a ſort of cover for a horſe.

CAPRIOLES differ from croupades in this, that in a croupade the horſe does not ſhow his

his ſhoes; and from a balotade in this, that in a balotade he does not yerk out.

CARACOL, is an oblique piſte or tread traced out in a ſemi-round, changing from one hand to another, without obſerving a regular ground.

CAREER; this word ſignifies both the ground that is proper for the manage and courſe, and race of a horſe that does not go beyond two hundred paces.

CAVALCADOUR, is a word uſed at the court of *France*, and among the families of the blood, ſignifying the querry; that is, maſter of the horſe.

CAUTING-IRON, an iron with which farriers ſear thoſe parts of a horſe that require burning.

CHANFRIN, is the fore-part of a horſe's head, extending from under the ears, along the interval, between the eye-brows, down to the noſe.

CHANGE a horſe, or change hand, is to turn, or bear the horſe's head from one hand to another, from the right to the left, and from the left to the right.

CHANNEL of a horſe, is the hollow between the two bars, or the nether jaw-bones, in which the tongue is lodged.

CHAPELET, is a couple of ſtirrup-leathers, mounted each of them with a ſtirrup, and joined at top in a ſort of leather buckle, called the head of the chapelet, by which they are made faſt to the pommel of the ſaddle.

CHAPERON of a bit-mouth, is a word only uſed for ſcatch-mouths, and all others that are not cannon-mouths.

CHARBON, an obſolete French word, ſignifying that little black ſpot or mark, that remains after a large ſpot, in the cavity of the corner teeth of a horſe, about the ſeventh or eighth year.

CHASTISEMENTS, or corrections, are the ſevere and rigorous effects of the aids; for when the aids are given with ſeverity they become puniſhments.

CHAUSSE trop-haut; a white-footed horſe is ſaid to be ſuch, when the white marks run too high upon the legs.

CHEVALER (a French word): a horſe is ſaid to be chevaler, when in paſſaging upon a walk or a trot his far fore leg croſſes or overlaps the other fore leg every ſecond motion. See to PASSAGE.

CHOPS, CLEFTS, RIFTS, are maladies in the palate of an horſe's mouth, cauſed either by eating coarſe or rough hay full of thiſtles and other prickly ſtuff; or by foul provender full of ſharp ſeeds, which by frequent pricking of the bars of his mouth cauſes them to wrankle and breed corrupt blood.

CLAMPONNIER, or Claponnier; an obſolete word ſignifying a long jointed horſe.

To CLOSE *a paſſade juſtly*, is when the horſe ends the paſſade with a demivolt, in good order, well narrowed and bounded, and terminates upon the ſame line upon which he parted, ſo that he is ſtill in a condition to part from the hand handſomely at every laſt time or motion of his demivolt.

CLOYED, ACCLOYED, a term uſed by Farriers of a horſe, when he has been pricked by a nail in ſhoeing.

COFFIN, or hoof of a horſe.

COILING *of the Stud*, is the firſt making choice of a colt, or young horſe, for any ſervice.

COLT, a word in general, ſignifying the male and female of the horſe kind.

COLT-EVIL, a diſeaſe to which both ſtone-horſe and gelding are ſubject.

To COMMENCE, or *initiate, a horſe*, is to put him to the firſt leſſons, in order to break him.

CORNERS, or angles of the volt, are the extremities of the four lines of the volt when you work in ſquare.

CORONET, or cronet of a horſe, is the loweſt part of the paſtern which runs round the coffin, and is diſtinguiſhed by the hair which joins and covers the upper part of the hoof.

CURVET, (*in the Manage*) an air, when the horſe's legs are more raiſed than in the *demivolts*, being a kind of leap up, and a little forward, wherein the horſe raiſes both his fore-feet at once, equally advanced, (when he is going ſtrait forward, and not in a circle) and as his fore-legs are falling, he immediately raiſes his hind-legs, as he did his fore; that is, equally advanced, and not one before the other: ſo that all his four legs are in the air at once.

CRAPAUDINE, or *tread upon the coronet*, is an imperfection in a horſe's foot.

CREPANCE, is a ſcratch or chap in a horſe's legs, given by the ſpunges of the hinder feet croſſing and ſtriking againſt the other hinder foot.

CRESCENT (among *Farriers*): a horſe is ſaid to have *creſcents*, when the point, or that part of the coffin bone, or little foot, which is moſt advanced, falls down, and preſſes the ſole outwards; and the middle of the hoof above the toe ſhrinks and becomes flat by reaſon of the hollowneſs beneath it.

CREST FALLEN is an imperfection or infirmity in a horſe, when the upper part of his neck, on which his mane grows, called the creſt,

creſt, hangs either on the one ſide or the other, not ſtanding upright as it ought to do.

CROUP *of a horſe* ought to be large and round, ſo that the tops of the two haunch bones be not within view of each other; the greater diſtance between theſe two bones the better.

A racking CROUP, is when a horſe's fore quarters go right, but his croup in walking ſwings from ſide to ſide.

CROWNED; a horſe is ſaid to be crowned, when, by a fall or other accident, he is ſo hurt or wounded in the knee, that the hair ſheds and falls off without growing again.

CRUPPER, the buttocks of a horſe; the rump: alſo a roll of leather put under a horſe's tail.

CURB is a chain of iron made faſt to the upper part of the branches of the bridle.

To CURTAIL *a horſe, i. e.* to dock him, or cut off his tail.

To CUT *the round,* or CUT *the volt,* is to change the hand when a horſe works upon volts of one tread; ſo that dividing the volt in two, he turns and parts upon a right line to recommence another volt.

D.

DEVUIDER, a term, in the academies, applied to a horſe, that in working upon the volts, makes his ſhoulders go too faſt for the croupe to follow; ſo that inſtead of going upon two treads, as he ought, he endeavours only to go upon one: which comes from the reſiſtance he makes in defending againſt the heels, or from the fault of the horſeman, that is too haſty with his hand. See HASTEN.

DISARM; to diſarm the lips of a horſe, is to keep them ſubject, and out from above the bars, when they are ſo large as to cover the bars, or prevent the true preſſure, or *appui* of the mouth, by bearing up the bitt, and ſo hindring the horſe from feeling the effects of it upon the bars.

To DISGORGE, is to diſcuſs, or diſperſe an inflammation or ſwelling.

DISUNITE; a horſe is ſaid to diſunite that drags his haunches; that gallops falſe, or upon an ill foot.

DOCK (or *Trouſſequeue*) is a large caſe of leather, as long as the dock of a horſe's tail, which ſerves as a cover to the tails of leaping horſes.

DOCK-PIECE *of a horſe,* ſhould be large and full, rather than too ſmall: if a horſe gall beneath the dock, greaſe the part every day, and waſh it with ſalt and water, or good brandy: the latter is the moſt effectual remedy.

DRAUGHT *horſe,* a horſe deſtined for the cart, plough, *&c.*

DRENCH, is a ſort of decoction prepared for a ſick horſe.

DRINKING *of horſes* immediately after hard riding, is very dangerous.

DRY, to put a horſe to dry meat is to feed him with corn and hay after taking him from graſs, or houſing him.

DUST *and* SAND will ſo dry the tongues and mouths of horſes, that they loſe their appetite.

E.

EBRIDLADE, is a check of the bridle which the horſeman gives to the horſe, by a jerk of one rein, when he refuſes to turn.

ECAVESSADE, is a jerk of the caveſſon.

ECHAPE; an echape is a horſe got between a ſtallion and a mare of a different breed, and different countries.

ECHAPER, to ſuffer a horſe to eſcape or ſlip from the hand.

ECOUTE; a pace or motion of a horſe.

ECURIE, is a covert-place for the lodging and houſing of horſes.

ECUYER, a *French* word, (in *Engliſh* querry) has different ſignifications in *France.*

EEL-BACK'D *horſes,* are ſuch as have black liſts along their backs.

ENLARGE a horſe, or make him go large, is to make him embrace more ground than he covered.

ENTABLER; a word uſed in the academies, as applied to a horſe whoſe croupe goes before his ſhoulders in working upon volts.

ENTERFERING; a diſeaſe incident to horſes.

ENTREPAS is a broken pace or going, and indeed properly a broken amble.

EPARER; a word uſed in the manage, to ſignify the flinging of a horſe; or his yerking or ſtriking out with his hind legs.

ERGOT, is a ſtub like a piece of ſoft horn about the bigneſs of a cheſnut, placed behind and below the paſtern joint, and commonly hid under the tuft of the fetlock.

ESQUIAVINE an old *French* word ſignifying a long and ſevere chaſtiſement of a horſe in the manage.

ESTRAPADE is the defence of a horſe that will not obey; who to get rid of his rider, riſes mightily before; and while his fore-hand is yet in the air, yerks out furiouſly with his hind legs, ſtriking higher than his head was before, and during his counter time goes back rather than advances.

To EXTEND *a horſe*, ſome make uſe of this expreſſion, importing to make a horſe grow large.

F.

FALCADE; a horſe makes falcades when he throws himſelf upon his haunches two or three times, as in very quick curvets; which is done in forming a ſtop, and half-ſtop.

FALLING-EVIL a diſeaſe proceeding from ill blood.

FALSE QUARTER is a cleft, crack, or chink, ſometimes on the outſide, but for the moſt part on the inſide of his hoof.

FARCIN, FARCY, FASHIONS, a creeping ulcer.

FEATHER *in a Horſe's forehead*, &c. is nothing elſe but the turning of the hair.

FEATHER alſo upon a horſe, is a ſort of natural frizzling of the hair, which in ſome places riſes above the lying hair, and there caſts a figure reſembling the top of an ear of corn.

FEEL; to feel a horſe in the hand, is to obſerve that the will of a horſe is in the hand, that he taſtes the bridle, and has a good *appui* in obeying the bitt.

FERME *a ferme*; a word peculiar to the manage ſchools, ſignifying in the ſame place, without ſtirring or parting.

FETLOCK is a tuft of hair as big as the hair of the mane, that grows behind the paſtern joint of many horſes.

FIG [*in Horſes*] a diſeaſe that takes its name from a wart or broad piece of fleſh growing upon the fruſh towards the heel, reſembling a fig in ſhape.

FILLETS, the loins of a horſe.

FIRE, to give the fire to a horſe, is to apply the firing iron red hot to ſome preternatural ſwelling in order to diſcuſs it.

FIRING IRON is a piece of copper or iron about a foot long, one end of which is made flat, and forged like a knife, the back of it being half an inch thick, and the fore edge about five or ſix times thinner.

FLEAM, is a ſmall inſtrument of fine ſteel, compoſed of two or three moveable lancets for blooding a horſe.

To FLING, is the fiery and obſtinate action of an unruly horſe.

To FLY *the heels*: a horſe is ſaid to fly the heels when he obeys the ſpur.

FONCEAU, is the bottom, or end, of a cannon-bitt-mouth; that is, the part of the bitt that joins it to the banquet.

FOOT of a horſe, conſiſts of the hoof or coffin; which is all the horn that appears when the horſe's foot is ſet on the ground.

FORE-LEGS of a horſe, conſiſt of an arm, a fore-thigh and the ſhank.

To FOUNDER a horſe, is to over-ride him, or to ſpoil him with hard working.

Cheſt FOUNDERING, a diſtemper proceeding from crudities in the ſtomach, or other weakneſſes obſtructing the paſſage of the lungs.

G.

GALLOP, is a motion of a horſe that runs at full ſpeed.

GALLOP, or *Canterbury-rate*, is a pace between a full ſpeed and a ſwift running.

GALLOPADE; the fine gallopade, the ſhort gallop, the liſtening gallop, the gallop of the ſchool: 'Tis a hand gallop, or gallop upon the hand, in which a horſe galloping upon one or two treads, is well united, well *raccourci*, knit together, well coupled, and well ſet under him.

GASCOIN, the hinder thigh of an horſe, which begins at the *ſtifle*, and reaches to the *ply*, or bending of the ham.

GATE, is the going, or pace of a horſe.

GAUNT BELLY'D, or *light belly'd horſe*, is one whoſe belly ſhrinks up towards his flanks.

GENET, a kind of *Spaniſh* horſe.

GIGS, otherwiſe called bladders, or flaps, are a diſeaſe in the mouth of a horſe.

GIRTH, a kind of ſaddle buckled upon a horſe's belly; alſo a ſaddle that is buckled and compleat for uſe.

GLANDERS, a diſtemper in horſes, proceeding, according to the *French* accounts, from corrupt humours about the lungs and heart, ariſing neither from the blood nor phlegm, but from the one and the other *bile*, and therefore it is called dry.

GOING, is the pace or gate of a horſe.

GORGED, *i. e.* ſwelled.

GOURDY LEGS, a diſtemper in horſes, cauſed by pains and other fleſhy ſores.

To GRAPPLE; a horſe is ſaid to grapple, either in one or both legs; the expreſſion being peculiar to the hinder legs.

GRAVELLING, a misfortune that happens to a horſe by travelling, by little gravel-ſtones getting

getting between the hoof and the ſhoe, which ſettle at the quick, and there feſter and fret.

GREASE MOLTEN, a diſtemper in a a horſe, when his fat is ſaid to be melted by over hard riding or labour. See the *Index*.

GROOM, a man who looks after horſes.

GROUPADE a lofty kind of manage, and higher than the ordinary curvets.

H.

HALBERT is a ſmall piece of iron one inch broad, and three or four inches long, ſoldered to the toe of a horſe's ſhoe, which jets out before, to hinder a lame horſe from reſting or treading upon his toe.

HALTER CAST is an excoriation of the paſtern, occaſioned by the halter being entangled about the foot; upon the horſe's endeavouring to rub his neck with his hinder feet.

HALTING happens ſometimes before, and ſometimes behind; if it be before, the ailment muſt of neceſſity be in the *ſhoulder*, *knee*, *flank*, *paſtern*, or *foot*.

HAM, HOUGH of a horſe is the ply or bending of the hind legs, and likewiſe comprehends the point behind, and oppoſite to the ply, called the hock.

HAND is a meaſure of a fiſt clinched, by which we compute the height of a horſe.

HAND-HIGH is a term uſed in horſemanſhip, and peculiar to the *Engliſh* nation.

HARD *Horſe*, is one that is inſenſible of whip or ſpur.

HARNESS GALLS; ſometimes the breaſts of coach-horſes are galled by the harneſs.

HAUNCH, or hip of a horſe.

HEARTS; a horſe of two hearts, *i. e.* a horſe that works in the manage with conſtraint and irreſolution, and cannot be brought to conſent to it.

HEAVY; to reſt heavy upon the hand, is ſaid of a horſe, who, thro' the ſoftneſs of his back, and weight of his fore-quarters, or thro' wearineſs, throws himſelf upon the bridle, but withal, without making any reſiſtance, or any effort to force the horſeman's hand.

HEEL *of a horſe*, is the lower hinder part of the foot.

HIDE-BOUND, a diſtemper in horſes when the skin ſticks ſo faſt to the back and ribs, that you cannot pull it from the fleſh with your hand.

HIP-SHOT; a horſe is ſaid to be ſuch, when he is wrung, or has ſprained his haunches or hips, ſo as to relaxate the ligaments that keep the bone in its due place.

HOOF of a horſe, is all the horn that appears when his foot is ſet to the ground.

HOOF-BOUND, is a ſhrinking of of the *hoof* at the top, and at the heel, which makes the skin ſtare above the *hoof*, and ſo grow over it.

HOOF-BRITTLE, an infirmity in horſes, proceeding either naturally or accidentally; naturally from the ſire or dam; accidentally from a ſurfeit, that falls down from the feet; or elſe from the horſe's having been formerly foundered.

HOOF-CAST, or, *caſting of the hoof*, is, when the coffin falls clean away from a horſe's foot.

HOOF-SWELLED; an infirmity that ſometimes happens to young horſes by being over-ridden, or too hard wrought, which cauſes them to ſwell in that part, by reaſon of the blood falling down and ſettling there, which, if not ſpeedily removed, will beget a wet ſpavin.

HOOF-LOOSENED, is an infirmity in a horſe, it is a diſſolution or dividing of the horn or coffin of his hoof from his fleſh, at the ſetting of the coronet. See more upon the *Articles of Diſeaſes*, &c. in the *Index of Diſeaſes*.

HORSE-MEASURE, a rod of box to ſlide out of a cane, with a ſquare at the end, being divided into hands and inches, to meaſure the height of horſes.

HORSE-SHOE; of theſe there are ſeveral ſorts. See the *Supplement*.

HORSE-RACING; a diverſion more uſed in *England* than in all the world beſide, and for which the *Engliſh* horſes are better than any other.

HOUGH, or *ham of a horſe*, is the joint of the hinder quarter, which joins the thigh to the leg.

HUNGRY EVIL, is an inordinate deſire, in horſes, to eat.

I.

JARDES, JARDONS, are callous and hard ſwellings in the hinder legs of a horſe, ſeated on the outſide of the hough, as the ſpavin is on the inſide.

IMPOSTHUME in horſes, is an unnatural ſwelling of humours or corrupt matter in any part of the body.

INSTEP, is that part of the hinder leg of a horſe that correſponds to the ſhank in the fore-leg, extended from the ham to the paſtern-joint.

INTERFERE, or *Cut*; to knock or rub one heel againſt another in going.

JOCKEY, one that trims up horſes, and rides about with horſes for ſale.

ITCH [*in Horſes*], a diſtemper which may be perceived by their rubbing their legs till the hair comes off.

K.

KNEE of a horſe, is the joint of the fore-quarters, that joins to the fore-thigh in the ſhank.

L.

LAMPAS, LAMPERS, LAMPRASS, is a ſort of ſwelling in the palate of a horſe's mouth, *i. e.* an inflammation in the roof of his mouth behind the nippers of his upper jaw; ſo called, becauſe it is cured with a lamp or hot iron.

LARGE; a horſe is ſaid to go large and wide when he gains or takes in more ground in going wider off the center of the volt, and deſcribing a greater circumference.

LASSITUDE, or *Wearineſs* in a horſe.

LEAD; a horſe going in a ſtrait line, always leads and cuts the way with his right foot.

LEAPING-HORSE, one that works in the high manage, a horſe that makes his leaps in order, with obedience, between two pillars, upon a ſtrait line, in volts, caprioles, balotades, or croupades.

LEGS *of the Horſeman*, the action of the horſeman's legs given ſeaſonably, and with judgment, is an aid that conſiſts more or leſs with the calf of the leg to the flank of the horſe, and in bearing it more or leſs off, as there is occaſion.

LENGTH; to paſſage a horſe upon his own length, &c.

LESSONS *for a Horſe*; when your horſe will receive you to and from his back gently, trot forward willingly, and ſtand ſtill obediently, then he is ſaid to have learnt his leſſons for what purpoſe ſoever he is intended.

LIGHTEN; *to lighten a horſe, to make a horſe lighter in the fore-hand*, is to make him free and lighter in the fore-hand than behind.

LIGS *in a Horſe*, are little puſhes, wheals, or bladders, within the lips of a horſe.

LISTENING; a horſe is ſaid to go a liſtening pace.

LOCKS, are pieces of leather two fingers broad, turned round, and ſtuffed on the inſide, to prevent their hurting the paſtern of a horſe.

LONG-JOINTED *Horſe*, is one whoſe paſtern is ſlender and pliant.

M.

MALANDERS, MALENDERS, a diſeaſe in horſes.

MALT-LONG, MALT-WORM, is a cankerous ſorrance about the hoof of an horſe, juſt upon the cronet, which breaks out into knobs and bunches that run with a wateriſh, ſharp lee, and humour, which will, if let alone, envenom the whole foot.

MANAGE, is a word that ſignifies a place, not only ſet a-part for the exerciſe of riding the great horſe, but likewiſe the exerciſe itſelf.

MANE, the hair hanging down on a horſe's neck.

MANGER, is a little raiſed bench under the rack in the ſtable, made hollow, for receiving the grain or corn that a horſe eats.

MARES, the female of the *horſe kind*.

MARK; a horſe marks, that is, he ſhews his age by a black ſpot, called the bud or eye of a bean, which appears at about five and a half, in the cavity of the corner teeth.

MARTINGAL, a thong of leather, faſtened to one end of the girths under the belly of a horſe, and at the other end to the muſs-roll, to hinder him from rearing.

MASTIGADOUR, or *Slabbering-bitt*, is a ſnaffle of iron, all ſmooth, and of a piece, guarded with *paternoſters*, and compoſed of three halfs of great rings, made into demi-ovals, of unequal bigneſs, the leſſer being incloſed within the greateſt, which ought to be about half a foot high. A *maſtigadour* is mounted with a headſtall and two reins.

MELLIT, a diſtemper in a horſe, being a dry ſcab growing upon the heels of his forefeet.

MES-AIR, is a manage half *terra a terra*, and half corvet.

MIDDLING-TEETH *of a Horſe*, are the four teeth that come out at three years and a half, in the room of other four foal-teeth, ſeated between the nippers and the corner-teeth.

MOLTEN GREASE, is a fermentation or ebullition of pituitous and impure humous, which precipitate and diſembogue the guts, and oftentimes kill a horſe.

MONTER *a dos*, or, *a poil*; a *French* expreſſion, ſignifying, to mount a horſe bare backed, or without a ſaddle.

MOON-EYES; a horſe is ſaid to have moon-eyes when the weakneſs of his eyes increaſes or decreaſes, according to the courſe of the

the moon; ſo that in the wane of the moon his eyes are muddy and troubled, and at new moon clear up; but ſtill he is in danger of loſing his eye-ſight quite.

MOUTH *of a Horſe*, ſhould be moderately well cloven; for when it is too much, there is much difficulty to bitt a horſe ſo as that he may not ſwallow it, as horſemen term it.

MULE, MOIL, is of two ſorts, the one engendred of a *horſe* and a *female aſs*, and the other of a *male aſs* and a *mare*.

N.

NAG, *Little Nag*, or *Tit*, is a horſe of a ſmall, low ſize.

NARROW, a horſe that narrows, is one that does not take ground enough; that is, does not bear far enough out to the one hand or to the other.

NAVEL-GALL, is a bruiſe on the back of a horſe, or pinch of a ſaddle behind, which if let alone long will be hard to cure.

NEEZINGS; helps to purge a horſe's head when it is ſtopped with phlegm, cold, and other groſs humours.

NEIGHING, is the cry of a horſe. Such a horſe neighs.

NIGHT-MARE, a malady incident to horſes as well as human bodies, proceeding from a melancholy blood oppreſſing the heart.

NIPPERS, are four teeth in the fore-part of a horſe's mouth, two in the upper and two in the lower jaw.

NOSE-BAND, or *Muſ-roll*, that is, the part of a head-ſtall of a bridle that comes over a horſe's noſe.

NOSTRILS *of a Horſe*, ſhould be large and extended, ſo that the red within them may be perceived, eſpecially when he ſneezes: the wideneſs of the noſtrils does not a little contribute to the eaſineſs of breathing.

O.

OBEY; a horſe is ſaid to obey the hands and the heels, to obey the aids and helps, (*i. e.*) to know or anſwer them according to demand.

OPENING *of a Horſe's heels*, is when the ſmith, in paring the foot, cuts the heel low, and takes it down within a finger's breadth of the coronet, ſo that he ſeparates the corners of the heel, and by that means impairs the ſubſtance of the foot, cauſing it to cloſe, and become narrow at the heel.

OSSELETS, (i. e.) *little Bones*, are hard excreſcences in the knees of ſome horſes.

OVER-DONE, *over-rid*, or *over-worked*; a horſe is ſo called, when his wind and ſtrength are broke and exhauſted with fatigue.

OVER-REACH, a horſe is ſaid to over-reach when he brings his feet too far forwards, and ſtrikes his toes againſt the ſpunges of his fore-ſhoe.

OX-FEET *in a Horſe*. See *Index of Diſeaſes*.

OX-LEGS, an imperfection in ſome horſes, which, tho' they have the back-ſinew of their fore-legs ſomewhat ſeparate from the bone, yet their ſinews are ſo ſmall, and ſo little ſet off, that their legs will become round after ſmall labour.

P.

PACES *of a Horſe*; the natural paces of a horſe's legs are three, *viz.* a *walk*, a *trot*, and a *gallop*; to which may be added, an *amble*, becauſe ſome horſes have it naturally; and ſuch horſes are generally the ſwifteſt *amblers* of any.

PAINS *in Horſes*, is a diſtemper, a kind of ulcerous ſcab, full of a fretting mattery water, breeding in the paſterns, between the fetlock and the heel; which comes for want of clean keeping and good rubbing, after the horſes are come off a journey, by means of which, ſand and dirt remaining in the hair, frets the skin and fleſh, which turns to a ſcab.

PALATE, the upper part or roof of the mouth.

PALSEY *in Horſes*, a diſeaſe that ſometimes deprives the whole body of ſenſe.

PANNELS *of a Horſe*, are two cuſhions or bolſters, filled with cow's, deer's, or horſe-hair, and placed under the ſaddle, one on each ſide, touching the horſe's body, to prevent the bows or bands from galling or hurting his back.

PANTONS, or *Pantable-ſhoes*, are a ſort of horſe-ſhoes that ſerve for narrow or low heels, and to hinder the ſole from growing too much downwards, ſo that the foot may take a better ſhape.

PARE; to pare a horſe's foot, is to cut his nails, that is, the horn and ſole of the foot, with a buttrice, in order to ſhoe him.

PARTS of a horſe's body proper to bleed in:

1. It is uſual to bleed *horſes* in the *jugular veins*, which lie on each ſide the neck, for the *farcy*, *mange*, *repletion*, and ſeveral other diſtempers; and alſo by way of evacuation twice

 a-year,

a-year, to all horſes that feed well and labour but little.

2. Blood is uſually taken from the temples, with a ſmall lancet, for bites or blows on the eyes.

3. *Farriers* have a lancet made on purpoſe for opening of veins beneath the tongue, for *head-aches*, or for being diſguſted or over-heated by exceſſive labour, or for *cholics*, and the *vives*.

4. It is uſual to bleed horſes in the griſtle of the noſe, without any regard whether they hit the vein or not; and this is alſo for *cholics*, *vives*, and being much over-heated.

5. Horſes are let blood in the middle of the palate, above the fourth bar, with a lancet or ſharp horn, when they have been diſguſted, harraſſed, or over-heated and dull.

6. Blood is taken from the *baſilisk*, or thigh-veins of horſes, for ſtrains in the ſhoulders, or the mange in thoſe parts.

7. Horſes are blooded in the paſterns, with a fleam or a lancet, for ſtrains or infirmities in the hams or knees.

8. They are let blood in the toes, with a buttrice, or drawing iron, for beating in the feet, and infirmities in the legs, ſuch as ſwellings and oppreſſions of the nerves.

9. The flank-veins are ſometimes opened, with a ſmall lancet made for that purpoſe, for the *farcy*.

10. Blood is drawn with fleams in the flat of the thighs, for blows and ſtrains in the *haunches*.

11. They bleed in the tail or dock, with a long lancet, for a fever and purſineſs.

PASSADE is a tread, or way, that a horſe makes oftener than once upon the ſame extent of ground, paſſing and repaſſing from one end of its length to the other; which cannot be done without changing the hand, or turning and making a demi-tour at each of the extremities of the ground.

PASSAGE; to paſſage a *horſe*, is to make him go upon a walk or trot upon two piſtes or treads, between the two heels, and ſide-ways, ſo that his hips make a track parallel to that made by his ſhoulders.

PASTERN *of a Horſe*, is the diſtance between the joint of that name and the coronet of the hoof.

PATIN-SHOE, a horſe-ſhoe ſo called, under which is ſoldered a ſort of half ball of iron, hollow within: 'Tis uſed for hip-ſhot horſes, and put upon a ſound foot, to the end that the horſe, not being able to ſtand upon that without pain, may be conſtrained to ſupport himſelf upon the lame foot, and ſo hinder the ſinews from ſhrinking, and the haunch from drying up.

PAW *the Ground*; a horſe paws the ground, when his leg being either tired or painful, he does not reſt it upon the ground, and fears to hurt himſelf as he walks.

PESATE, or *Peſade*, or *Poſade*, is when a *horſe* in lifting or raiſing his fore-quarters, keeps his hind-legs upon the ground without ſtirring, ſo that he marks no time with his haunches till his fore-legs reach the ground.

PIAFFEUR, is a proud ſtately horſe, who being full of mettle, or fire, reſtleſs and forward, with a great deal of motion, and an exceſſive eagerneſs to go forwards, makes this motion. The more that you endeavour to keep him in, he bends his leg the more up to his belly: He ſnorts, traverſes, if he can, and by his fiery action ſhews his reſtiveneſs.

PICKER, is an iron inſtrument five or ſix inches long, bent or crooked on one ſide, and flat and pointed on the other, uſed by grooms to cleanſe the inſide of the manage horſes feet.

PILLAR; moſt great manages have pillars fixed in the middle of the manage-ground, to point out the center; but all manages in general have upon the ſide or circumference, other pillars placed two and two, at certain diſtances, from whence they are called the two pillars, to diſtinguiſh them from that of the center.

PINCHING is when a horſe ſtanding ſtill, the rider keeps him faſt with the bridle-hand, and applies the ſpurs juſt to the hair of his ſides.

PISSING *of Blood*, may proceed from divers cauſes; for which, with the Cure, ſee the *Index*.

PISTE, is the tread, or track, that a horſe makes upon the ground he goes over.

PLANET-STRUCK, or *ſhrew-running*, as it is called by ſome, is a diſtemper in horſes, being a deprivation of feeling or motion.

PLANTED [*with Farriers*], a term uſed of a horſe, who is ſaid to be *right planted on his limbs*, when he ſtands equally firm on his legs, and not one advanced before the other; his legs ſhould be wider above than below, that is, the diſtance between his feet ſhould be leſs than between his fore-thighs, at that part next to the ſhoulders; the knees ought not to be too cloſe, but the whole leg ſhould deſcend in a ſtrait line, to the very *paſtern-joint*, and the feet ſhould be turned neither out nor in, the paſtern being placed about two fingers breadth more backwards than the coronet.

PLATE-LONGE, is a woven ſtrap, four fathom long, as broad as three fingers, and as thick as one, made uſe of in the manage for rai-

ſing

ſing a horſe's legs, and ſometimes for taking him down, in order to facilitate ſeveral operations of the Farrier.

PLAT-VEIN, is a vein on the inſide of each fore-thigh, a little below the elbow.

POGE, a cold in a horſe's head

POINSON, is a little point, or piece of ſharp-pointed iron, fixed in a wooden handle, which the cavalier holds in his right hand when he means to prick a leading-horſe in the croupe, or beyond the end of the ſaddle, in order to make him yerk out behind.

POINTS, or *Toes* of a bow of a ſaddle.

POINT; a horſe is ſaid to make a point, when in working upon volts he does not obſerve the round regularly, but putting a little out of his ordinary ground, makes a ſort of angle, or point, by his circular tread.

POLL-EVIL, is a ſort of *fiſtula*, or deep ulcer between the ears of the poll, or in the nape of the horſe's neck, which proceeds from corrupt humours falling upon it.

PONT-LEVIS, is a diſorderly reſiſting action, in diſobedience to his rider, in which the horſe rears up ſeveral times running, and riſes ſo upon his hind-legs that he is in danger of coming over.

PORTER, [*to carry*], uſed in the *French* manage, for directing or puſhing on a horſe at pleaſure, whether forwards, upon turns, &c.

PRESS *upon the Hand*; a horſe is ſaid to reſiſt, or preſs upon the hand, when either thro' the ſtiffneſs of his neck, or from an ardour to run too much a-head, he ſtretches his head againſt the horſe's hand, refuſes the aid of the hand, and withſtands the effects of the bridle.

To PRICK, or *pinch*, is to give a horſe a gentle touch of the ſpur, without clapping them hard to him.

PRICKER, [*Hunting-Term*], a hunter on horſeback.

PRICKT, otherwiſe called *accloyed*, *cloyed*, or *retrait*, &c. in reſpect to horſes, ſignifies only the having a prick by the negligence of the Farrier in driving the nails, by their weakneſs, ill pointing, or breaking them; which, if not preſently taken out, will, in time, break out into a foul ſore. You may diſcern it by the horſe's going lame; but if you would know it more certainly, pinch him round the hoof with a pair of pincers, and when you come to the place aggrieved he will ſhrink in his foot; or elſe you may try where he is pricked by throwing water on his hoof, for that place where he is hurt will be ſooner dry than the reſt.

PUNCH; a well-ſet, well-knit horſe, is ſhort backed, and thick ſhouldered, with a broad neck, and well lined with fleſh.

PURSINESS *in Horſes*, is a ſhortneſs of breath, either *natural* or *accidental*. The *natural* is when the horſe is cock throppled; for that his thropple or wind-pipe being ſo long, he is not able to draw his breath in and out with ſo much eaſe as other horſes do which are looſe throppled, becauſe the wind-pipe being too ſtreight, which ſhould convey the breath to the lungs, and vent it again at the noſe, makes him pant and fetch his breath ſhort; and in like manner when his pipe is filled with too much fat, or other phlegmatic ſtuff, which ſuffocates him, and makes his lungs labour the more.

PUT; 'tis uſed for the breaking or managing of a horſe; as, *Put your horſe to corvets*, *put him to caprioles*.

PYE-BALD *Horſe*, is one that has white ſpots upon a coat of another colour.

PYROET; ſome are of one tread or piſte, and ſome of two.

Thoſe of one tread are otherwiſe called, *Pirouettes de la tete a la queve*.

Pyroets de la tete a la queve, are entire and narrow turns made by the horſe upon one tread, and almoſt in one time, in ſuch a manner, that his head is placed where his tail was, without putting out his haunches.

Q.

QUARTER; to work from quarter to quarter, is to ride a horſe three times in end, upon the firſt of the four lines of a ſquare; then changing your hand, and riding him three times upon a ſecond; at the third line changing your hand, and ſo paſſing to the third and fourth, obſerving the ſame order.

QUARTERS *of a Saddle*, are the pieces of leather, or ſtuff, made faſt to the lower part of the ſides of a ſaddle, and hanging down below the ſaddle.

QUARTERS. *Fore-Quarters*, and *Hind-Quarters*; the fore-quarters are the ſhoulders and the fore-legs; the hind-quarters are the hips and the legs behind.

QUITTER-BONE, a hard round ſwelling upon the coronet, between a horſe's heel and the quarter, which moſt commonly grows on the inſide of the foot.

QUITTER, the matter of an ulcer or ſore.

R.

RACK, a wooden frame made to hold hay or fodder for cattle.

RACKING, a certain pace of a horſe, or a motion in going, in which he trots nor gallops, but is between both.

RAGOT, is a horſe that has ſhort legs, a broad croupe, and a ſtrong thick body.

RAISE; to raiſe a horſe upon corvets, upon caprioles, upon peſades, is to make him work at corvets, caprioles, or peſades.

RAISE is likewiſe uſed for placing a horſe's head right, and making him carry well; and hindering him from carrying low, or arming himſelf.

RAISTY, RESTIVE, a term uſed in reſpect of a horſe, when he will go neither backwards nor forwards.

RAKE; a horſe rakes, when being ſhoulder-ſplait, or having ſtrained his fore-quarters, he goes ſo lame, that he drags one of his fore-legs in a ſemicircle, which is more apparent when he trots than when he paces.

To RAKE *a Horſe*, is to draw his ordure with one hand out of his fundament, when he is coſtive, or cannot dung; in doing this the hand is to be anointed with *ſallad oil*, *butter*, or *hog's greaſe*.

RAMINGUE; a horſe called in *French ramingue*, is a reſtive ſort of a horſe, that reſiſts the ſpurs, or cleaves to the ſpurs, that is, defends himſelf with malice againſt the ſpurs, ſometimes doubles the reins, and frequently yerks, to favour his diſobedience.

RASE; to raſe, or glance upon the ground, is to gallop near the ground, as our *Engliſh* horſes do.

RATS-TAILS, a moſt venomous diſeaſe in horſes.

RAT-TAIL; a horſe is ſo called when he has no hair upon his tail.

RAZE; a horſe razes, or has razed, that is, his corner teeth ceaſe to be hollow, ſo that the cavity where the black mark was, is now filled up.

REARING *an End*, is when a horſe riſes ſo high before, as to endanger his coming over upon his rider.

RECHEAT, a leſſon which huntſmen wind upon the horn when the hounds have loſt their game, to call them back from purſuing a counter game.

RHEUM, is a flowing down of humours from the head, upon the lower parts.

RHEUMATIC *Eyes in Horſes*, are cauſed by a flux of humours from the brain, and ſometimes by a blow.

REINS, two long ſlips of leather faſtened on each ſide the curb or ſnaffle.

REMOLADE, is a leſs compounded *honey charge* for horſes.

RENETTE, is an inſtrument of poliſhed ſteel, with which they ſound a prick in a horſe's foot.

REPART, is to put a horſe on, or make him part a ſecond time.

REPOLON, is a demi-volt; the croupe is cloſed at five times.

REPOSTE, is the vindictive motion of a horſe, that anſwers the ſpur with a kick of his foot.

REPRISE, is a leſſon repeated, or a manage recommended.

RESTY, a reſty horſe, is a malicious unruly horſe.

RETRAITS, or *Pricks*; if a prick with a nail is neglected, it may occaſion a very dangerous ſore, and feſter ſo in the fleſh, that the foot cannot be ſaved without extreme difficulty.

RIBS *of a Horſe*, ſhould be circular and full, taking their compaſs from the very backbone.

RIDGES, or *Wrinkles of a Horſe's mouth*, are the riſings of the fleſh in the roof of his mouth, which run a-croſs from one ſide of the jaw to the other.

RIDGELING, the male of any beaſt that has been but half cut

RIG, a horſe that has had one of his ſtones cut out, and yet has got a colt.

RING-BONE *in a Horſe*, is a hard, callous, or brawny ſwelling.

RIVET, is that extremity of the nail that reſts or leans upon the horn when they ſhoe a horſe.

ROAN; a *Roan* horſe is one of a bay ſorrel, or black colour, with grey or white ſpots interſperſed very thick.

ROPE, *Cord*, or *Strap*, is a great ſtrap tied round a pillar, to which a horſe is faſtened when we begin to quicken and ſupple him, and teach him to fly from the chambriere, and not to gallop falſe.

ROPES *of two pillars*, are the ropes or reins of a caveſſon, uſed to a horſe that works between two pillars.

ROUND, or *volt*, is a circular tread.

ROUSSIN, is a ſtrong, well knit, well ſtowed horſe.

ROWEL, the goad or pricks of a ſpur.

S.

SACCADE, is a jerk more or leſs violent, given by the horſeman to the horſe in pulling or twitching the reins of the bridle all on a ſudden, and with one pull, and that when a horſe lies heavy upon the hand, or obſtinately arms himſelf.

SADDLE, is a ſeat upon a horſe's back, contrived for the conveniency of the rider.

SADDLE-GALL; when a horſe's back is hurt or fretted by the ſaddle.

SALLENDERS, are chops or mangy ſores in the bending of the horſe's hough.

SAULTS, the leaping or prancing of horſes, a kind of curveting.

SCAB, or *itch*, a diſtemper in horſes, proceeding from their being over-heated, and corrupt blood.

SCABBARD, is the skin that ſerves for a ſheath or caſe to a horſe's yard.

SCABBED HEELS *in Horſes*, a diſtemper, called alſo the *fruſh*.

SCATCH-MOUTH, is a bitt-mouth, differing from a cannon-mouth in this, that the cannon is round, and the other more oval.

SEAMS, SEYMES, *in Horſes*, are certain clifts in their quarters, cauſed by the dryneſs of the foot, or by being ridden upon hard ground.

SEAT, is the poſture or ſituation of a horſeman.

SEELING; a horſe is ſaid to *ſeel*, when, upon his eye-brows, there grow white hairs, mixed with thoſe of his uſual colour.

SEVIL *of the branches of a bridle*, is a nail turned round like a ring, with a large head made faſt in the lower part of the branch, called *gargouille*.

SHAMBRIER, or *Chambriere*, is a long thong of leather, made faſt to the end of a cane or ſtick, in order to animate a horſe, and puniſh him if he refuſes to obey the rider.

SHANK, *in a horſe*, is that part of the fore-leg, which is between the knee and ſecond joint, next to the foot, called a fet-lock, or paſtern joint,

SHORT-JOINTED; a horſe is ſaid to be ſhort-jointed that has a ſhort paſtern.

SHOULDER *of a Horſe*, is the joint in the fore-quarters that joins the end of the ſhoulder-blade with the extremity of the fore-thigh.

SHOULDER-PIGHT *in a Horſe*, is a malady, being the diſplacing of the point of the ſhoulder by ſome great fall, rack, or pain, which may be known by one ſhoulder-point's ſticking out farther than its fellow.

SHOULDER-PINCHING, a misfortune that befals a horſe by labouring or ſtraining when too young, or by being over-loaded.

SIDE; to ride a horſe ſide-ways, is to paſſage him, to make him go upon two treads, one of which is marked by his ſhoulders, and the other by his haunches.

SIGUETTE, is a caveſſon with teeth or notches; that is, a ſemi-circle of hollow and vaulted iron, with teeth like a ſaw.

SINEW, to *unſinew a horſe*, is to cut the two ſinews on the ſide of his head.

SINEW *ſprung*, is a violent attaint, or over-reach, in which a horſe ſtrikes his toe, or hinder-feet, againſt the ſinew of his fore-leg.

SKITTISH *Horſe*, is one that leaps inſtead of going forward, and does not ſet out or part from the hand freely, nor employ himſelf as he ought to do.

SLACK *a leg*, is ſaid of a horſe, when he trips or ſtumbles.

SNAFFLE, or *ſmall watering bitt*, is commonly a ſcatch-mouth accounted, with two very little ſtrait branches, and a curb, mounted with a head-ſtall, and two long reins of *Hungary* leather.

SNORT, is a certain ſound, that a horſe, full of fire, breaths through his noſtrils, and ſounds as if he had a mind to expel ſomething that is in his noſe, and hindred him from taking breath.

SOLE *of a Horſe*, is a nail, or ſort of horn, that is much tenderer than the other horn that encompaſſes the foot, and by reaſon of it's hardneſs, is properly called the horn or hoof.

SORRANCES; maladies incident to horſes.

SPAVIN, a diſeaſe among horſes, which is a ſwelling or ſtiffneſs in the hams.

SPEAR; the feather of a horſe.

SPLENTS; a diſeaſe in horſes, which is a callous, hard, inſenſible ſwelling, or a hard griſtle, breeding on the ſhank bone. It ſpoils, in time, the Shape of the Leg.

SPUNGE *of a Horſe-ſhoe*, is the extremity or point of the ſhoe that anſwers to the horſe's heel.

STARS, are diſtinguiſhing marks in the fore-heads of horſes.

STEP *and* LEAP, is one of the ſeven airs, or artificial motions of a horſe.

STIFLE *in a Horſe*, a large muſcle, or that part of the hind-leg which advances towards his belly, and is a moſt dangerous part to receive a blow upon.

STONE-BRUISING, a misfortune that befals the cods of a horſe.

STOP, is a pauſe or diſcontinuation.

STRAIN, SPRAIN, a misfortune that befals a horſe when his ſinews are ſtretched beyond their due tone.

STRING-HALT [*in a Horſe*], an imperfection which is a ſudden twitching or ſnatching up of his hinder leg.

STUD; a place where ſtallions and mares are kept to propagate their kind.

SUMPTER-HORSE; a horſe that carries proviſions and neceſſaries for a journey.

SOLE *of a Horſe*, is, as it were, a plate of

 horn,

horn, which encompaſſing the fleſh, covers the whole bottom of the foot.

SORREL, is a reddiſh colour, with which the mane ought to be red or white; it is diſtinguiſhed, according to the degrees of it's deepneſs, into a burnt ſorrel, and a bright or light ſorrel; but, generally ſpeaking, 'tis the ſign of a good horſe.

SOUND; a horſe is ſuch that does not halt.

T.

TEDDER, TETHER, a rope wherewith the leg of a horſe is tied, that he may graze within a certain compaſs.

TEETH, are little bones in a horſe's jaws, which ſerve not only to facilitate the nouriſhment, but likewiſe to diſtinguiſh the age of horſes.

TERRA A TERRA, or *terre a terre* is a ſeries of low leaps, which a horſe makes forwards, bearing ſide-ways, and working upon two treads.

TERRAIN, is the managed ground upon which the horſe marks his piſte or tread.

THIGHS *of a Horſeman:* The effect of the rider's thighs is one of the aids that ſerves to make a horſe work vigorouſly in the manage.

TICK, an infirmity in an horſe, when he preſſes the edge of the manger with his upper teeth.

TOE *before, and quarter behind,* [*with Farriers*] a rule which they obſerve in ſhoeing horſes.

TRAMEL, a machine for teaching a horſe to amble.

TRANCHE-FILE, is the croſs-chain of a bridle that runs along the bitt-mouth from one branch to the other,

TRAVES, a kind of ſhackles for a horſe that is in teaching to amble or pace.

TRAVERSE, a horſe is ſaid to traverſe when he cuts his tread croſs-wiſe, throwing his croupe to one ſide, and his head to the other.

TRAVICE, is a ſmall incloſure or oblong quadrangle, placed before a farrier's ſhop.

TREPINGER, is the action of a horſe, who beats the duſt with his fore-feet in managing, without imbracing the volt; and who makes his motions and times ſhort, and near the ground, without being put upon his haunches.

TRIP, a ſtumbling, a falſe ſtep.

TRUSSED; a horſe is ſaid to be well truſſed, when his thighs are large, and proportioned to the roundneſs of the croup.

TUEL; the fundament of a horſe.

TURN, is a word commonly uſed by the Riding-Maſters, when they direct their ſcholars to change hands.

TURNING *ſtraight* [*in the Manage*], an artificial motion of a horſe.

TUSHES, are the fore teeth of a horſe, ſeated beyond the corner teeth, upon the bars.

TWIST; the inſide, or flat part of a man's thigh; upon which a true horſeman reſts upon horſe-back.

TROT, is one of the natural paces of a horſe.

V.

VARISSE, [*in Horſes*] an imperfection upon the inſide of the ham, a little diſtant from the curb, but about the ſame height.

To VAULT *a ſhoe*, is to forge it hollow, for horſes that have high and round ſoles.

UNITE; a horſe is ſaid to unite, or walk in union, when in galloping the hind-quarters follow and keep time with the fore.

VOLT, ſignifies a round or circular tread.

URINE; a ſerous or wateriſh excrement derived from the blood, which paſſes from the reins, and is diſcharged through the bladder.

W.

WALK, is the ſloweſt, and leaſt raiſed of a horſe's goings.

WIND-GALLS, a diſeaſe, being bladders full of a corrupt jelly.

WIND-GALL, is a ſoft ſwelling, occaſioned bp over-working, juſt by the horſe's fetlock.

WITHERS *of a Horſe* begins where the mane ends, being joined to, and ending at the tip of the ſhoulder-blades.

WITHER-WRUNG; a horſe is ſaid to be wither-wrung when he has got a hurt in the withers.

Y.

YARD-FALLEN; a malady in a horſe which proceeds from want of ſtrength to draw it up within the ſheath.

YIELD, is to ſlack the bridle, and give the horſe head.

Z.

ZAIN, is a horſe of a dark colour, neither grey nor white, and without any white ſpot or mark upon him.

F I N I S.

AN

INDEX

TO

VOL. I.

Which contains the Duke of *Newcastle's* New Method of dressing Horses.

change

FINIS.